P9-CMA-954

NATIONS OF THE MODERN WORLD

AUSTRALIA	O. H. K. Spate *Director, Research School of Pacific Studies, Australian National University, Canberra*
CEYLON	S. A. Pakeman *Formerly Professor of Modern History, Ceylon University College; Appointed Member, House of Representatives, Ceylon, 1947–52*
CYPRUS	H. D. Purcell *Lecturer in English Literature, Queen's University, Belfast*
MODERN EGYPT	Tom Little *Managing Director and General Manager of Regional News Services (Middle East), Ltd., London*
ENGLAND	John Bowle *Professor of Political Theory, Collège d'Europe, Bruges*
FINLAND	W. R. Mead *Professor of Geography, University College, London; Formerly Chairman, Anglo-Finnish Society*
MODERN GREECE	John Campbell *Fellow of St. Antony's College Oxford*
	Philip Sherrard *Assistant Director, British School of Archaeology, Athens, 1958–62*
MODERN INDIA	Sir Percival Griffiths *President of the India, Pakistan and Burma Association*
MODERN IRAN	Peter Avery *Lecturer in Persian and Fellow of King's College, Cambridge*
ITALY	Muriel Grindrod *Formerly Editor of* International Affairs *and* The World Today *Assistant Editor of* The Annual Register

JAPAN	Sir Esler Dening *H.M. Ambassador to Japan, 1952–57*
KENYA	A. Marshall MacPhee *Formerly Managing Editor of* The East African Standard Group*; producer with British Broadcasting Corporation*
LIBYA	John Wright *Formerly of the* Sunday Ghibli, *Tripoli*
MALAYSIA	J. M. Gullick *Formerly of the Malayan Civil Service*
MOROCCO	Mark I. Cohen and Lorna Hahn
NEW ZEALAND	James W. Rowe *Director of New Zealand Institute of Economic Research, Inc.* Margaret A. Rowe *Tutor in English, Victoria University, Wellington*
NIGERIA	Sir Rex Niven *Colonial Service, Nigeria 1921–59; Member of Northern House of Assembly, 1947–59*
PAKISTAN	Ian Stephens *Formerly Editor of* The Statesman *Calcutta and Delhi, 1942–51; Fellow of King's College, Cambridge, 1952–58*
SOUTH AFRICA	John Cope *Formerly Editor-in-Chief of* The Forum*; South African Correspondent of* The Guardian
SUDAN REPUBLIC	K. D. D. Henderson *Formerly of the Sudan Political Service; Governor of Darfur Province, 1949–53*
TURKEY	Geoffrey Lewis *Senior Lecturer on Islamic Studies, Oxford*
THE UNITED STATES OF AMERICA	H. C. Allen *Commonwealth Fund Professor of American History, University College, London*
WEST GERMANY	Michael Balfour *Reader in European History, University of East Anglia*
YUGOSLAVIA	Muriel Heppell and F. B. Singleton

NATIONS OF THE MODERN WORLD

LIBYA

LIBYA

By

JOHN WRIGHT

FREDERICK A. PRAEGER, *Publishers*
New York · Washington

BOOKS THAT MATTER

Published in the United States of America in 1969
by Frederick A. Praeger, Inc., Publishers
111 Fourth Avenue, New York, N.Y. 10003

Library of Congress Catalog Card Number: 79-79075

Printed in Great Britain

FOR

MARIATERESA

Preface

WHEN I first arrived in Tripoli in 1965 I tried without success to find a general history of Libya, although several useful books were on sale: Haynes on the antiquities of Tripolitania, Evans-Pritchard on the Sanussis, Khadduri on modern political development, Kubar on the oil industry. A search through the libraries of the Municipality, the Antiquities Department, the Italian Cultural Institute, the British Council, and some of the oil companies in Tripoli showed that the book I had in mind apparently did not exist, at least not in any European language. I therefore decided to write it myself.

About a third of it was written in a flat in Sciara Ghat in the centre of Tripoli. After interruptions caused by the birth of a son and the outbreak of the Middle East War of June 1967, further chapters were written in a villa on the Italian side of Lake Lugano, in Milan (where the Brera and Ambrosiana libraries provided much useful material on medieval and Italian Libya), in Twickenham, and in Kensington.

I have reviewed the years 1911–51 at length, for Libya was then the subject of such unique social and political experiments as the Italian 'demographic colonisation' of the late 1930s and constitutional development under UN supervision after the Second World War. And, because of their greater importance in the story of modern Libya, the discovery and exploitation of oil resources are given more attention than the nation's political development since independence.

London J.L.W.
February 1969

Contents

Maps

List of Illustrations

[All are inserted between pages 144 and 145]

Acknowledgements

ACKNOWLEDGEMENT for kind permission to reproduce illustrations is made to the following, to whom the copyright of the illustrations belongs:

Rosario Casella: 1, 2, 5, 6, 8, 9, 10, 16, 20, 22, 23.
Esso Petroleum Company, Limited: 3, 4, 7, 14, 15, 17, 18, 19, 21.

Note on Transliteration

LIBYA is unique among Arabic-speaking countries in having followed rules of Italian orthography for the transliteration of Arabic into Roman script. French rules were imposed in other Arab Maghrib countries and in Syria-Lebanon; English became the standard in Egypt, Sudan, Palestine, and Iraq.

Starting with the disadvantages of their rigid orthography and alphabet of only twenty-one letters, the Italian soldiers and administrators who went out to Libya from 1911 onwards did their best to reduce the subtleties of Arabic pronunciation to the simplicity of Italian phonetics. In 1915 the Ministry of Colonies brought some order out of chaos by issuing a forty-page booklet setting out rules for the transcription of Tripolitanian and Cyrenaican place-names. After pointing out that Arabic makes great distinction between long and short vowels and has a dozen consonants unknown in Italian, the author, C. A. Nallino, ruled that neither Classical nor Tripoli Arabic, but local dialect, was to be the guide to pronunciation. Arabic names were preferable to Berber ones, and names that had already passed into Italian and general European usage – Augila, Bengasi, Homs – were not to be changed. Classical place-names, and not their Arabic derivatives or equivalents, were to be used; thus Tripoli, Sirte, and Cirene for Arabic Tarablus, Surt, and Shahat. Nallino's instructions were that the letter *'ayn* – 'which has no equivalent in our language' – was to be completely ignored. *Thā'* was to be treated as a plain 'T' (to save the Italians their customary difficulty in pronouncing 'Th' in any form), and local speech was to be followed in the rendering of *qāf* as 'G' (as in 'Garabulli') or 'Gh' before 'I' or 'E' (as in 'Ghibli').

Although Nallino tended to over-simplify (Marayid became Mraed; Tolmaitha, Tolmeta; Al-Zuwaitina, Ez-Zuetina) at least his standards remained in force for almost thirty years. But from 1942–3 onwards British occupation forces in Cyrenaica and Tripolitania introduced English standards in a country familiar with Italian ones, a process that was continued when American oilmen and experts started arriving in Libya in the 1950s and English ousted Italian as the country's second language. The French occupation of Fezzan in the Second World War added further complications by offering a third standard. The two Fezzanese oases known as 'Gat' and 'Gadames' to the Italians, and as 'Ghat' and 'Ghadames' to the English, were to the French administrators and map-makers 'Rhat' and 'Rhadames'. Italian 'Uadi' and English 'Wadi' became 'Ouadi', and the Anglo-Italian 'Gasr' (a word believed to derive from the Latin 'Castrum') became 'Qçer'. Thus, one of the main depressions of Fezzan could be rendered 'Uadi esc-Sciatti', 'Wadi al-Shatti', or 'Ouadi ech-Chatti' depending on the nationality of the writer.

In this book the spelling of place-names is based on the 1 : 3,000,000 Esso Road Map of Libya. But 'common usage', which tends towards Italian orthography, sometimes takes over. Thus 'Zuara', as written on Libyan signposts, is preferred to Esso's 'Zuwārah'; the Esso map in fact keeps such Italian spellings as 'Agedabia', 'Gefara', 'Augila', and 'Uaddan'.

Personal names are written in the simplest form consistent with reasonable accuracy. Again, 'common usage' is the rule where applicable and 'Omar Mukhtar' is preferred to the more scholarly ''Umar al-Mokhtar'. (The Esso map marks one of the main streets in each of Tripoli, Benghazi, and Baida as 'Omar el Muktar', 'Omar al Mukhtar', and 'Omar el Mukhtar' respectively.) Such Italian transliterations as 'Sef en-Nasr' and 'Hag ben Mohamed' are given as 'Saif al-Nasir' and 'Haj bin Mohammad' for the sake of English orthography and a questionable increase in accuracy.

This problem of transliteration is a bilateral one: an international oil company is known in Libya and the Arabic-speaking world as 'Bee-Bee' for the Arabic alphabet, while enjoying three variations on the letter 'H', has no 'P'; which also explains why the first Indian Prime Minister was once welcomed in Cairo as Bandit Nehru.

The Parts of Libya

All North Africa west of Egypt was known by the Ancient Greeks as *Libye*. Only once before this century was the name 'Libya' given to specific territories, when the emperor Diocletian created the Provinces of *Libya Superior* and *Libya Inferior* in northern Cyrenaica about the year A.D. 300. But Libya was always accepted as an alternative geographical expression to *Tripoli* or *Barbary* for central North Africa. It was in 1934, after the completion of the Italian conquest of Cyrenaica and Tripolitania, that the two Provinces were united as the colony of *Libia*, and the independent federal kingdom comprising Tripolitania, Cyrenaica, and Fezzan that was established in 1951 kept the name associated with the region since ancient times.

The kingdom of Libya (*Al-Mamlakah al-Libia*) has a Mediterranean coastline (for the most part exposed, featureless, and dangerous) of 1,200 miles. On the east it has a frontier of 800 miles with the United Arab Republic (Egypt) and on the west one of 250 miles with Tunisia and another of over 600 miles with southern Algeria. In the south-east there is a common frontier with Sudan, and in the south with the republics of Chad and Niger.

Libya lies across sixteen full degrees of longitude (9° to 25°) and more than fourteen of latitude (18° 45′ and 33°). With an area of 680,000 square miles, it is the fourth largest country in Africa; it is more than two and a half times the size of Texas and seven times bigger than Great Britain and Northern Ireland.

Ninety-five per cent of this vast area is classified as 'desert', part of which actually consists of featureless and dreary pre-desert steppe. The remaining 5 per cent is judged fit for 'economic use', but only one half of one per cent of the total land area is now cultivated, a proportion that could possibly be doubled. Settled farming is restricted by climate and availability of water to the coastal strips and the hill ranges of northern Tripolitania and Cyrenaica, and to some inland oases. There are no perennial rivers, and few streams.

In northern Tripolitania a fertile coastal strip, nowhere more than seven miles wide, and with a typical 'Mediterranean' climate, merges with the Gefara Plain, sometimes called a 'miniature Sahara'. The plain ends at the steep northern escarpment of the Gebel Nefusah, a range of hills rising no higher than 3,000 feet, which curves round to meet the sea at Homs. To the south the *Gebel* gives way to broken country, the Ghibla, which merges into the great stony plateau of the Hammadah al-Hamra. The *Hammadah* extends about 200 miles to the south until the level drops to the three great oasis-systems of western Fezzan, the Wadis Shatti and Ajal, and the Murzuk Depression, where water tables lie only a few feet below the surface.

The Gebel Akhdar (Green Mountain) of northern Cyrenaica rises in two narrow steps from the coast to a 2,000 foot high plateau, relatively well-wooded and fertile. To the east the hills fall away towards the Egyptian frontier across a barren, stony region, the Marmarica. Southwards, the land slopes into the Libyan Desert, the largest 'true' desert in the world. Cyrenaica has three main oases: Gialo, Giarabub, and the widespread Kufra group. In the far south of Cyrenaica and Fezzan the Tibesti Mountains form a barrier between Libya and Central Africa.

The settled areas in the north of the country are separated from each other by 300 miles of wilderness, the Sirtica, whose sands meet the waves of the Mediterranean. The Sirtica is one of the world's greater natural barriers and, until the building of the Libyan coast road in the 1930s, overland travel between Tunisia and Tripolitania, or Egypt and Cyrenaica, was easier than the journey across this 'abomination of desolation' between Tripolitania and Cyrenaica.

None of the hill ranges is high enough to upset the opposing climatic influences of the Mediterranean and the Sahara. Libyan weather is characterised by sudden, and sometimes violent, changes. In winter the northern coastlands can be miserably wet and stormy: the war correspondent Alan Moorehead, reporting the British advance across the uplands of northern Cyrenaica in the winter of 1941–2, noted a marked similarity of climate and scenery to the Yorkshire moors. Snow may fall on both the Gebel Nefusah and the Gebel Akhdar, and Sebha, in Fezzan, often records winter temperatures below freezing. Although the northern hills receive up to 20 inches of rain a year (compared with the London average of 23·5 inches) most of it falls between December and March. Showers are usually so short and heavy that most of the water floods straight off the land into the sea, carrying with it any fertile topsoil there may happen to be. Further south rainfall is scantier and more erratic, and in Fezzan the very rare storms, which melt the mud-brick buildings and cause sudden floods, are considered more of a curse than a blessing. Once in every five or six years a drought, sometimes lasting through two seasons, affects all, or most, of the country.

The hot, southern wind, the *Ghibli*, which is known as the *Khamseen* in Egypt and which reaches Italy as the *Scirocco* and France as the *Mistral*, may blow at any time of the year, but is most common in April, May, and June, and at the end of the summer. A classic *Ghibli*, bringing sand and dust with it from southern Algeria, can raise the temperature on the coast by 30 or 40° Fahrenheit in a few hours, hide the sun, destroy growing crops, and sprinkle layers of fine dust inside tightly-shuttered buildings. In Tripoli, the effects rarely last more than three days, but in Fezzan, where the discomforts are greater, there are some lugubrious adages about the disasters it is supposed to cause: 'If the *Ghibli* blows forty days – God preserve us from the evil! – the camel becomes pregnant without the intervention of the male.'[1]

Libyan summers are hot and, on the coast, humidity in August may rise to 90 per cent. The world's highest-recorded shade temperature, of 136° Fahrenheit, was registered at Azizia, on the northern edge of the Gefara Plain, in September 1932. But the northern hills, and particularly the Gebel Akhdar, are cool and breezy. For the greater part of the year the climate of Tripoli is idyllic and, taken as a whole, the climate of Libya is a healthy one.

Article Three of the amended constitution of 1963 describes the kingdom of Libya as 'a part of the Arab Home-Land and a portion of the African Continent', thus recognising the two main ethnic characteristics of the country. Libya is 'Arab' by virtue of its conquest by Arabs and adoption of the 'Arab' religion of Islam; the additional common factor that confers membership of the 'Arab Home-Land' on Libya, Morocco, Lebanon, and a dozen other states of North Africa and western Asia, but denies it to a country like Iran, is that the majority of their populations speak Arabic. Cyrenaica has actually been more genuinely 'Arab' than any other country

[1] Lethielleux, *Le Fezzan*, etc. Tunis, 1948.

outside the Arabian Peninsula since the eleventh century, when earlier inhabitants were overwhelmed by masses of pure Arab migrants.

Racially, Tripolitania is more truly 'a portion of the African Continent'. In the west the Arab newcomers mixed with, but did not submerge, the fairer-skinned Berbers, who have certainly been in North Africa since the end of the Old Stone Age. In Tripolitania small communities of Berbers live as settled farmers along the northern fringes of the Gebel Nefusah between Yefren and Nalut, and on the coast at Zuara; they make up an estimated 4 per cent of the total population of Libya. Among themselves they still speak Berber, a branch of the widely-spoken Hamitic language group to which Ancient Egyptian, Coptic, Somali, Galla, and Ethiopian also belong. Berber place-names are still common in areas where Berber is no longer spoken; they survive in Arabic-speaking Libya as Celtic place-names survive in English-speaking Britain. Many 'Arab' inhabitants of Tripolitania still show traces of their mixed Berber ancestry.

The population of southern Cyrenaica and Fezzan is mixed. There are people of Arab and Berber origin, as well as mixed and pure negroes, whose ancestors were brought from Central Africa as slaves.

The Tuareg, the race of desert warriors who reverse Islamic custom by wearing the veil while their women's faces remain uncovered, are thought to be descended from an ancient Fezzanese people, the Garamantes, or from refugees from Roman or Arab invasion. The oases of Ghat and Ghadames are outposts of the Tuareg homeland that covers western Fezzan and parts of the Sahara down to Timbuctu. The Tuareg are an aristocratic people, tall, lithe, and handsome. They speak a form of Berber and a high proportion is literate in the Tuareg script, *Tifinagh*. Their society is matriarchal and the nobles, who do no work, are expected to live by fighting; but the ending of the Saharan caravan trade and the pacification of the desert have taken away their livelihood.

The dark-skinned Tebu, who live in southern Cyrenaica and Fezzan, are believed to be descended from an ancient Saharan race. The Greek historian and geographer Herodotus recorded that the 'Ethiopian' troglodytes were 'exceedingly swift on foot' and that their language 'might be the screeching of bats'. The modern Tebu are also noted for their powers of endurance and, according to the eighteenth-century German explorer, Frederick Hornemann, the Tebu speech was described by Arabs as 'like the whistling of birds'.

It would seem that the same race of people had sweetened their language (now recognised as a Sudanic dialect) from bat-like to bird-like sounds in the twenty-two centuries between the Libyan visits of Herodotus and Hornemann. The Tebu are smallish people, svelte and lightly-built, and with almost aquiline noses, thin lips, and straight hair; they are Muslims, and many live in round huts with pointed roofs.

There is in all Libya no stranger or remoter community than the *Dawada*, the 'worm-eaters' who live, and have apparently lived for centuries, in three villages in the Ramla al-Dawada between the Wadis Ajal and Shatti in western Fezzan. Also known as 'The Forgotten of God', the 400 Dawada live mainly on a 'worm' found in three of several salt lakes that lie miraculously amidst the sand dunes. According to the writer James Wellard, who is one of the few outsiders ever to have visited the community, the 'worms' are a type of not unpalatable brine shrimp (*artemia salina*), which are mashed to a paste, formed into cakes, and dried in the sun ready for eating.

So very few people live in Libya that it is not only a desert country, but a deserted one. According to the Ministry of Planning's figures, 1,559,399 people were counted in the 1964 census, which gives an overall density of 2·3 people per square mile. (In 1967 the population was estimated at 1,700,000.) About 60 per cent of the population lives in the cities of Tripoli (235,000) and Benghazi (140,000) and fourteen other towns and large villages. There are over one million people in northern Tripolitania, but barely 70,000 in the whole of Fezzan, at a density of about one person per 3 square miles. Surprisingly, in a desert country, the combined nomadic and semi-nomadic populations account for perhaps one-sixth of the national total.

The Italians form the largest foreign community. Cyrenaica has very few, but in Tripolitania there are nearly 30,000. About 5,000 live on farms near Tripoli or Misurata, and the rest in Tripoli itself. Tripoli has a small, but long-established, Maltese community, and there are Greek communities in Tripoli and Benghazi. There are also thousands of foreign oilmen, businessmen, teachers, 'experts' and advisers, and their families, representing so many nationalities that when the first Venezuelan ambassador to Libya took up his post early in 1966 even he found himself at the head of a little community of his fellow-nationals.

Chapter 1

The Hunter-Artists

HISTORY has been imposed on Libya. It is a country many times invaded and occupied, but its people have rarely invaded or occupied other lands. Throughout the ages foreigners have settled in its wide, lonely spaces, or have used them as convenient battlefields. Libya has been more conquered than conquering, for there has always been *lebensraum* in this big, empty land. Foreigners were accepted; if they withdrew after a period of occupation, it was usually because other foreigners had evicted them.

The earliest recorded foreign settlement was by the Phoenicians. The founding of their trading stations on the coast of Tripolitania in the first millennium B.C. marks the first certain arrival of a known people, and a little history starts with it; some of the prehistory of Libya is to be read in the pictures drawn on the rocks in the desert interior of the country.

Some of the finest of all ancient rock-art is still to be seen in Libya. Literally thousands of pictures have been found at more than twenty sites. Most of these are in Fezzan: to the north of Brak: in the triangle Brak–Murzuk–Sebha; and in the Acacus and Tibesti Mountains. There is one site in Cyrenaica, near the borders of Egypt and Sudan, and four in the Tripolitanian *Gebel*. The significance of this rock-art was first recognised by the German explorer Heinrich Barth in 1850, but only in the past thirty years has it been studied in detail. There are so many drawings that not for decades will all the known sites have been examined and many more have surely to be found yet. After studying rock-art in the Acacus for ten years, the archaeologist Professor Fabrizio Mori estimated in 1966 that he could profitably spend another ten there.

The prehistoric artists worked on smooth, flat rock-faces, engraving deep, bold lines with sharpened flints. They drew from life the wild animals they hunted, and made up scenes of little naked men shooting arrows at huge beasts. Whether these pictures were intended to be merely decorative, and are therefore remote forerunners of the English hunting print, or whether they were some sort of graphic prayer for successful hunting, is not very important. What is striking is that all the animals shown are now found not in Libya, but in tropical Africa, many hundreds of miles to the south.

The ancient hunter-artists covered rock-faces with closely-observed, confident drawings of elephants, giraffes, crocodiles, rhinoceroses, hippopotami, and other animals that once lived in what has since become the greatest desert in the world. The Sahara (the word is Arabic for sand sea) is not old. Ten thousand years ago most of North Africa must have been an almost ideal centre of amenity for primitive hunting and food-gathering Man. The fauna and flora were probably similar to those of parts of East Africa today, with splendid herds of wild animals pasturing on open savannah and bush-country. Water must have been plentiful for the hippopotamus to have thrived there, and fossilised trees have been found in parts of the desert where no plant, let alone a proper tree, now grows. These fossils, much sought-after as 'conversation-piece' paper-weights in air-conditioned Tripoli offices, show how completely the climate and life of the country have changed.

Small groups of men must have prospered on the rich game lands and some had time enough to spare from the hunt to take up art and gouge on suitable rock-faces along the river valleys impressive portraits of the prolific wild-life all around. So far, next to nothing has been discovered of these hunter-artists' homes, but Saharan prehistory is a new study and much may yet be found. Certainly, that untidy character Early Man has scattered amazing quantities of his stone tools and weapons over parts of the country. The workmanship shows that by the end of the Old Stone Age, about 10,000 years ago, the people of Libya were members of a 'Mediterranean' brown-skinned, black-haired race, one among the many ancestors of the modern Libyans.

The early rock-art of Libya tells of a well-watered land supporting herds of wild animals with Man, the vegetarian and carnivore, living off both. But the climate and the land were slowly becoming drier and Man was passing through one of his great revolutions: he was ceasing to be a gatherer of wild plants and a parasitic hunter, and was learning to be a farmer and stockbreeder, a keeper and not merely a consumer of plants and animals. The results of this revolution were recorded by a new school of rock-artists. Domesticated cattle take their place in pictures alongside the 'traditional' subjects of wild animals. Cattle, some with collars, and often in big herds, are frequently shown, and there are occasional drawings of sheep as well. An ass-like horse is a rare subject; it is doubtful if he was domesticated and the true horse was not to appear from Asia until many centuries later. The men in the drawings are no longer naked, but wear animal skins and feathers.

As drawings of domestic animals became more frequent, so those of wild animals became rarer, for Man was taking over the best pastures and watering-places for his herds, and the wild animals were being driven off to find grazing and water where they could. Domestic animals, protected by Man, prospered at the expense of the wild. This process is being repeated in parts of Africa today as cattle pastures and cultivation spread out into traditional game-lands.

Beyond the swamps and river-valleys, wild animals would have found a land that was going dry and barren as a result of climatic changes at the end of the last Ice Age. Down the centuries the rainfall dwindled and the desert crept over bush and savannah. In trying to escape from this increasingly hostile environment, some wild-life slowly retreated to the 'good lands' to the south of the desert, which to this day support quantities of game. But many animals must have been cut off in shrinking islands of vegetation in the desert. The last survivors of this once prolific tropical life, a few frogs and an occasional crocodile, still exist in some oases and are dying out even now. The ostrich lived on for many centuries after other animals and birds had disappeared. Late rock pictures show that this bird flourished in the desert in Roman times, and it still survived in the early nineteenth century; but not since 1914 has a wild ostrich been seen in Libya. Large antelopes and giraffes managed to withstand the ever more desperate drought until early in the Christian era. Elephants, the rhinoceros, and the hippopotamus became extinct in Libya before that, although elephants were certainly living in Algeria and Morocco in the first centuries A.D.

Although wild-life was the first to suffer from this desiccation, domestic animals were eventually to fare no better. There came a time when rain was so rare and all surface water so scarce that even the river-valleys were too dry to support cattle. By the final centuries B.C. the animals of the pastoral people had largely died out or had moved on. Artists stopped drawing cattle as the herds disappeared from all but a few oases. The cow was replaced by hardier animals: the goat and, much later, the camel.

At the end of the Old Stone Age North Africa had been invaded and occupied by a brown-skinned race, closely related to other peoples scattered around the Mediterranean basin. A fair-skinned, fair-haired, blue-eyed people came in with later invasions and it was these 'white' Caucasians living in Africa north of the Sahara that the Greeks called 'Libyans'.

The name came from the Ancient Egyptian. Tribes of the deserts west of the Nile Valley are described as 'Lebu' or 'Rebu' in Egyptian inscriptions of the second millennium B.C. and centuries later the Greeks gave the name 'Libyan' to all the people of North Africa, apart from the Egyptians. The Greek name 'Ethiopian' ('the burnt-faced men') was applied to the Sudanese peoples living in and to the south of the great desert.

There were skirmishes and minor engagements between the armies of Old Kingdom Egypt and the desert tribesmen to the west not long after 3000 B.C. The Libyans made swift plundering raids into the Nile Valley. This was the old war between the pastoral nomad of the desert and the settled farmer on its fringes. To the XXIst Dynasty of Egypt the Libyans were a serious menace, but to the greater Egyptian dynasties they were merely a pest, to be dealt with by an occasional show of force in the form of a punitive expedition. Many hardy tribesmen of the Western Desert served with distinction in the New Kingdom armies on campaign in Asia.

Egypt had considerable economic and social influence on the primitive desert tribes. There was trade between the Nile Valley and the country to the west and south-west, where the people seem to have adapted Egyptian religion and burial rites to their own needs. It was through Egypt that a new animal, the horse, was introduced into North Africa about 1500 B.C. The domesticated horse had come to Egypt from Asia, and with it the chariot; both may well have come to North Africa together. The horse chariot was a formidable weapon and in the open desert it was to become supreme. From about 1000 B.C. onwards a race of Libyan herdsmen, the Garamantes, used the chariot to conquer other desert tribes and to build a loose empire in and beyond Fezzan: the Greek historian and geographer Herodotus tells how the Garamantes used to hunt the 'Ethiopian troglodytes' in chariots drawn by four horses.

There is a model reconstruction of one of these chariots in the Castle Museum in Tripoli. The model is of a bare skeleton of a vehicle. The two massive, six-spoked wheels were attached with pegs to a solid, unsprung axle. The driver and spearman balanced themselves on rough foot-holds chopped out of the top of the axle. Stout shafts, braced by a single cross-bar, were fixed to the axle. At the ends of the shafts, curved wooden collars fitted over the necks of the horses. Reins and harness passed through iron rings on the shafts and cross-bar and two horses were harnessed on both sides of each shaft. The full strength of all four must have been needed to drag the heavy, unsprung vehicle across country at speed.

In the first millennium B.C. the interior of North Africa must have been sadly depopulated, compared with three and four thousand years before. Negroes, who had moved northwards into the savannahs during the wet period, seem to have slowly retreated southwards again as the climate and land became drier. The wildlife had decreased, although in some *wadis* and oases there was still pasture for what Herodotus describes as the 'backward-grazing cattle' of the Garamantes. If these cattle moved forward across the pasture while grazing, Herodotus explains, the curving horns on the lowered heads would dig into the ground. The cattle overcame this embarrassment by stepping backwards while grazing, and the long horns merely scraped the earth. This account has been substantiated by rock-drawings of such cattle recently found in the desert.

Nothing is known of the origins of the Garamantes who herded the long-horned cattle on the dry grazing grounds of ancient Fezzan. It is likely that they had originally penetrated southwards from the coast, and it was probably they who introduced the horse and chariot from Egypt; iron-working was another wonder they may have brought to New Stone Age Libya.

In time, the Garamantes came to control the trade routes from the Mediterranean coast across the desert to Central Africa. They dominated the desert interior for well over a thousand years. The Phoenicians and Greeks who settled on the coasts traded through them, the Romans fought them and later became their allies. With their chariots, superior weapons, and organisation, the Garamantes were able to overcome other desert tribesmen, who were disorganised, unmounted, and armed only with Stone Age weapons.

Chapter 2

The Phoenicians

THE COAST of North Africa to the Phoenicians of 3,000 years ago, like the coast of West Africa to fifteenth-century Portuguese navigators, was a useful guide and a possible refuge on long journeys into the unknown. The Phoenicians were great sailors, but like all sailors of antiquity they would never willingly sail out of sight of land, or at night, or in winter. Phoenician merchants who first sailed westwards across the Mediterranean from Levantine ports to trade for the metals of Spain cautiously groped their way past the shores of North Africa, and the Portuguese *caravels*, seeking the sea route to the Indies twenty-five centuries later, hugged the coasts of West Africa almost as closely. Phoenicians and Portuguese alike considered Africa only as a useful handhold on long voyages through the unknown to distant sources of profitable trade, and not until later did they investigate the commercial possibilities of the continent.

With their practice of anchoring close in-shore or even beaching their ships at night, the Phoenicians soon found the few safe anchorages along the southern Mediterranean coast. In time, perhaps when ships were caught away from home at the approach of winter, temporary settlements were made at these anchorages and sailors were forced to turn farmers for the season. The Phoenicians, then, were the first known people to settle in Libya, if only seasonally at the beginning.

These settlers came from the centre of the eastern Mediterranean coast, roughly modern Lebanon and northern Palestine. They were a Semitic people, influenced by the earlier civilisations of western Asia, and they had that special talent for business that the modern Levantine has inherited. Their homeland, the narrow coastal strip squeezed between the Mediterranean and the steep Lebanon ranges, was surrounded by strong, aggressive neighbours and the Phoenicians expanded by the easiest route open to them, the sea. By 1000 B.C. they were active throughout the eastern Mediterranean; in time they sailed westwards to the Balearics and Spain; they may have

opened up a trade in British ores; later still, according to certain accounts, they sailed round Africa. The metals they brought from the western Mediterranean were then as much sought-after as were spices in medieval Europe, or as petroleum is today.

Phoenician ships began to put in regularly at the North African harbours while on voyages between the eastern and western Mediterranean. The settlements that grew up around these havens were at first simple victualling stations, like the original Dutch settlement at Cape Town, which was established to service East Indiamen at mid-point on the long voyages between Europe and the east. They were strongholds on small, easily-defended peninsulas overlooking a safe anchorage. But the Phoenicians were always ready to develop new business ties, and before long these settlements were busy trading posts. Carthage, on the coast of Tunisia, was traditionally founded in 814 B.C. by emigrants from Tyre and was to become a thriving colony, a greater commercial centre than Tyre itself, and eventually the capital of a line of Phoenician trading posts and colonies that spread westwards along the North African coast to the Atlantic and eastwards into Tripolitania.

At least three such posts were established on the coast of Tripolitania. A temporary one, which later became permanent, was founded at Sabratha. There was another at Tripoli (Phoenician Ui'at, later Oea) where a line of rocks and shoals extended from a peninsula to form a sheltered anchorage that could be readily defended from landward attack. Leptis Magna (Phoenician Lpqy, Lepcis to the Romans) was established on a small, sheltered estuary and was probably the most easterly of the permanent posts, although the town of Sirte, about 200 miles to the east, may have been founded by the Phoenicians.

It is not known when the Phoenicians settled permanently in Tripolitania. Sabratha may have been used from time to time from the eighth century B.C. onwards, but finds on the site suggest there was no permanent occupation until two or three centuries later. Settlements seem to have been made with the approval of the natives. The Phoenicians were more interested in trade than colonisation, and even when the settlement expanded into colonies the settlers and the native population seem to have co-existed successfully.

Phoenician civilisation was an offshoot of the older civilisations of the Near East and the Phoenicians acquired considerable sophistication through trade contacts with many lands and peoples. It was these traders who brought the international 'Mediterranean' civilisation of the first millennium B.C. to the backwaters of Tripolitania and the North African coast westwards. The primitive Berber tribesmen had so much to gain from the higher civilisation of the settlers. On the narrow coastal plains and in the terraced hills of their native Lebanon, the Phoenicians had developed an intensive and efficient agriculture, and they applied their knowledge on the broad coastal plains of North Africa with impressive results. They are credited with introducing the olive, the vine, the peach, the fig, and other Asiatic plants. It was with the olive, well-suited to the climate and light, sandy soils of Tunisia and Tripolitania that the settler-farmers had their greatest success.

The cities the Phoenicians founded thrived on trade and farming. The local influence of the great city of Carthage was tremendous; that of the settlements in Tripolitania must have been considerable and Sabratha was an object-lesson to the Berber tribesmen in ordered, civilised, and settled living. While the hinterland of Carthage in northern Tunisia virtually became a Phoenician province, with Berbers working the land for their foreign overlords, the same happened on a lesser scale in Tripolitania. Punic, a Semitic language, became the business, cultural, and administrative speech of coastal North Africa. Upper-class Berbers adopted Phoenician manners and culture, and the civilising influence of the colonies filtered out to the desert tribesmen, many of whom ceased to be semi-nomads and settled on the land as farmers.

By the fourth century B.C. the North African colonies had broken most of their links with the mother-country after a series of disasters had overtaken Phoenicia. The sacking of Tyre by Alexander the Great in July 332 was the final blow. Carthage, by this time a greater city than Tyre had ever been, carried on the traditions of the originally Asian Phoenician civilisation for a further two centuries.

The Carthaginians were as enterprising in business as the Phoenicians had been. From Carthage and from their towns along the coasts of Tripolitania, Tunisia, Algeria, and Morocco they carried on trade with Central Africa and around the central Mediterranean basin. They did not control the desert trade routes as they controlled the Mediterranean shipping lanes, and although the writer Athaneus says the Carthaginians crossed the desert regularly, it is more likely that untrusting merchants sometimes accompanied caravans from the Mediterranean coast to Central Africa. These merchants would have travelled as passengers, for the caravans would then, as now, be under the command of a native guide. The Carthaginians were content, wisely enough, to leave the desert transport business in the hands of the desert peoples, for the sea was the medium the Carthaginians knew and could best exploit.

The *Emporia* (markets), as the Greeks called the trading towns of North Africa, did not expand as Carthage did. They were tightly ruled by the capital and only in domestic affairs were they allowed any self-government. To maintain the trade monopoly, Carthage banned all ships but her own from North African waters. The *Emporia* were heavily taxed. They paid tribute to Carthage in cash or goods, customs dues were levied on them, and they were expected to provide the capital with troops during wars, or pay for the hire of mercenaries. Nevertheless, they managed to achieve moderate prosperity.

Goods were carried from Tripolitania to Central Africa by way of two great trade routes which met up about 250 miles south of Ghadames and continued as a single route to the River Niger. Sabratha, Oea, and Leptis had the advantage over other Carthaginian towns of being at least 100 miles further south, and therefore that much nearer to the inland markets of Africa. Travellers taking the shortest route from the Niger to the Mediterranean went via Ghadames to Sabratha. A series of rock-drawings of the Garamantes' chariots marks the great trans-Sahara trade routes from Fezzan to the Niger. The first series of drawings starts about 100 miles south of Ghadames and continues to the Niger, reaching it at a point about 150 miles east of Timbuctu. A second line of drawings runs southwards from Germa, the Garamantean capital in Fezzan, and joins the first line at a point about 300 miles to the south-west. The Garamantes carried the manufactured goods of the Mediterranean world deep into Africa and returned with silver, gold, tin, iron, and precious stones, and from the desert itself brought such products as ostrich feathers and dates.

The Carthaginians probably paid the caravan men either in cash, which would then be spent, sailor-fashion, in town before the caravan started out again, or in the form of perishable goods, such as food, drink, and clothing. Certainly, few objects imported from the north at this period have been found in the desert. From their capital at Germa, the Garamantes probably ruled a limited area of the desert, but as traders they probably dominated all the country from the Atlantic to the Nile and from the steppes of Sudan to the coasts of the Mediterranean.

Herodotus visited Libya about 450 B.C. He described the Greek colonies on the coast of Cyrenaica and listed the native tribes of the country in some detail. The tribal geography that Herodotus describes seems to have changed little between his day and Roman times. When he wrote, the desert must have been rather as it is now, although neither as extensive nor as barren, for the lions and other animals that lived in what he called 'the wild-beast tract' were numerous enough to be notorious. These animals have since been hunted into extinction by Man, and not starved out of existence by the desiccation of the land.

According to Herodotus, the Libyan tribesmen were pastoral nomads living off the meat and milk of their flocks and herds. Many of them were probably seasonal nomads who worked the land as farmers for part of the year. Hunting and gathering of insects, especially locusts, provided additional sources of food.

The Libyans were still making stone tools and weapons well into the Roman era, for metalwork of any sort was an imported luxury. Even the Garamantes, who had used the chariot for centuries, do not seem to have known the potter's wheel. Homes were either tents, crude stick and grass huts, or a series of rooms dug out of the earth like the surprisingly comfortable troglodyte dwellings still used in the Tripolitanian *Gebel*. Marriage in most tribes was polygamous and descent was traced through the mother. Nothing is known of tribal organisation. Tribes occasionally joined forces against a common enemy, but none of these weak, loosely organised federations lasted for long.

Religion was primitive. Herodotus says the only gods to which offerings were made were the sun and the moon. Funeral ritual and the cult of the dead were more elaborate and tombs of the Garamantes, in particular, have been found by the thousand. Religion seems to have become a little more polished under the influence of New Kingdom Egypt: the sun-worshipping eastern Libyans took enthusiastically to the cult of Amon-Ra, the Egyptian solar ram-god, when it was introduced in the sixth century B.C. A sanctuary of Amon-Ra, founded at Amonium (Siwa Oasis), was soon widely famed for its oracle.

The tribes known collectively to the Classical world as 'Libyans' lived in what is now Libya, Tunisia, Algeria, and Morocco and were the ancestors of the modern Berbers. Few in number, widely scattered across the vast bulk of North Africa, they had little culture; they were content to call themselves *Imazighen*, the free men. There were no centres of settled population, apart from the oases, and no cities until the Phoenicians and the Greeks established them. The steppes and deserts of North Africa were not suitable as a cradle of civilisation. There were no centres of amenity like the Nile Valley or the Mesopotamian flood-plain to support dense urban populations. At the same time, life was not so hard as in the rocky, narrow valleys of Greece that men were driven to migrate elsewhere.

Chapter 3

The Greeks

THE GREEKS have long been enthusiastic emigrants. Overpopulation, poverty, and other troubles have driven a hundred generations of them from their homeland in search of a better life in Asia or Africa, America or Australia. Cyrenaica was an obvious choice for early Greek settlement. Only 250 miles from the Peloponnese and under 200 miles from Crete, it was once a land as full of promise as was North America to European immigrants. Northern Cyrenaica, a shoulder of handsome country rounded by the Mediterranean, its well-watered, fertile highlands rising in tiers from the coast, its summer climate perfect and its winter tolerable, was literally a promised land to the first Greek migrants from the Aegean.

Legend quoted by Herodotus tells that Cyrenaica had been promised these first settlers by the Oracle of Delphi. The settlers came from the island of Thera, the modern Santorini, where overpopulation and a seven-year drought in the middle of the seventh century B.C. had caused much distress. Emigration was the only solution and, following the Oracle's advice, some 200 young men led by one Aristocles sailed to Africa with a Cretan guide and settled on the island of Plateia in the Gulf of Bomba. Aristocles, according to the legend, had asked the Oracle to recommend a cure for his stammer, and had been advised to found a colony in Libya. This would seem to have been typically irrelevant oracular advice had he not lost his stammer through the shock of suddenly meeting a lion soon after his arrival in Africa.

The settlement on Plateia was not a success. Two years after landing there, and encouraged by further advice from the Oracle, the Greeks moved to Aziris on the mainland. After six not very prosperous years there they were invited by local tribesmen to inspect a better site, that of the future city of Cyrene. Rainfall was plentiful for, as the Libyans pointed out, 'here the sky leaks': rainfall charts show the area of Cyrene as still the wettest part of Libya.

It was there, 10 miles from the sea, on a plateau 2,400 feet high, and beside a perennial spring that Cyrene was founded, traditionally in 631 B.C., and Aristocles, as Battus I, became its first king.

He was succeeded by his son, Arcesilaus I, who reigned for sixteen years, and he by Battus II Eudamon, during whose reign new immigrants began to arrive from southern Greece and the Aegean islands. The growth of the colony alarmed the neighbouring Libyan herdsmen, who were willing to share their grazing lands with the foreigners, but were not willing to be driven off them. Relations between the Greeks and the Libyans, which had been cordial, rapidly deteriorated. The Libyans turned to Egypt for help and in 570 B.C. the Pharaoh Apries (Ua Ha Bra) answered the call by marching into Cyrenaica with a great army. The Greeks won a surprising victory and Apries was killed; his successor improved relations with Cyrenaica by marrying a daughter of Battus.

The reign of Arcesilaus II marked the start of the senseless and seemingly endless internal quarrels that plagued Greeks wherever they settled, and about 560 B.C. dissident citizens of Cyrene founded the new city of Barce 60 miles to the west.[1]

Reforms by Battus III, son of Arcesilaus II, brought a period of political stability that ended with the accession of his son, Arcesilaus III. After being forced to flee the country, he recruited an army and reconquered Cyrene. Forced to leave again, he took refuge in Barce, but was strangled there.

In 525 B.C. Egypt was occupied by the Persians and queen Pheretina, the mother of Arcesilaus III, asked for their help in avenging her son's murder. The Persians invaded Cyrenaica, left Cyrene untouched, but attacked Barce. After a long siege the city was taken in 515 B.C. The invaders marched as far west as the site of Benghazi, but lost many men to marauding tribesmen on the way back to Egypt. Queen Pheretina later died, like Herod Agrippa, of worms.

As its most westerly and remote outpost, Cyrene was only nominally part of the Persian empire, but was forced to pay tribute and provide troops. When, after some years, Egypt drove the Persians out, Cyrenaica quietly regained its independence as well.

The city of Euesperides was founded about 515 B.C. by settlers from Cyrene or Barce. The site was beside a lagoon, latterly a salt

[1] Cyrene gives its name to Cyrenaica, and eastern Libya is still so called by Europeans. The Arabs know Cyrenaica as Barca, after Barce.

marsh, near modern Benghazi. No part of Libya is as rich in mythology, and near Euesperides were the supposed sites of the Gardens of the Hesperides, the River of Lethe, and Lake Tritonis.[2]

Other Greek cities had also been founded along the coast. Teuchira (Tocra) was the port of Barce; Tolemaide (Tolmayta) lay to the north-east; Apollonia (Marsa Susa) was the port of Cyrene. By 500 B.C. Apollonia had reached its greatest splendour and Tolemaide was rapidly developing.

Cyrene's seventh king, Battus IV (515–470 B.C.), came to the throne after the Persian invasion. He was succeeded by the eighth and last king of Cyrene, the unhappy Arcesilaus IV. The fate of the Cyrenean monarchy had been settled long before when the Delphic Oracle had warned that only eight kings, four named Battus and four named Arcesilaus, would rule over Cyrene. Most of the known actions of Arcesilaus IV during his thirty-year reign seem to have been performed in the hope of thwarting the Oracle's prophecy. The Oracle had its way in the end: Arcesilaus was assassinated at his 'safe' retreat of Euesperides, and a republic was declared at Cyrene.

During the early republican era the quarrels of the half-dozen Cyrenaican cities worsened. Each city was virtually an independent state and city matched itself against city; ever-changing alliances of cities bickered in endless and petty rivalry. But they managed to unite for war against Carthage which had always resented the Greek colonisation of Cyrenaica and Greek trans-Saharan trade. Although Carthage never officially recognised Greek trading rights in North Africa, trade between Carthage and Cyrenaica was carried on both by desert tribesmen and by Greek and Carthaginian merchants who used to meet quietly at Charax, a trading post on the Wadi Caam between modern Homs and Zliten.[3] But Carthage also interfered with Greek trade links with the interior and this commercial rivalry, coupled with a territorial dispute, worsened relations between the two states.

The territorial dispute between Cyrenaica and Tripolitania was at least settled, and in a way that makes good legend, even if the facts are suspect. After the founding of Euesperides, the Greeks had slowly penetrated south and west round the shores of the Gulf of

[2] The lake was the favourite home of the merman Triton, son of Poseidon.
[3] About 510 B.C. the Carthaginians destroyed a Greek colony only three years after its establishment in the Wadi Caam area.

Sirte and eventually made contact with Carthaginian patrols sent out from Tripolitania. There was no question of either side colonising the grim Sirtica desert region, but both wanted to control as much of it as possible as a buffer zone against the other. War was avoided when both sides acknowledged a common frontier.

Legend says the issue was decided by a running race. It was agreed that the frontier would be at the meeting point of two pairs of long-distance runners starting simultaneously from Carthage and Cyrene. The Carthaginian runners, the brothers Philaeni, had covered about three-quarters of the way from Carthage to Cyrene when they met the Greek team. The meeting took place near the most southerly curve of the Gulf of Sirte. The Greeks had plainly done so badly in the contest that they at once accused the Carthaginians of cheating. This the Philaeni denied, and offered to be buried alive on the spot on condition that it was recognised as the frontier. Both sides agreed and the Philaeni (the name means Lovers of Fame in Greek) were duly put living into their graves and covered with sand. Mounds, known as the Altars of the Philaeni, were raised over them, and the supposed site of the altars is still the frontier between Tripolitania and Cyrenaica. Mussolini had the towering Arch of the Philaeni built there and this landmark is now known by the name British troops gave it in the Second World War, Marble Arch.

Although the frontier agreement seems to have held good, there were no other grounds for accord between Carthage and Cyrenaica. The war that broke out between them about 500 B.C. was the most bitter Cyrene ever fought and all the cities of Cyrenaica seem to have supported her.

By the end of the sixth century the Cyrenaican cities had become important trade centres, although never on the same scale as Carthage. Cyrene traded with other Greek cities on the Mediterranean and in nearer Asia. Land trade with Central Africa was carried on through Augila, 150 miles south of Agedabia. From there, trade routes reached out south-westwards across the desert to Murzuk and south-eastwards to Siwa Oasis. Yet the real wealth of Cyrene came from the farms on the well-watered highlands of northern Cyrenaica. The Greeks, unlike many races past and present, considered farming honourable work. Within a century of the Greeks settling there, Cyrenaica was becoming famous for its agricultural produce, and Herodotus says that the land yielded three harvests a year.

The crops along the coastal strip were brought in first, then those in the coastal hills, and finally those on the plateau round Cyrene. Eight full months separated the first harvest from the last. The water supplies were tended as carefully as the crops and herds, and effective irrigation systems were devised. Every year the entire population had to turn out in a body to help destroy invading locusts and their eggs; those who failed to perform this duty earned the same punishment as army deserters.

Like the Carthaginians, the Greeks introduced new crops. Cyrenaica grew quantities of barley; corn and olive oil were exported and the apples of Cyrenaica were as famous as the saffron and essence of roses. The country supported great herds of sheep and cattle, and the horses were prized for their speed: 'breeder of flocks' and 'abounding in fleeces' were two ancient attributes of Cyrenaica, and even in the Middle Ages the Genoese were still importing the fine wools of the region, valued since the earliest times.

One product, above all others, brought Cyrene fame and fortune. The Silphion plant, at one time so important to the economy that it was shown on Cyrenean coins, is now utterly extinct and botanists have been unable to identify it. It was, ancient writers maintain, an excellent cattle fodder and a medicine; its sap cured the ills of men and animals and trees. It was valued as a flavouring, especially of fish dishes. Silphion was in demand throughout the ancient world, yet it was peculiar to Cyrenaica, where its export was probably a royal, and later a state, monopoly. There was a rival Asiatic plant, but the true Cyrenaican variety was always considered to be superior. By late Roman times it was becoming a rarity. Barbarian raiders, realising its importance to the economy, destroyed all they found. Farmers, forced to pay taxes on its growth, tore it up and fed it to their cattle.

By the beginning of the fifth century B.C., Cyrene was one of the greater capitals of the Greek world. The site was superb, with views down the terraced folds of the hills to the sweep of the coast and the sea, often so intensely blue as to be almost purple. Most of the public buildings were in the Doric style, in which the Cyreneans continued to build for hundreds of years, but the finest work, noble, chaste, and disciplined, was done in the fourth and early third centuries B.C. Even in ruins, Cyrene is still an example of Hellenistic architecture at its best. This must indeed have been Pindar's 'city founded on a golden crown'.

The city produced several brilliant minds, and although intellectually never up to the standards of Athens, it was acknowledged by Athenians and Greeks everywhere as a centre of high learning. Cyrene and Athens exchanged scholars and Plato himself helped to draw up Cyrenean laws. Later, when Alexandria became an intellectual capital, Cyrenean scholarship was well regarded there. The mathematician Theodorus lived at Cyrene, where there was a flourishing school of philosophy, founded probably by the Cyrenean Aristippus (435–356 B.C.). The city was a famous medical centre (the pure air and good climate probably effected the best cures) and there was at least one shrine of Aesculapius, the god of medicine, in the surrounding hills. The geometrician Eratosthenes was a Cyrenean, and Plato studied with, if not under, him.

Cyrene was as famous for its chariots as for the horses harnessed to them. Even the women, Pindar records, were beautiful.

Yet for all their ability and the resources of their country, the Cyrenaican Greeks never had the influence, either political or military, economic or cultural, they should have had. Cyrene, standing near important trade routes, could have rivalled Carthage, yet never did. Although they had a common religion, language, and culture, the cities of Cyrenaica were more or less politically independent of each other. What centralised authority there had been under the monarchy was lost when the republic was declared. Relations between the Greeks and the native Libyans were not particularly good. While Carthage kept her subject towns firmly under control, and at the same time co-existed with the Libyans, the Greeks were continually fighting the tribesmen, who sometimes took advantage of inter-city quarrels to invade Greek territory. The Libyans were taught many skills by the dull, stolid Carthaginians, but seem to have learned little from the Greeks.

In the autumn of 332 B.C. news of another invasion of Egypt reached Cyrenaica. The invader was Alexander the Great, then in mid-career of conquering the known world. In 331, after founding the city of Alexandria on the Canopus mouth of the Nile, he went into the Libyan desert to interview the Oracle of Zeus Ammon at Siwa Oasis. He was met on the way by a mission from Cyrene which presented him with chariots and horses. The world conqueror is said to have refused an invitation to visit Cyrene and, although he did not occupy Cyrenaica, he seems not only to have considered it one of his conquests, but also to have been planning the incorporation of more of Africa than Egypt alone into his empire. When he died in 323 B.C. at the age of thirty-three, the empire was broken into three parts. Egypt went to Ptolemy, one of Alexander's generals, and unrest in Cyrenaica gave him the excuse to annex the territory to Egypt.

The Ptolemies were not popular and there were at least two bitter revolts in Cyrenaica in the first twenty years after the loss of independence. But at least Cyrene had been given a constitution (there is a copy in the Cyrene Museum) that helped the city to settle its own political differences for the first time in generations.

Cyrene won back some of its freedom when Magas, the stepson of the first Ptolemy, became governor in 300 B.C. By 283 he was calling himself 'king' and nine years later he even tried to invade Egypt. After dominating Cyrene for fifty years, and becoming gross in the process, Magas died, suffocated by his own fat, as ancient writers claim. Accord between Cyrene and Egypt was renewed when the daughter of Magas, Berenice, married Ptolemy III. The union was celebrated by renaming Cyrenaican cities: the port of Barce became Tolemaide and Euesperides, as the new city of Berenice, was moved a mile or so to the site on which the centre of Benghazi now stands. It is after Ptolemy's Cyrenaican bride that Berenice's Hair in the night sky is called.

Cyrenaica as a whole prospered under the Ptolemies, and it was at this time that colonies of Jews began to settle there. After Apollonia, Berenice, Cyrene, Teuchira, and Tolemaide federated as the *Pentapolis*, or Five Cities, there was little further political trouble between them, but it was also under the Ptolemies that they were given defensive walls, most probably the first they had ever had.

In the 160s B.C. Ptolemy VII Euergetes and his brother Philometer, the joint rulers of Egypt, quarrelled. Philometer, after losing the throne to his brother, sought the help of an old ally of the Ptolemies, the Roman republic. Rome settled the dispute by reinstating Philometer in Egypt and giving Cyrenaica to his brother. Euergetes had by his Cyrenean mistress a son, Ptolemy Apion. Euergetes died in 116 and in his will, made years before, he left Cyrenaica to the Roman people, if he had no heir. He did in fact leave a legitimate heir, who took the throne of Egypt, while Apion became the last Greek ruler of Cyrenaica. He reigned for twenty years and on his death in 96 B.C. he, too, bequeathed the country to the Romans.

Cyrenaica indulged in a final twenty-two years of characteristic civil discord before being brought under the firm control of the Roman Senate with the appointment of Cornelius Lentulus Marcellinus as Governor in 74. During the Roman civil wars which broke out shortly after, Pompey's followers used Cyrene and Berenice as bases for their march across the Sirtica to join up with the main Pompeian forces in Tunisia. The Roman world was stabilised again after the Battle of Actium in 31 B.C. and so decisive was the battle that for three centuries afterwards the Cyreneans dated their monuments from it. Octavian came to power: with the title of Augustus he was to be the first of the Roman emperors. It may well have been a Cretan pilot who guided the first Greek settlers to Plateia 600 years before; it was with Cretans that the Cyrenaicans were to share their fortunes for the next 300 years, for Rome united Cyrenaica and Crete as a single province.

Chapter 4

The Numidians

TRIPOLITANIA became Roman through war. In 289 B.C. Carthage took Messina in Sicily from the Greeks and in doing so came into conflict with Rome, the major power on the Italian mainland. During the first Punic War (264–241 B.C.) a Roman fleet raided the Carthaginian cities on the North African coast, and Carthage lost Sicily. The Second Punic War broke out in 218 and Italy was invaded and terrorised by Hannibal. The war ended when the Romans landed in North Africa and defeated the Carthaginians at the Battle of Zama, on the modern Algerian–Tunisian frontier, in 201 B.C. Libyans fought on both sides in this campaign and the Romans probably only won at Zama because one Masinissa, head of the Numidian Massyli tribe, brought 4,000 horsemen into the battle on the Roman side at a decisive moment.

Masinissa was well rewarded for his help. According to the terms of the peace of 201 B.C., Carthage was to cede to him all lands that had ever belonged to him or his ancestors. To Masinissa, the terms justified his continual seizing of tracts of Carthaginian territory, to be added to the extraordinary Numidian kingdom he was creating. Masinissa was a leader of genius, and he had the ability to unite the primitive, nomadic Numidian tribesmen of the desert fringes into a great nation on the Carthaginian model. It was a formidable achievement, this making of the Sahara's first real native state.

The Carthaginians were powerless against Masinissa, for the peace terms did not allow them to make war without Rome's consent, and Rome tacitly approved the looting of land from the conquered enemy. About 165 B.C. he seized Tripolitania. Refused permission to hunt a rebel across what was still Carthaginian territory, he made war and occupied the Gefara Plain. When he started to besiege Leptis, Oea, and Sabratha, Carthage appealed to Rome for just treatment. A Roman senatorial commission settled the dispute by ordering Carthage not only to surrender the cities to Masinissa, but to pay him compensation for having failed to do so sooner! The cities had been powerless to resist him as they were wholly dependent on Carthage for their defence, and had no initiative of their own. Masinissa thereby gained all coastal Tripolitania, and by 161 his kingdom reached from western Algeria to the fringes of the Sirtica.

Ten years later the North African question reached a crisis. Rome was by then aware that the fiercely nationalistic Numidian kingdom was potentially as dangerous as Carthage had ever been and when, in 150, the Carthaginians in desperation went to war against Masinissa, Rome intervened. As Carthage had broken the terms of the peace of 201 by attacking the Numidians, Rome was technically justified in declaring war on her. But Rome also went to war to frustrate Masinissa's life-long ambition of making Carthage the capital of his kingdom. After four years of fighting and siege, Carthage was taken, the people were enslaved, and the great city was destroyed (146 B.C.). Remaining Carthaginian territory in northern Tunisia was annexed as the new Roman province of *Africa* to prevent Masinissa occupying it.

Rome thereby acquired her first small, and rather reluctant, hand-hold on the very tip of a strange and almost unknown continent. And if the sprawling Numidian kingdom was a potentially troublesome neighbour, it was also a bulwark against the roaming desert tribes to the south. Masinissa had died aged over ninety and Rome, in the first year of the final war with Carthage, had arranged for control of the Numidian kingdom to be divided between his three legitimate sons, with Micipsa taking the treasury, Gulussa the armed forces, and Mastanabal administering the law. The kingdom prospered in peace for a generation. The cities of Tripolitania, free from the cramping control of Carthage, became more mature and enterprising. They were far from the Numidian capital at Cirta, the modern Constantine in Algeria, and although they paid the same taxes they had paid to Carthage, they were otherwise self-governing. Growing trade with Italy brought them under Roman influence, but Tripolitania as a whole was still an undeveloped, thinly populated, and backward province.

Carthage had been destroyed, but what civilisation there was in the Numidian kingdom, and it was mainly confined to the cities, was Carthaginian. The old social and political systems continued unchanged. Religion, apart from the official abolition of human sacrifice, was Carthaginian. Neo-Punic, a development of the old Carthaginian speech, was the official language.

Micipsa, eldest son of Masinissa, became the sole ruler of the Numidian kingdom when his brothers died. More of a student than an administrator, he left most of the actual work of government to Jugurtha, his bastard nephew. Jugurtha was an able ruler and had great influence over the Numidian tribesmen. He persuaded his uncle to adopt him and when, in 118, Micipsa died, the kingdom was left jointly to Micipsa's sons, Adherbal and Hiempsal, and to Jugurtha. This 'troika' was not to last long. Jugurtha, beginning to show his true character, had Hiempsal murdered and went to war against Adherbal. Rome failed to make Jugurtha honour a compromise settlement. When Jugurtha killed Adherbal and, worse in Roman eyes, also massacred a number of Italian settlers, a Roman army was sent to Africa to bring the prince to heel.

Leptis Magna, and probably Oea and Sabratha as well, now risked shaking off Numidian rule by making an alliance with Rome, and Roman troops were sent to Leptis to suppress a pro-Jugurtha faction in the city. Although Tripolitania's role in the war was slight, the province was forced to supply Jugurtha with recruits. The war ended in 104 with Jugurtha's betrayal to the Romans and his death in Rome. Gauda, Jugurtha's half-brother, was put on the Numidian throne as a Roman puppet.

For the next fifty years Leptis Magna seems to have been the trusted friend and ally of Rome, and the Romans must have helped Leptis, Oea, and Sabratha defend themselves against desert raiders and the Numidians. Although the other two cities had followed the lead of Leptis in seeking friendship with Rome, they were nominally still part of the Numidian kingdom, which tried from time to time to bring them back under its control.

The cities' state of semi-independence ended in 49 B.C. when civil war broke out between Julius Caesar and Pompey. The reigning king of Numidia, Juba I, was a strong supporter of Pompey and Leptis Magna, at least, became involved with Pompey's cause when Juba's troops seized the city and forced it to supply troops and equipment. After Pompey's defeat at Pharsalus in 48 B.C. and his death, his followers rallied in Africa and Leptis became a base of the Pompeian forces. Julius Caesar landed in Africa late in 47 and the following year annihilated the Pompeian army.

Now came the reckoning. Rome annexed the Numidian kingdom as the province of New Africa (*Africa Nova*). The original Tunisian province became known as Old Africa (*Africa Vetus*). As a punishment for helping the Pompeian cause, Leptis Magna was made a subject city of Rome and was fined one million litres of olive oil a year. Probably not only Leptis, but Oea, Sabratha, and even Tripolitania as a whole, had to pay this heavy tax. Tripolitania had unluckily, and most likely unwillingly, supported the losing side in the civil war. Led by Leptis, the province had been on excellent terms with Rome in pre-war days; it was in thorough disgrace when, after the war, it became part of the Roman empire.

Chapter 5

The Romans

TO THE ROMANS, the only people ever to unite all the lands around it, the Mediterranean was *Mare Nostrum*, Our Sea, common to all the people of the empire. On the southern shore of *Mare Nostrum*, Roman Tripolitania matured for two centuries before entering into a brief golden age in the late summer of the empire. Nearly 4,000 miles of the North African coastal fringes became Roman just as Rome was becoming an empire. Augustus, the first emperor, put Africa under the rule of a proconsul, whose capital was at the rebuilt city of Carthage, and a new legion, the *Legio III Augusta*, was formed to police the long and troubled southern frontier of the otherwise remarkably peaceful province. For some 260 years this force, generally 5,000 men, with some auxiliaries, represented Roman military power from the Sirtica to the Atlantic, a situation similar to the more recent policing of extensive African colonial territories by small armies of native troops under European command.

From the beginning of their occupation the Romans were on the offensive against the desert tribes. When in 20 B.C. war broke out on the southern frontier, the Spanish-born proconsul of Africa, L. Cornelius Balbus, attacked the main source of trouble, the Garamantes. Setting out from Oea or Sabratha, he marched with his army first to Ghadames, 250 miles from the coast. This oasis, a junction of caravan trails, was an important Garamantean trade centre. The Romans, aware of its strategic and commercial value, made it an 'allied city', and it was for centuries an outpost of the empire. From Ghadames, Balbus marched 350 miles south-east to Germa, the Garamantean capital in the Wadi Ajal.

The Romans hailed the expedition as a great victory and Balbus was granted a triumph. In fact, Roman propaganda probably exaggerated the military successes, and the captured places, listed at length by Pliny, were most likely poor oasis villages, a few natural strongholds, and wells used by the desert nomads; only

Ghadames and Germa were real prizes. The tribesmen were an elusive foe and although the Roman forces may have killed at least 5,000, thereby meeting one of the conditions of being granted their triumph, there was probably no decisive battle. Balbus must in time have come to realise what another desert fighter, T. E. Lawrence, was to grasp 2,000 years later: that desert warfare is like war at sea; occupation of any area of sea or desert is meaningless so long as the enemy remains whole and undefeated.

The Balbus expedition was a show of strength by Rome, but it did not pacify the frontier, and the tribes continued to raid Roman territory. Five years after the expedition there was another big campaign against the Garamantes, and yet another in A.D. 6. The Garamantes also supported a later revolt, organised by a Roman army deserter, Tacfarinas, that kept the frontier in a state of uproar for eight years. The revolt ended with the capture of Tacfarinas in A.D. 24, and the Garamantes hastily sent a mission to the emperor Tiberius to beg pardon for having supported the wrong side.

While the empire was being shaken by the events of the year 68–9, when four emperors were proclaimed in quick succession, Oea and Leptis started a private war between themselves. The reason was officially given as the pilfering of one city's crops and cattle by the other, but the real cause was business rivalry, for there was always competition between the coastal cities for the greatest share of the Saharan and Mediterranean trade. Oea unwisely asked the help of the Garamantes, who were at that time active on the frontier. While the citizens of Leptis cowered behind hastily built defences, tribesmen invaded and devastated the surrounding countryside. Leptis was finally relieved by a strong Roman force under Valerius Festus, the Garamantes were driven off, leaving much loot behind, Oea was subdued, and peace was made between the cities. Festus then mounted a campaign against the Garamantes, but instead of following the route taken by Balbus ninety years before, he marched into Fezzan 'past the head of the rock', a phrase of Pliny's that despite much thought by scholars still tells nothing certain of the route taken. What is known is that Festus reached Fezzan four days faster than Balbus had done, caught the Garamantes unawares, and soundly beat them in battle. For more than a century after the Festus campaign there was peace, co-operation, and trade between the Garamantes and the Romans, to their mutual benefit.

The Garamantes, the most powerful of Roman Tripolitania's neighbours, were a mysterious race. The few ancient writers who mentioned them for the most part repeated the little that the two main authorities, Herodotus and Pliny, had to say. The Romans seem to have known next to nothing of the people beyond the southern frontier, and the first-century geographer Strabo admits his ignorance with the comment: 'For the most part the nations of Libya are unknown'. But knowledge of the Garamantes has been increased by modern archaeological research. Their homeland was the Wadi Ajal, a 100-mile long chain of oases on the southern edge of the Ubari Sand Sea, relatively fertile, protected by sand dunes, and ideally placed for the control of the Saharan trade routes. Their commercial empire stretched far across the desert south of the line Ghadames–Kufra, and possibly reached Lake Chad. In the oases and at the desert wells they built forts to protect the trade routes, and caravanserais for men and animals; presumably they policed the desert with their formidable four-horse chariots. The Garamantes were horse-breeders, and Strabo tells how they raised 100,000 foals in a year. They are also credited with digging the *foggars*, the underground water channels that still irrigate the gardens of the Wadi Ajal. Around Germa, the capital, almost 60,000 tombs have been counted; the actual total is far greater. The contents of excavated tombs show that the Garamantes prospered on trade with the Romans from the late first century onwards and came under the cultural influence of Rome, using Latin script alongside their own *Tifinagh*. Germa was a surprisingly large town of stone buildings, in contrast to the mud brick now in use, and Garamantean rulers were buried in large tombs, two-step pyramids of stone, in which the corpse was supplied with moderately rich trappings for use in the after-life. The Garamantes carried across the desert the manufactured goods of the Roman world, which they traded with the peoples of western Sudan for slaves, gold, and ivory, ostrich feathers and hides, and wild beasts for the games in the arenas of the empire. From the Sahara itself they exported salt, a necessity rarely found in the Sudan, and which the Sudanese bought with alluvial gold.

It was almost certainly in company with their Garamantean allies that the Romans made two expeditions deep into the Sahara, and even beyond, late in the first century. The first marched south for three months until it reached 'the land of the Ethiopians', which might have been anywhere in north Central Africa. The second, which may have been a trade rather than a military mission, pushed southwards until it reached 'Agysimba' where the rhinoceros roamed, presumably deep in the Sudan.

The Romans completed the occupation of all northern Libya in A.D. 85–6 when they overcame a revolt by the great Nasamonian tribe living in eastern Tripolitania and along the Gulf of Sirte. The tribe was driven into the desert and the emperor Domitian was able to claim that the Nasamonians no longer existed; the opening of a safe land route between Tripolitania and Cyrenaica probably dates from this time.

For all his acquired sophistication, the Roman never lost his peasant-like love of the land. Under the empire the farmlands of Tripolitania reached a level of prosperity equalled neither before nor since. With their amazing capacity for hard work and, more telling, their ability to organise and direct the work of others, the Romans made Tripolitania a moderately rich province that sent huge surpluses of olive oil to Italy. The province was not a granary of the empire, for little corn was exported. But the remains of Roman olive oil presses tell of a vast output of low-grade oil used not for cooking but for lighting and cleaning.

It is now believed that the spread of the desert over the farmlands of North Africa from the third century onwards was not due to climatic changes. Two thousand years ago North Africa was as dry, or nearly so, as it is today. But the tendency of the desert to spread was checked by the Romans' careful treatment of the light, sandy soils, and by water collection and conservation schemes on a wide scale; when later these defences collapsed the desert, held back for centuries, broke through with greater effect than ever and farmland that had supplied oil for an empire became a vast dust-bowl. Water holds back the desert and across the *wadis* of the Tripolitanian hinterland dams were built; fine pieces of hydraulic engineering, they were sited to check the heavy, irregular rushes of storm-water and lead them off into storage basins and cisterns. Silt brought down by the floodwater was collected and built up into terraced fields. Underground water was raised through wide, stone-lined wells and most buildings had means of collecting rainwater from the roof and storing it in tanks.

The economy of Roman Tripolitania, like that of Greek Cyrenaica, was agricultural and was enriched by Saharan trade. There were few Italian colonists, for with the population of Italy actually decreasing, there were no surplus peasants to send to North Africa as settlers. Under the early empire the land was farmed by Berber peasants and by smallholders, many of them ex-soldiers who had been granted plots of land on retirement. But, in time, taxation tended to force the small farmer off the land and increasingly large areas became the property either of the state or of fewer and greater landowners. The big estates were worked by gangs of landless Berber serfs whose only benefit from Roman rule was the better organisation of their labour and who, under the later empire, were to become a dangerously subversive element in North African society.

Life was different in the cities. The Roman empire has been called 'a federation of municipalities' and the Tripolitanian townsmen derived more benefit from Roman rule than the countryman. There grew up an urban élite, a well-mixed society of Italians and Romanised Afro-Phoenicians. The Romans rarely interfered with local government or daily life and Carthaginian customs were observed in the cities where Neo-Punic was more usually spoken than Latin. Apuleius wrote that his son-in-law, of a good Oea family, neither knew Latin nor wished to know it, and this was not a rare case. The old Carthaginian religion was still followed in the country and in the towns.

The Roman development of the cities of Leptis, Oea, and Sabratha started at the time of Augustus. In due course they were made 'free cities' and started to mint their own rather crude coinage. By the end of the first century A.D. they must have had an 'international Roman' appearance and atmosphere, and public buildings were faced with Italian marble imported as ballast in the oil ships. The wealth of the cities was not the result of an economic boom, but had been built up through decades of painstaking work. The cities dominated the countryside. The three ports had no rivals and the name 'Tripolis', the Three Cities, was first used at the end of the second century.

Probably no part of the empire gained more than Africa from the *Pax Romana* of the first two centuries A.D. There was a quickening of life and intellect as waves of 'foreign' influence washed across *Mare Nostrum* into such cultural backwaters as Tripolitania. During the Golden Age of the second century, when nearly every part of the empire was peaceful and prosperous, the wellbeing of

Tripolitania was undisturbed. For three or four generations no writer recorded any troubles there; indeed there was little to say about this model and very provincial province.

For generations, Jews had been migrating into Cyrenaica where, with Libyan converts, they formed communities of solid and valued citizens. Many more came in after the destruction of Jerusalem in A.D. 70. The end of the first century was a time of unrest among Jewish communities everywhere, and in Cyrenaica a wandering Jew named Jonathan stirred up much trouble. He was arrested and later executed in Rome. The harsh treatment of his followers, among them many leading Jewish citizens, caused strong and lingering anti-Roman feeling. In 115 the Jews of Cyrenaica began a general revolt, organised on military lines, and it rapidly spread to the large Jewish communities in Egypt and the Near East. The effects of the year-long rebellion were felt all over the empire and it is said that the transfer of troops to put it down caused the loss of newly-won lands in the east and revolts by tribes on the Danube and in Britain.

The Jews took over Cyrene and raged through the holy and venerable city in an orgy of vandalism and energetic destruction. Many of the oldest and finest buildings were reduced to rubble. Troops under Marcius Turbo were sent to stamp out the revolt, and Cyrene was recaptured. The Romans crushed resistance mercilessly, for they were weary of the troubles caused by this 'hot-headed race', as a contemporary writer called the Jews. Almost 250,000 people are said to have died in the revolt in Cyrenaica alone, and the damage was such that the country never fully recovered.

The emperor Hadrian took a personal interest in the reconstruction and was for some time hailed as the 'founder' of Cyrene. Troops were settled on abandoned farmland and others were sent to the new city of Hadrianopolis, between Benghazi and Barce. Cyrenaica made a slow, half-hearted recovery, but not for seventy or eighty years were some of Cyrene's public buildings restored; others were never rebuilt. The country was still convalescing in an age when Tripolitania and the rest of the Roman world were 'on holiday', as the second-century Greek rhetorician Aelius Aristeides enthused in his *Encomium of Rome*: 'If there are still unhappy people, they are those not included in the Empire....'

*

Writing in the 1930s, the Italian historian Roberto Paribeni said of Libyans ancient and modern: 'While we make our [Libyan] subjects petty officials, drivers and janitors, the Romans raised one of their provincials to the Imperial throne.' The 'provincial' was Septimius Severus, one of the few great rulers of the later empire. He was born into an upper-class Romanised Libo-Punic family at Leptis Magna in A.D. 146, and was proclaimed emperor by the troops he commanded in Pannonia in 193. He was both a Roman and an African. Stories are told of his liking for African vegetables and cooking, and of how he spoke Latin with a strong Punic accent.

While troubles were menacing many parts of the empire at the end of the second century Africa, and particularly Tripolitania, were enjoying the personal attention of the emperor, and rose to their most prosperous state under his rule. Africans took important posts in the administration and the army, and Punic, as well as Latin, was spoken at court. The emperor visited Leptis in 203 and while there mounted a campaign against the desert tribes that had invaded Roman territory for the first time in a century. This was perhaps the first slight but ominous sign of the dangerous new mood of restlessness that was to drive the desert peoples on their invasions of the coastal belt in generations to come. After defeating the invaders, the emperor ordered a complete reorganisation of the southern defences. Tripolitania was given more independence and the cities were granted new privileges.

Septimius Severus made Leptis one of the foremost cities of the empire. The great African port, developed during one of Rome's last outbursts of energy, became a model of the Severan achievement, the fusing of the cultures of Roman Africa, Europe, and Asia. Some of the late work at Leptis looked far ahead. New ideas in sculpture were tried out. Some *avant-garde* panels on the Severan Arch, hastily built in honour of the emperor's visit in 203, anticipated Byzantine style and composition. Sculptors from Asia Minor, working with African assistants on both the arch and on the pilasters of the Severan Basilica, put a novel emphasis on light and shade by deep incutting, with results as close to medieval as to classical sculpture. The aristocratic colonnaded street that Septimius Severus made the main thoroughfare of the new Leptis recalled streets of Roman cities in Syria. The Severan Forum and the attached Severan Basilica were superb examples of late and already decadent Roman building. The harbour of Leptis was remodelled and protected by colossal stone breakwaters. Ships of up to 1,000 tons unloaded onto wharves provided with colonnaded warehouses; at night mariners were guided into port by a great beacon atop a one-hundred foot lighthouse. Septimius Severus has been criticised for overdeveloping, for prestige purposes, a city neither great nor wealthy enough to justify its being turned into a lesser Rome. He died in York in 211, but his work in Tripolitania was carried on by his son and successor, Caracalla (211–17), and Alexander Severus (222–35).

Tripolitania is not easily defended from invasion from the south. Even the Gebel Nefusah is not rugged enough to stop invaders who, should they cross the hills to the final northern escarpment, may then dominate the Gefara coastal plain. For the first two centuries A.D. Rome had defended the province mainly by bold attack. Flying columns moved deep into the desert to disperse tribesmen wherever and whenever they massed for possible raids into the settled lands. Later, this simple, aggressive strategy was not enough to counter the increasing pressure of the tribes on the long, open frontier. Septimius Severus therefore started a new defensive system that Caracalla and Alexander Severus continued and that was completed in 238 when the *Legio III Augusta*, after defending the frontier for 250 years, was disbanded.

Since there were no natural lines of defence on the southern frontier, the Severans made artificial ones, the *Limes*, which were a co-ordinated system of static defence in depth, intelligently adapted to the lie of the land and to the main lines of communication. Both Septimius Severus and Caracalla pushed the vague imperial frontier southwards, the first time in over one hundred years that it had been moved. That this was done at a time when strategic withdrawals were being made on many frontiers of the empire shows just how much importance the Severans attached to their desert defences.

The *Limes* were organised in successive lines of defence. Along the actual frontier were built three great strongholds to control the movement of men, animals, and goods to and from Roman territory. One was at Bu Najim, on the road from Leptis to Fezzan; a second fort at Gheria al-Garbia controlled the wells of Al-Tabunia which were a vital halt for caravans on the direct north–south route from Oea to the Garamantean capital at Germa; a third was built at Ghadames, on the great trans-Saharan trail ending at Sabratha.

North of the outposts was the core of the *Limes* system, the *Limitanei* settlements. Alexander Severus had encouraged the system of granting tax-free holdings near the frontier to army veterans at the end of their service in Africa. These hardy, fighting frontiersmen were both farmers and defenders of the land. Ruins of their fortified farms, austere, cube-shaped stone buildings, still stand on the eastern ranges of the Gebel Nefusah, along the great Wadis Sofeggin and Zemzem and their tributaries, and in the Sirtica coastal area. The biggest-known *Limitanei* settlement was at Ghirza on the Zemzem, where there are the remains of at least thirty large farms. There, and at other sites on the desert fringes, still stand many of the funerary monuments, most of them of a gargoyle ugliness, built by the *Limitanei*.

The *Limes* system of three concentric lines of defence was completed by a road, 605 Roman miles long, following the crescent curve of the *Gebel* from Tacapis (Gabes) in Tunisia, to Leptis Magna, and enclosing most of the best farmland in Tripolitania. It was built primarily for the fast lateral movement of troops at the rear of the main lines of defence.

For over a century this well-organised system protected the fertile heartlands of Tripolitania from outside attack. A less elaborate *Limes* system in Cyrenaica relied mainly on castles placed at strategic points, and on garrisons in the larger towns.

Chapter 6

Christians and Barbarians

THE SPAN BETWEEN the formal Roman annexation of Tripolitania and the Vandal conquest was about 470 years, or roughly the same length of time that Europeans (Vikings excluded) have known America. For 150 years, perhaps for two centuries, Tripolitania lived under a genuine and fairly benign *Pax Romana* while Cyrenaica, having lost much of its old personality and *joie de vivre*, was not a very happy part of the empire.

Early in the third century Africa started to show symptoms of the vague but awful malaise that was spreading through the empire. There were many complex causes, properly understood neither then nor now, for the long vigorous decline of Roman Africa after the Severan Golden Age, but what was remarkable was how the African provinces continued to hold together for a further 200 years.

Tripolitania, a minor and remote frontier region, was one of the first parts of the empire to be harmed by the fifty years of general chaos that followed the murder of Alexander Severus in 235. The main wealth of the country was in the farmland won from the fringes of the desert, but only under good and regular government could it be given the exacting care it needed if the desert was to be held back. In Tripolitania, as in Cyrenaica and throughout the empire, there was economic collapse, wild inflation, a slump in trade, and crippling taxation. The upper classes moved from the cities to country estates that in time tended to become almost independent communities, while Roman urban civilisation declined. Leptis, first among the Tripolitanian cities, suffered most, for its wealth had never been as great as the architectural and other splendours flaunted under the Severans had implied. The city was soon in serious economic straits. The great public buildings were not kept up and by the year 300 many were in ruins. A special tax overseer was appointed to the city in 238, a sure sign that citizens were having more trouble than usual in paying their dues. A similar official was appointed to Oea later in the century, but Sabratha's economy was more resilient and, surprisingly, demand continued for the trans-Saharan luxury goods that were still being exported through the port of Sabratha at a time when shipments of staple produce from Leptis were actually declining.

At the turn of the third and fourth centuries the emperors Diocletian and Constantine gave the empire fifty years of order, and one of their reforms was to make Tripolitania a separate province, extending from the traditional frontier with Cyrenaica to the Shott al-Gerid salt lake in modern Tunisia. Diocletian ended the 300-year-old link between Crete and Cyrenaica as a single province. The *Pentapolis*, and with it the north Cyrenaican plateau, was renamed the province of Upper Libya, with Tolemaide its capital, and the mostly barren coastlands between Derna and Alexandria became the province of Lower, or Dry, Libya.

Christianity came to Libya, and particularly to Cyrenaica, in its very early years, but not until the late empire had it become well established. Simon of Cyrene helped carry the Cross to Calvary and Cyrenaican Jews, the 'inhabitants of parts of Libya about Cyrene', were among the crowd of many nations who heard the Apostles preach 'with divers tongues' in Jerusalem after Pentecost. Jews of Cyrene took part in the dispute with, and the stoning of, St Stephen the first martyr. Lucius, a Cyrenaican Jew who was in Antioch when Paul and Barnabas started their mission there, was traditionally the first bishop of Cyrene. There is a legend that St Mark, the founder of the Alexandrine Church, made a missionary journey to Cyrenaica, and the Muslim Berbers of the Gebel Nefusah have a tradition that Tripolitania and the lands to the west were evangelised by St Philip the Apostle. Both stories are probably untrue, and the nearest any Apostle is likely to have gone to Libya was St Paul when he was shipwrecked on Malta.

Word of the new faith, and actual converts, reached Cyrenaica as a result of local Jews' many contacts with Palestine and Syria, and arrived later in Tripolitania from both Cyrenaica and Rome. Most early converts were made among members of the large Jewish communities. As their numbers grew, the Cyrenaican Christians periodically 'purified' the pagan temples of Cyrene and other cities with typical Judaeo-Hellenic zeal, in many cases completing, or repeating, the damage done during the Jewish revolt of 115.

By the reign of Septimius Severus Christianity had become a considerable movement in Roman Africa, but Tripolitania played a minor part in its development. There were no great Tripolitanian Fathers of the Church and there are no records of Tripolitanian martyrs. Catacombs found at Sabratha and Sirte may or may not have sheltered Christians during persecutions. The influence of the new religion on the un-Romanised, Libo-Punic Tripolitanians was far less than on other North Africans. Archaeus of Leptis is the first known Tripolitanian bishop, and he was not consecrated until the end of the second century. Four Tripolitanian bishops, those of Oea, Girba (modern Jerba in Tunisia), Leptis Magna, and Sabratha, were among the eighty-five from all Africa who were called by St Cyprian to the Council of Carthage in 256. Records of attendance, or representation, at councils of the African Church over the next 150 years show that no new bishoprics were created in Tripolitania, yet during that period the total number of African bishoprics rose to 690. Only three bishops of Upper Libya, those of Berenice, Teuchira, and Barce, attended the Council of Nicaea in 325, although there were by then many urban and rural bishoprics in the province. Among the few known Cyrenaican martyrs was a bishop of Cyrene who died during the persecutions of Diocletian.

It was after the emperor Constantine in 313 recognised Christianity as the official religion of the empire that the Donatist schism started to split the African Church, although in Tripolitania the split was narrower than in other parts of north-west Africa. The Donatists held that Christians who had lapsed during persecutions could be readmitted to the Church only after a second baptism. The Catholics took the opposite view and the result was the development of two rival Churches, each complete in its separate organisation, but with no doctrinal differences. In time, the split widened into a political one and while the conservative Catholic Church, which condoned slavery and other of what are now considered social injustices, became the official Church of the Roman establishment, the Donatist Church tended to attract anti-Roman elements, colonists, small landowners, dispossessed Berbers, and other malcontents. They joined the Donatist Church less out of religious conviction than as a gesture of revolt against the totalitarian Roman state that overtaxed and exploited, apparently without conferring any benefits in return. The Donatist revolt was put into action by the *circumcelliones*, meaning not 'those who prowl round barns', as many authorities have it, but 'those who prowl around shrines', that is, the martyrs' tombs where food was handed out to them. This extremist sect of outlaw terrorist gangs burned and looted Catholic and pagan farms alike. This was the revolt of the Berber peasant landworker, or serf, against the Roman, or Romanised landowner, that helped to ruin the North African countryside, but never achieved complete revolution. Donatism was not only a rural movement. Of the Tripolitanian cities, both Oea and Leptis were represented by Donatist bishops, and Sabratha by a Catholic, at the Council of Carthage where in June 411 St Augustine had the Donatists formally condemned as heretics. The Donatist schism hardly touched Cyrenaica, but other heresies, including the Arian and the Sabellian, had a following there.

The Sirtica Desert is one of the more fearsome quarters of this earth, although its reputation is worse than the reality. The Ancients imaginatively filled it with 'a numerous host of monsters dire', but not so much with perils in human form. This was an oversight, for it was the barbarous tribes of the region who raided, but never wholly conquered, both Roman Tripolitania and Cyrenaica. In the summer of 363 Tripolitania was invaded by the Austurians, a large tribe, or group of tribes, whose homeland was almost certainly in the Sirtica. They lived, an ancient writer noted, by 'robbery and slaughter', but knew the value of reconnaissance and subversion in preparing their campaigns. Their first attack on Tripolitania was supposedly to avenge the execution by the Romans of an Austurian *agent provocateur*. The barbarians were not opposed by the panic-stricken farmers, and they spent days roaming the country around Leptis, smashing, burning, and looting. Great walls, completed a few years earlier, kept the invaders out of the city, but the unprotected suburbs were ravaged.

The fine *Limes* system, built up over the previous 150 years, had not kept the barbarians out, for the *Limitanei* had let the invaders pass unchallenged. The people of Leptis were helpless against future invasions, and they asked count Romanus, commander of the Roman forces in Africa, for protection. He marched to Leptis in strength but demanded as his 'fee' for driving off the Austurians quantities of stores and 4,000 camels. These the citizens were unable to deliver and Romanus left the city to fend for itself. Appeals to the emperor brought no satisfaction, and such by then was the rottenness of Roman government that blackmail and bribery prevented the investigation of Tripolitania's case.

In the autumn of 365 the Austurians invaded again, pushing across the country to Oea, and possibly as far as Sabratha. During a third invasion the following summer they made the country around Leptis a wasteland by cutting down trees and destroying vines and other crops. The city was besieged for eight days, but was again saved by its walls. No further Austurian invasions are recorded, one likely explanation being that the barbarians, having moved permanently with their flocks into the Gefara coastal plain, needed to invade no more. Thereafter, there was little contact between the coast and the semi-Romanised farmers living in the Gebel Nefusah and on the *Limes* settlements in the great *wadi* system to the south-east.

Christianity started spreading through the Gebel Nefusah in the late fourth century, with the Donatists claiming the majority of converts. By the fifth century there were scattered across the hills and the pre-desert lowlands large, vigorous, and mainly Christian communities, so isolated that they had their own ecclesiastical organisation and a social and economic system that foreshadowed medieval European feudalism. These communities, whose sculpture and monumental architecture were gross but energetic, achieved a crude prosperity at a time when the coastal cities were becoming semi-deserted ruins.

Leptis lost its main source of income when the Austurians cut down the olive-trees that took fifteen unproductive years to mature. After years of physical and moral collapse in the late third century, the city had been partly restored in the first half of the fourth. Public buildings had been repaired and the great walls that kept the barbarians out were raised. But after the Austurian invasions Leptis sank faster than before. The population, which may have risen to 100,000 in the period of the Severan Dynasty, fell to a few thousand. Buildings still in use were not repaired and, as the ruined fields turned to semi-desert, drifting sand slowly heaped itself up against the city walls. Because there was no maintenance, the diversionary dam on the Wadi Lebda burst, the waters returned to their old course, spilled through the centre of the city, and filled the wide harbour with silt and rubble. At the end of the fourth century St Girolamus was calling Leptis a 'half-barbaric city'.

*

In 365, an earthquake jolted Cyrenaica and the whole of the eastern Mediterranean, toppling venerable buildings at Cyrene, where crushed skeletons have been found beneath fallen masonry. Even the task of clearing up after the earthquake was too great for the demoralised citizens, and although parts of Cyrene were painstakingly rebuilt, the horror had shocked much of the life out of the ancient city. More disasters pressed on the land: locust swarms darkened the sky; desert barbarians attacked the cities and overran the country estates. The Austurians started invading Cyrenaica in 395 and the province, like Tripolitania thirty years before, was left with no formal defence when the *Limitanei* failed to stand against the invaders. There were three main Austurian invasions, each lasting for three or four years. Cyrene itself was attacked in 405, and in 410 the barbarians pushed right across the mountains to the sea and the provincial capital at Tolemaide.

When, in 399, Synesius of Cyrene went to Constantinople to present the traditional golden crown to the new emperor, Arcadius, and to beg for a reduction of taxes, he reported: 'Cyrene, a Greek city, and one whose venerable and holy name the wise men of olden times praised in a thousand odes, is now poor and wretched, a pitiful ruin...'

Synesius was a rare and excellent man, the only one in the history of Roman Cyrenaica who stands out as a figure of his age. His writings (Gibbon calls him 'the polite and eloquent Synesius') have endured on their own merits, and not because their author was an early Father of the Church. He was born about 370 into a family claiming descent from Cyrenaica's first Greek colonists. He became a scholar in the best pagan Greek tradition; he was also a soldier, a gentleman landowner, and a nobleman of the Roman world. In 410 the bishop of Tolemaide and primate of Cyrenaica died and Synesius was appointed to the vacant see, although at the time he was married, had three sons, and was not even a baptised Christian.

His many surviving letters tell of a Cyrenaica still prosperous and beautiful, but shocked by waves of natural disasters and barbarian invasions. Before becoming bishop, Synesius and other landowners had organised a sort of home guard, and had fortified their country homes against the invaders, since there was no longer an effective frontier defence system. As primate of Cyrenaica, Synesius defended his people against the corrupt bureaucrats who were exploiting them. He yearned for the countryside, since civilised life had ended in the cities, and perhaps the most peaceful and stable communities in Cyrenaica in his lifetime were the simple, bucolic tribes on the southern and eastern desert fringes. By the time he died in 414, his country's horizons had greatly narrowed. Egypt and Constantinople were the centres of a smaller world. The city of Rome, which Synesius never mentioned in his writings, and indeed the whole of the western empire, were forgotten, as Cyrenaica itself was probably forgotten in the west.

Chapter 7

Vandals and Byzantines

ROMAN NORTH AFRICA west of the Sirtica was overrun early in the fifth century, not by the desert tribes who had been tormenting it for 200 years, but by semi-barbarian invaders from Europe. The Vandals were a Germanic people, followers of the great Arian heresy of Christianity, who had acquired a little civilisation during their migration across France and temporary settlement in Spain, which the Arabs later called *Andalus* after them. In 429 count Boniface, the *comes Africae*, rebelled against imperial authority and invited the Vandal king, Geneseric, to come to Africa and support him. Geneseric landed in Morocco with 30,000 of his fighting men and 50,000 women, children, and old people. Some months later, Boniface ended his quarrel with Rome, but the Vandals would not return to Spain. Instead, Boniface was forced to flee, leaving the Vandals at large in Morocco and, like other barbarians called to fight within the empire at that time, Geneseric seized for himself the lands he was supposed to be defending. At the end of ten years of hard campaigning, he took Carthage and, although recognised as a 'tributary king' of the empire, he continued his offensive. In 455 his fleet landed at Ostia, Rome itself was sacked, and Tripolitania was occupied at about the same time, although Vandal authority was limited to the coastal cities. The walls of Leptis and Sabratha were demolished, but those at Oea were left standing, and the city's ascendancy over its two ancient rivals was assured from then onwards.

The Donatists welcomed the Arian Vandals as their champions against the Catholic, and Roman, Church. Catholics were persecuted under the new régime, their property was confiscated, their churches were desecrated, and the bishops of Sabratha and Oea were exiled. There were six Tripolitanians among 466 North African bishops called in 484 to a great council at Carthage, where eighty-eight anti-Arians were executed by order of Geneseric's son,

Huneric. This was very largely a persecution of the Roman establishment, lay and ecclesiastic, by its Vandal enemies, and in overthrowing Roman power in North Africa, Geneseric and his successors started something of a popular revolution. The results of the persecution were a revival of the Donatist schism and growing anarchy in the North African Church.

Despite their reputation, the Vandals seem to have been no more wantonly destructive than other contemporary invaders of the Roman empire; it was their inactivity and negative influence that were so harmful. Geneseric, who had experience only of tribal government, took over the Roman administrative system as he found it. Latin remained the official language of the state, and the non-literate Vandal language was used only by the ruling class and in Arian ritual. The Vandals ousted the Roman governing class and lived as a privileged and alien minority. They consumed the wealth of the country, but had no contribution of their own to make either to its economy or to its government. In Tripolitania, at least, no trace of their art or building has been found. Good living and an agreeable climate soon sapped their fighting strength and any homespun Germanic virtues they may once have had.

Their greatest disservice to North Africa as a whole, and to Tripolitania in particular, was their neglect of the desert frontier defences. It was the Roman army that had held Africa. The Vandals, when they had completed their conquest, disbanded their army and, like the Carthaginians, became a sea power; but while they sailed their ships on raids to Italy and the central Mediterranean islands, the desert frontier was left unguarded. The old Roman *Limes* system was far beyond the zone of Vandal occupation, but no attempt was made to defend any fixed frontier against the desert tribes. Geneseric took tribesmen with him on sorties across the Mediterranean and thereby successfully, but only temporarily, satisfied their need for war and its spoils. After his death raids by tribesmen on the undefended coastlands and the unwalled cities became increasingly frequent.

By the late fifth century the Vandals had virtually abandoned all former Roman territory, apart from some coastal strongholds, to the desert and its people. The Berber tribes, and the landless Berber serfs, were reverting to their traditional nomadic pastoralism and were joining together, on the pre-desert steppes, into powerful new tribal federations. The ancient battle between the people of the desert and the people settled on the desert's fringes that the Romans had for so long successfully fought on the latter's behalf, was by the fifth or sixth centuries being lost to the desert. Nomadism, Professor Richard Goodchild has pointed out, 'is contagious: it brings uncontrolled herds into planted areas and converts the planters into more nomads'. When he encroaches on the sown the nomad consumes, and never replaces, what years and even generations of work have produced. Rather than wait for the vintage, he feeds his goats on the vines; the maturing olive tree is useful to him only as fuel for tonight's camp fire; he lives in his tent, and the farmhouse, the villa, and the church become stables for his cattle.

Although they neglected the frontier defences, the Vandals can hardly be held responsible for so great a social movement as the resurgence of North African nomadism. But they are very much to blame for the destruction of much of the remaining Roman farmlands and cities, and Roman North African civilisation in general, that resulted from their neglect. The introduction of the camel into North Africa in the first centuries of the Christian era and its adoption by the nomads gave the restless desert peoples the absolute command of the Sahara and military superiority in most of the undefended lands bordering it. The result was a complete social and political revolution that seems to have been stimulated by migrants who penetrated the Sahara from the Red Sea area, and who helped to prepare North Africa ethnically, socially, and psychologically for the coming of the Arabs in the seventh century.

The camel, which the Ancients counted as one of the Seven Wonders of Nature, is not a native of Africa. Only at the beginning of the Christian era were small numbers first introduced from Arabia by the Romans. For the next two centuries camels were, despite their known advantages in the desert, a rarity in Africa. They were probably unknown outside Tripolitania, where they seem first to have become established, but there may have been problems of acclimatisation and handling. Septimius Severus, as an African, could appreciate their military and commercial value in the desert, and encouraged breeding. The merchants of Leptis Magna were probably the first in Africa to use camel caravans, a means of transport far superior to the pack-horse, pack-ass, or unwieldy cart. The people of Leptis were unable to consign the 4,000 camels asked for by count Romanus in 363 because the herds had been driven off by the Austurian raiders, but that the city was asked to supply such a quantity at short notice shows how important the camel must have become to the Tripolitanian economy.

The Vandals fought on horseback, using the light, wiry, and incredibly tough Barbary breed. About the year 500, in the course of a rebellion in Tripolitania, they met camel-mounted nomads in battle for the first time, and were given a practical demonstration of the superiority of the camel in desert warfare. The tribesmen adopted the simple tactic of lying their mounts down in a defensive ring, a posture that also suited the animals' unco-operative and unpredictable nature. Inside the ring the tribesmen awaited the Vandal attack, which broke up in chaos when the horses refused to charge the solid bank of camels. The camel ring, which remained in use in Saharan warfare until this century, could only be effectively broken by a camel-mounted enemy, and none was to challenge the desert tribes until the coming of the Arabs.

On the pre-desert steppes of southern Tunisia and Tripolitania there appeared in the fifth and sixth centuries the great Berber tribal confederation of the Zenata, camel-mounted nomad pastoralists who augmented their meagre resources by frequent pillaging raids into the settled lands along the coast. Nomads have always been obliged to widen their margin of survival by raiding richer, settled communities on the fringes of the deserts or the steppes and taking the necessities, weapons, metal products, and certain foodstuffs, as well as a few non-essential luxuries, that their own environment could not provide. The Zenata probably roamed southwards into the desert grazing grounds after the first winter rains and spent the summers in the mountains: the Gebel Nefusah of Tripolitania is named after an important Jewish tribal element in the Zenata confederation. Indeed, Jewish influence and possibly leadership are thought to account for the extraordinary political coherence of the Zenata, extraordinary, that is, by the standards of factious Saharan tribalism. Jewish refugees who fled south and west into the desert from Cyrenaica after the revolt of 115 may very well have formed the nucleus of the Roman-hating, camel-mounted Zenata of later centuries. Kahina, the Zenata queen who fought so violently against the Arabs in the seventh century, had a Jewish name, possibly an early version of Cohen. Various groups of outlaws and refugees from justice, or injustice, or persecution, in the Roman territories must have had considerable influence in the organisation of the camel tribes with whose rise the entire balance of power in

North Africa shifted away from the coast and into the desert. The movement was far advanced when the Arabs started their conquest in the seventh century, but in the meantime Roman power was re-established on the coast for another century.

North Africa was liberated from the Vandals at the command of the emperor Justinian who, from his capital at Constantinople, ruled the still largely intact eastern, and Greek, half of the Roman empire; an attempt by the emperor Heraclius in 460 to oust the Vandals had failed after Tripolitania had been temporarily occupied. Besides winning back extensive provinces for the empire, Justinian saw reconquest as a praiseworthy crusade of the true Faith against the heretics who were persecuting the North African Catholics.

Belisarius, the finest general of the age, was put in command of the expedition and while it was being prepared certain Tripolitanians, under a leader called Pudentius, proclaimed their independence from the Vandals and asked Justinian for help. The emperor quickly sent troops to the province, which was occupied without difficulty in 533. In June the same year Belisarius landed in North Africa, took Carthage, and within six months had crushed all opposition. The Vandals entirely disappeared as a nation (although individuals were assimilated into the local population) and their century of rule was revealed as an altogether negative and sorry interlude that had only hastened the ruin of Roman Africa.

Reconquest had been easy, but Byzantine rule proved disagreeable to the majority of people in the vast and semi-derelict provinces. The Catholics, freed from persecution, hailed reconquest as a triumph for their Church, and in many cases their confiscated property was restored. But now it was the turn of the Arians, the Donatists, the Jews, and the pagans to be persecuted by vindictive ecclesiastical authorities. The Greek Byzantines, although they called and considered themselves 'Romans', were almost as alien in the Latinised provinces as the Vandals had been. The tribes had become far too independent to submit voluntarily to the new rulers; heavy taxation and a troublesome army caused an undercurrent of discontent among Justinian's new, but very quickly disillusioned, African subjects. Rebellions were frequent, and within one year of reconquest serious uprisings had to be suppressed in Tripolitania. Although the Byzantines realised there had to be peace with the tribes, they were not always tactful in their dealings with them, as in the year 544 when eighty tribal notables, guests at Leptis Magna, were massacred.

The Tripolitania taken over by the Byzantines was ruined and depopulated. Most of the country was dominated by the nomadic Leuatha tribes and Justinian's rule was very strictly limited to the coastal cities and the coastal routes. After a century of raids and neglect, Sabratha and Leptis were mere ghost towns where perhaps a few hundred miserable squatters lived in squalor among the ruins. Only at Oea were the city walls still intact and the port in working order. The most prosperous communities were those on the old Roman frontier and others that had been established later in the Gebel Nefusah. Isolated, Christian, semi-feudal, and self-sufficient, they seem to have co-existed with the Berber tribes around them.

Justinian took a personal interest in Tripolitania's recovery. Organised civil and religious life started again, but Byzantine Tripolitania was a shadow of the old Roman province. Efforts were made to restore Sabratha and Leptis, empty and sand-covered though they were. New defensive walls were built, but only around small areas of the old city centres. At Leptis the Byzantine walls, built with cemented blocks and rubble from the Severan city, merely enclosed the Old Forum, the Severan Forum, and the port area. That the eastern mole of the port was also fortified shows that the town was not even safe from attack by pirates. Byzantine Leptis was in fact little more than a heavily fortified naval dockyard with a small civilian population. Inside the new walls, buildings were restored with rubble and carelessly matched masonry salvaged from the ruins. Workmanship was often shoddy and showed signs of haste, and the best Byzantine work at Both Leptis and Sabratha was the interior fittings brought ready-made from Constantinople. A few fine pieces, such as the stupendous 'Tree of Life' mosaic from the floor of one of the churches at Sabratha, were created on the spot by imported artists. The magnificent Severan basilica at Leptis, foot-deep in sand and rubbish, had long since ceased to be used as a public building, and was cleaned out and rebuilt as a church dedicated to the Mother of God. Four other buildings at Leptis were turned into lesser churches.

According to the historian Procopius, the emperor planned to Christianise all Tripolitania. Missionaries were sent into the interior and even reached Ghadames and the Garamantes of Fezzan. It is not known how successful these missions were; there may have been some conversions among the Garamantes, but there is no definite evidence of this. It is suggested that the cross-motif still common in Tuareg ornament may be a result of Byzantine missionary activity in the desert but, again, the evidence is vague. Christianity certainly advanced in North Africa, and especially in the interior, under Byzantine influence, but while there were two known Tripolitanian bishops in 525, nine years later, just after the reconquest, there were none.

Justinian and his successors never tried to resurrect the old Roman African empire. It would have been a political and a military impossibility, for there was no subduing the newly emerged camel tribes. These Saharans, mobile, daring, and relatively well organised, had made themselves far more formidable than any people the Romans had fought in Africa after the fall of Carthage. The eastern empire was a maritime and commercial power and the Byzantines in North Africa followed Carthaginian rather than Roman policy. After the occupation of the ports and their immediate hinterland, the Byzantines concentrated on reopening the trade routes across the Mediterranean and the Sahara. Leptis, Oea, and Sabratha regained a little of their old commercial vigour, but were continually menaced by the desert people. Saharan trade was falling off because the caravans could no longer be properly protected and because once important desert trading centres like the Garamantean capital of Germa were in decline. Tripolitania's slight recovery under the Byzantines was largely due to Justinian's personal interest; after his death in 565, Constantinople's hold on the territory became only nominal, but for two or three generations there was an exhausted peace and even a little prosperity. The desert tribes had firmly established themselves over nearly all inland Tripolitania which, by the end of the sixth century, had reverted to the old, pre-Roman nomadic pastoralism.

Cyrenaica had remained an imperial province and at the time of the empire's formal division into Greek eastern and Latin western halves in 395 had been incorporated into the eastern bloc ruled from Constantinople. For geographically, and as part of the Greek world for ten centuries, Cyrenaica belonged to the eastern Mediterranean rather than the western. The African land frontier between the two halves of the empire was the Sirtica Desert; since the Austurian invasions the overland route between Carthage and

Alexandria had been closed, and it remained closed even during the Byzantine occupation of Tripolitania.

At the end of the fifth century the cities of Cyrenaica were ruined and semi-deserted. The old city walls at Teuchira and Apollonia were still maintained, but at Cyrene and Tolemaide new walls, enclosing a much reduced area, had been built. Tolemaide was later entirely abandoned when its aqueduct broke down, for the skill and manpower needed to repair it were no longer available. Since the fourth century the townspeople had been moving to the country, where there was always some sort of a living to be made by farming. In doing so, the Cyrenaicans were following the trend in many parts of the empire, where the rural population and the villages were growing as the cities decayed. Northern Cyrenaica was rather better defended from the barbarians by the Byzantines than was Tripolitania by the Vandals, and scattered across the fertile uplands of the Gebel Akhdar are the remains of many Christian villages of the fifth and sixth centuries. The moderately prosperous, mixed Graeco-Roman and Berber, communities who lived in them continued to work the long-established Greek farms. The villages were built for defence and many of the churches were fortified, for the *Gebel* was frontier country, always liable to be invaded from the desert. Soldier-farmers provided a core of fighting men who, unlike the Tripolitanian *Limitanei*, defended the country as a whole rather than a fixed frontier. The Byzantine government also protected the hills with massive forts and watch-towers, well built of squared stone blocks, and there was a system of beacon signals to warn the country of barbarian raids. The Gebel Akhdar was not allowed to become an isolated zone of independent communities as the Tripolitanian *Gebel* had done. Its defences, which were the joint responsibility of the regular army, the Church, and the people, were fairly effective throughout the fifth and sixth centuries in preserving the crude bucolic culture that had superseded the unique civilisation of the Cyrenaican Pentapolis.

Some restoration and refortification of the Cyrenaican cities was done during Justinian's reign, and great new fortresses were built at Boreum, near modern Marsa Brega, and at Tobruk, to defend respectively the western and the eastern coastal approaches to the province. Another fortress built at Paraetonium (Marsa Matruh) protected the seaward end of the caravan route to Siwa Oasis.

Those were the last major works carried out by the Byzantines in

Libya, where the Mediterranean civilisation, to which Tripolitania and Cyrenaica had been subjected for the best part of ten centuries, was slowly coming to an end. The desert and its people were encroaching on the old Carthaginian and Roman, Greek and Byzantine, provinces and were reversing the processes of Semitic, Greek, and Latin civilisation. But the complete triumph of the Berber nomad over the 'foreign' presence on the northern fringes of his desert-steppe homeland was forestalled in the seventh century by the arrival of a new invader from the east, the Muslim Arab.

Chapter 8

The Arabs

THE ELEVENTH-CENTURY 'Wheel Map' that showed the Earth as a disc divided into three orderly parts, the eastern half representing Asia, the north-west quarter Europe, and the south-west Africa, was indicating divisions wider than mere continental ones. The Mediterranean was no longer the *Mare Nostrum* of the Romans, but a frontier disputed between the navies, pirates, and traders of Afro-Asian Islam on the one hand and European Christendom on the other. The loss of the provinces west of Cyrenaica to the Vandals and the desert peoples in the fifth century had started the separation of North Africa from the long influence of European, and latterly Christian, civilisation. It was a separation that nearly became absolute as a result of the Arab conquests of the seventh and eleventh centuries.

The recurring overpopulation crises of the Arabian desert tribes have throughout recorded history been solved by waves of mass migration into neighbouring, and richer, lands: the outcome of two early migrations was the settlement of the Jews and the Phoenicians in Palestine and coastal Syria. But the migration of the seventh century was altogether vaster, swifter, and more spontaneous than any other. The Arab warriors who in the 630s started on the conquest of half the known world were inspired and united by the new message of Islam that the Prophet Mohammad had preached in the last years of his life. By the time Mohammad died in 632 his new religion had converted and united the tribes of western Arabia. Still more phenomenal was the conquest and conversion of more civilised lands and peoples that followed. *Jihad*, or Holy War against the Infidel, inspired the tribesmen to make increasingly bold raids into the Fertile Crescent provinces of the Persian and Byzantine empires. Byzantine Syria fell to the Arabs after the Battle of the Yarmuk (636) and the Persian empire was overrun in the late 630s. Egypt, after the consolidation of its conquest by Omar Ibn al-As, became the base for an advance across North Africa in the early 640s. The lands between Egypt and the Atlantic were called by the Arabs *Jazirat al-Maghrib*, the Island of the Sunset, or the West. Tripolitania and Tunisia were, more specifically, the *Maghrib al-Wasith*, the Middle West.

Mounted Arab troops first crossed into Cyrenaica in 642. The Byzantine provincial governor withdrew with his army into the port of Teuchira, which was still walled and provided private baths for the governor and his staff and public ones for the troops. Elsewhere, the small Byzantine garrisons were overrun and the richest town in the province, Barce, or Barca, was taken after a siege, probably in the autumn of 642, although the sequence of events is not clear. The citizens submitted to an annual levy of 13,000 *dinars*, and paid so regularly that Arab historians called the Barcans the most generous of North African peoples. The last Byzantine stronghold in Cyrenaica, Teuchira, does not seem to have fallen until the second Arab offensive in 644–5. The provincial capital was established at Barca, which became the base for a new westward advance and gave Cyrenaica the name by which the Arabs still call it.

Between Barca and Tripoli was the Sirtica, the 300 miles of open desert that few armies had ever crossed. But the troops of Omar Ibn al-As, 'attended by their faithful camels', as Gibbon says, 'beheld without terror the familiar aspect of the soil and climate.' The Arabs' command of the desert was their vital advantage in their conquest of North Africa and there was no resistance until they reached Tripoli, where they camped on the hill of Dahra (now well within the city limits) and started to besiege the town. The Arab historian Abd-al-Hakim relates how, after a month of inactivity, a small hunting party happened to go down to the shore, and noticed a gap between the city walls and the sea, for there were no defences along the waterfront, a belated discovery that reveals a poor intelligence service. Tripoli was taken and sacked after the besieging army had crept into the city through the gap. The Byzantine army was evacuated by sea and most of the civilians fled to the mountains. As soon as Tripoli had fallen, Arab cavalry rode through the night to Sabratha. According to Abd-al-Hakim, it was taken when the Arabs, who were thought to be still at Tripoli, rode at dawn through the city gates that had been opened to let sheep out to pasture.

Tripoli (which the Arabs called *Tarablus al-Gharb*, Tripoli of the West, to distinguish it from Tripoli in Lebanon) may not have been permanently occupied until the second Arab offensive of 645, when

Rouifa Thabit was appointed governor. Under his reasonable administration refugees began to return and accept Islam. Meanwhile, invading troops had advanced southwards from Barca to the wealthy trading oasis of Augila. Fezzan was not penetrated until about 663 when the army of Okba bin Nafa overthrew what was left of the Garamantean empire. The king of Germa was captured and made a tributary, and the invasion of the Libyan Sahara ended when the Arabs took the word of a guide who assured them there were no more places to be conquered. For several centuries the Arabs, like the Carthaginians and the Romans, seem to have left trans-Saharan trade to the management of the Berbers who had fled into Fezzan as refugees.

Although a Byzantine rearguard action was fought in Tripolitania, the Arabs broke this resistance almost as easily as the Byzantines had overcome the Vandals a century earlier. In Tunisia, which the Arabs called *Ifriqiya*, a corruption of Africa, the defence was stronger, and there were some counter-attacks. But it soon became clear that the real opponents of the westward advance were not the Byzantine fleet and rabble army, but the Berbers, both the nomads of the interior and the Christian farmers of the coastlands. They were alternately co-operative and rebellious. Like all people conquered by the Arabs, they were encouraged to become Muslims, and there were distinct material advantages in doing so. But many Berber communities so frequently accepted and then rejected Islam, Arab historians claim, that some were reconverted twelve times over – probably only a numerical exaggeration.

The Berber revolt stemmed from the traditional xenophobia and independence of the race, characteristics stimulated by memories of Roman, Vandal, and Byzantine misrule. Few other races fought the Arabs so well or for so long. The settled, Donatist Christian Berbers were initially, at least, almost as hostile towards the Arabs and Islam as they had been in the past towards the Romans and Catholicism. More formidable opponents were the mountain and desert tribes, and particularly the Zenata confederation, whose qualities and fighting powers were so similar to those of the Beduin Arab.

Not until 670 was *Ifriqiya* effectively invaded by Okba bin Nafa, and the city of Kairouan founded as a base for further offensives against the Byzantines and the Berbers. Ten years later the advance westwards became a rout when the Berbers occupied Kairouan and a seaborne Byzantine force landed in Cyrenaica, for a time closing the route to Egypt. A great uprising was led by the Judaised prophetess-queen Kahina, who for three years united the mountain tribes from the Aures of western Algeria to the Gebel Nefusah of Tripolitania. Believing that the fertility of the coastal plains had attracted the invaders, she adopted a drastic scorched earth policy in the naïve hope that the complete destruction of farms, villages, trees, and crops would make the country so worthless that the Arabs would end their occupation. In fact, Kahina's main achievement was the further economic ruin of North Africa, and although the invaders were temporarily driven back to Cyrenaica in 694, Kahina was eventually defeated and killed. From then onwards the conquest of the Maghrib was consolidated and in 711 an Arab–Berber army crossed the Straits of Gibraltar into Spain, an invasion still recalled in the 'Andalusian' folk songs of Tripolitania.

North Africa underwent deep and lasting changes in the generations following the Arab conquest. The Arabs had brought with them little more than their religion, the language, and their own racial characteristics, but all three had an increasing influence on the people of the coast from the late seventh century onwards. In the mountains and in the desert, where the Berbers guarded their independence for centuries, Islam was accepted, but Arabic and the Arabs were not.

For the first time in their history, the Berbers were offered a faith, and with it a social system and a culture, that they could completely absorb. Their conversion, once their hostility had been overcome, was as much the result of past influences as of present convenience. Unlike contemporary Christianity, Islam was a simple faith with no great doctrinal differences, it was the religion of the conqueror, and converts were privileged. But Berber receptiveness was also due to the lasting influence of the Semitic Punic civilisation that still formed the background to the lives of the coastal North Africans when the Semitic Arab conquerors appeared, some eight centuries after the fall of Carthage. By contrast, the ease and speed with which Roman and Hellenic civilisation was thrown off and Christianity denied after the Arab conquest showed how relatively superficial their influence had been. The old faith did linger on until the tenth or eleventh centuries and seems to have died out just as the Church in Europe was becoming concerned for the fate of North African Christianity. A remarkable tenth-century Christian cemetery, with epitaphs in simple, ill-written Latin, has been found at Al-Ngila, near Tripoli, and shows that poor, isolated communities kept up the faith, spoke Latin, and used Christian names, for at least 300 years after the first Arab conquest. There were, besides, very large communities of Jews, who formed an influential and intellectual middle class.

By the eighth century the Muslim empire was disturbed by political and religious disputes that arose when the great early years of spiritual fervour, conquest, and unity ended. The Kharijites, who rejected the authority of the Caliph and elected their own leaders, were increasingly active in North Africa from the mid-eighth century onwards. Like Donatism, Kharijism was a politico-religious protest movement that appealed to the Berbers, and independent Kharijite tribal communities arose in the Gebel Nefusah and other corners of the Maghrib. These breakaway movements increased with the shifting of the central authority, when the Umayyad Caliphs, who had ruled from Damascus, were replaced by the Abbasids whose capital, the new city of Baghdad, was 500 miles further east. The Caliphs frequently lost control of North Africa, and Tripoli was sacked and partially destroyed during a temporary occupation in 758 by the Zenata Berbers of the Ibadite sect, an extreme form of Kharijism.

These invaders were later expelled and their elected leader, Imam Abu al-Khattab, was killed in battle in 761. Many of his followers fled into Fezzan and settled, not in the Wadi Ajal, the traditional commercial and political centre of Fezzan, but in the Murzuk Depression. At the ancient town of Zawila the Imam's followers established the dynasty of Bani Khattab. Despite internal quarrels and frequent raids by nomads, it survived for about two centuries and Zawila became one of the leading trade centres of the Sahara.

In the year 800 the great Caliph Harun al-Rashid appointed the Arab Aghlabite family his viceroys in Tunisia and Tripolitania. The Aghlabites became hereditary rulers, virtually independent of Baghdad. Arab historians record five major rebellions against Aghlabite rule in Tripolitania alone between 805 and 896. Meanwhile, the theocratic Rustemite state had been established over the pre-desert belt from Morocco to the Gebel Nefusah, and controlled the caravan routes from Tripoli to Egypt, but both Aghlabite and Rustemite rule was ended by a great new Berber dynasty, the Shi'ite Fatimites, who took Tripoli in 910. After the Fatimite conquest of Egypt and the founding of Cairo as a new capital in 969, power in the middle Maghrib was transferred to a Fatimite governor, Bulukin Ibn Zairi, who established the virtually independent Zairite Dynasty. Although direct Arab rule was over, the Berbers continued to rebel against the established government and Tripoli was taken by the Zenata in 1000 and again in 1022.

The country prospered under the Zairites until the mid-eleventh century, when the Amir al-Moia revolted against the Shi'ite Fatimites, nominal though their rule was, by returning to orthodox Sunnism and recognising the authority of the Caliph of Baghdad. The Fatimite Caliph of Cairo retaliated, with results he could hardly have foreseen. Some years before, the Bani Hilal and the Bani Sulaim and other primitive, predatory, and alarmingly aggressive tribes, had crossed from the Hijaz into the Nile Valley, where they had caused such damage and chaos that they had been banished to Upper Egypt. About the year 1050 the Caliph loosed these hordes on the Maghrib with the twofold purpose of ridding himself of them and of punishing Al-Moia's politico-religious desertion. The outcome, however, was rather more far-reaching.

Unlike the Arab warrior invaders of the seventh century, the newcomers took their families and their flocks with them. The historian Ibn Khaldun likened them to an army of locusts destroying everything in its path. It has been estimated that one million men, women, and children spent nearly a century travelling from the Nile Valley to Algeria, progress comparable to the Israelites' forty years of wandering in the desert. Cyrenaica was slowly overrun, probably in the 1060s, and settled life virtually ceased when great numbers of the Bani Sulaim nomads took over the northern part of the country, which is racially still one of the most completely Arab countries outside the Arabian peninsula. More Bani Sulaim settled in Tripolitania, while the rest of the migrants wandered westwards into Tunisia. In the two centuries before the coming of these people, Libya was perhaps as prosperous as in Carthaginian times; for the following 350 years, says Ibn Khaldun, the plains were ruined. The geographer Idrisi, writing of Tripoli in 1154, says: 'Before the present time, all the surroundings of the city were well cultivated and covered with fig plantations, olives, dates and every kind of fruit tree. But the Arabs [the Bani Hilal and Sulaim] destroyed this prosperity and the people were obliged to abandon the countryside. The plantations were devastated and the waters ceased flowing.' And a modern authority, Professor Bernard Lewis, affirms that 'it is to this invasion that the backwardness of North Africa can be attributed.'

After the first Arab conquest the Maghrib had remained overwhelmingly Berber. The Arabs were a small, mainly urban, élite, increasingly Berberised through intermarriage and the gradual rise of the Islâmic–Berber political power of the Fatimites and other dynasties. Islam was the predominant religion, but Berber, and not Arabic, was spoken by the majority of people. Some of the old Roman farmlands were still worked and gave the country a reputation for fertility, a reputation, that is, among people recently arrived from the deserts of Arabia.

It was the invaders of the eleventh century who so thoroughly Arabised the Maghrib. Zairite power in Tunisia and Tripolitania was shattered into numerous petty Arab–Berber clans. Berber tribes were assimilated by the newcomers and the old tribal groupings were broken up. From the Beduin Arabic spoken by the invaders are derived most of the modern Arabic dialects of the Maghrib. The Beduin spread themselves across the countryside, which became one vast open range for their flocks; except within sight of the sea and in the still strongly Berber Gebel Nefusah and other mountainous areas, settled agriculture ceased. Tripoli was left as the only inhabited settlement of any size between Egypt and Tunisia. This revolution was achieved over many generations but, even in its chaotic beginnings, during the actual invasion, it was not contested by a single pitched battle.

Chapter 9

European Intervention

THE INVASION of the Maghrib by Asiatic nomads in the eleventh century was one symptom of the decay of the Islamic world; another and slighter one was the capture of Tripoli by the Sicilian Normans in 1146, only forty-seven years after the fall of Jerusalem to the Crusaders. The Arabs had taken Sicily in the ninth century, but by 1087 the Normans had conquered it, and under the tolerant rule of Roger I and Roger II a unique and brilliant Norman–Arab culture flourished in the island. From Sicily, Norman power spread over the central Mediterranean: Malta was taken in 1091, and by 1135 Roger II had captured the island of Jerba, then considered part of Tripolitania. One assault on Tripoli ended in disaster. But in 1146 Roger II's great admiral, George of Antioch, with a fleet of 200 ships, stormed and sacked the city where, typically, the defenders had been fighting among themselves. Christian Arabs were sent from Sicily to garrison and repopulate the town, but there seems to have been no occupation of the interior. Before he died, Roger II had assumed the title of king of Africa, for he ruled the coast from Tripoli to Algeria. Norman expansion was in no way a crusade and, as in Sicily, there was complete respect for Islamic law and custom.

Roger II's heir, William, abandoned this policy of toleration and very rapidly lost his North African possessions to a new power that had arisen in the west. The Almohads had taken over Morocco in 1147, and five years later their conquests reached Tunis. Because Norman rule had become intolerable, the Almohads were welcomed as liberators. In 1158, after the governor of Tripoli had ordered the preaching of anti-Almohad propaganda in the city mosques, the people rose against the Normans, and massacred the Norman garrison. The twelve-year occupation had been the first serious attempt at North African conquest by a Christian power since the sixth century, but its only lasting achievement was the awakening of anti-Christian feeling in the Maghrib.

Tripoli submitted freely in 1160 to the Almohads, who by then had brought the Maghrib under a united Berber government. But Tripolitania was for the next fifty years disputed between the Almohads and Armenian adventurers from the Balearic Islands and benefited little from Almohad administrative and cultural achievements. In 1229 Tripoli came under the rule of the Hafsids when the Abu Hafs, the Almohad governors of Tunis, proclaimed their independence.

Meanwhile Cyrenaica, a forgotten backwater inhabited since the Hilalian invasion mainly by Arab nomads, was lightly ruled from Egypt, first by the Fatimites, and later by the Seljuk Turks who succeeded them. In the Tripolitanian hinterland the Arab–Berber struggle was periodically renewed, and in Tripoli itself there were throughout the late Middle Ages violent, but for the most part unrecorded, political changes.

The Arab penetration of Fezzan was slow. For centuries after the expedition of Okba bin Nafa Saharan trade was the monopoly of Berber tribes whose camel caravans and camel-mounted warriors had in the fifth and sixth centuries eclipsed the waning horse-borne commerce and cavalry of the Garamantes. Medieval Fezzan was ruled as an independent or semi-independent state with Saharan trade as its *raison d'être*. At the end of the twelfth and beginning of the thirteenth centuries the country was in turmoil and came for a time under the rule of a soldier of fortune, Karakush Sharif al-Din, who had been one of Saladin's lieutenants in the Palestine campaigns against the Crusaders. Unrest in Fezzan usually resulted in the intervention of an outside power that had no particular desire to rule the country but was concerned for the safe passage of caravans. Such was the case when, in the thirteenth century, king Dounama of Bornu, one of the Sudanese kingdoms, brought some order by establishing a puppet régime under a governor at the new capital of Traghen, a few miles east of Murzuk.

Islamic traders, operating mainly from Morocco, but also through Fezzan, slowly made an extended trade link with the Sudan and so brought Central Africa into contact with the Mediterranean. The Fezzanese oasis towns (most of them are now but poor mud villages) prospered on the exchange of goods between Negroland and the Islamic and Christian worlds. In the eleventh century towns on the great Fezzanese trail from the Mediterranean to Central Africa,

Hon, Uaddan, Sebha, and Zawila, impressed the visitor with their markets, mosques, caravanserais, and baths. Doctors of law, poets, and holy men frequented Uaddan and the desert was criss-crossed with caravan trails carrying local and international traffic. The Spanish–Arab geographer Idrisi who worked at the court of Roger II saw Zawila at the height of its prosperity in the mid-twelfth century. He found it small, but full of bazaars. He described it as the 'gateway to the country of the Blacks', and met there merchants of the cities of Khorasan in Central Asia and Kufa and Basra in Iraq. Even Jadu, a fairly unimportant town on the edge of the Gebel Nefusah, traded with Benghazi, Siwa, Kufra, the Fezzanese oases, and Wadai in Sudan.

Tripoli in the ninth and tenth centuries was one of several North African bases of the Muslim fleets raiding Sicily and southern Italy, and in the tenth century had a reputation as one of the best markets for Christian slaves, and especially for women. But sporadic warfare between Christendom and Islam barely affected the commercial relations between the Maghrib ports and the Italian maritime states. About the year 1000 the naval forces and merchants of Sicily, Naples, Amalfi, Gaeta, Bari, and Otranto united to dominate the North African seaborne trade.

A document of 971 shows that Venetian ships often called at Tripoli with, in particular, European timber, iron, and arms, exports strictly forbidden by the Church and the Christian powers, including Venice itself. There were severe penalties for supplying Muslim states with the strategic materials they lacked and could be expected to use against Christendom when provided with them. Christian slaves from the Dalmatian coast and from Italy were also illegally exported to the Maghrib by the Venetians, and as far back as 748 the Pope had tried to stop the trade.

In his *Description of Africa*, the tenth-century Arab geographer Ibn Haukal called Tripoli: 'A most wealthy and powerful city, with vast markets... Merchandise is plentiful there, as, for example, local wool and vivid blue and fine black stuffs of great value. These goods are loaded onto ships that call continuously from Europe and the Arab lands with cargoes of merchandise and livestock.' He found the people outstanding among North Africans for their dignity, for the elegance of their clothes and food, for their physical beauty, and for their 'heightened sentiments'; they were charitable, judicious, pious, and orderly, dutiful subjects and friendly towards foreigners, even to the extent, Ibn Haukal remarks, of piloting foreign ships into the difficult anchorage free of charge.

By 1100 the town had regular trade with Amalfi, Gaeta, Trani, and Bari, which paid small amounts of 'tribute' for the privilege of maintaining *fonduks* (warehouses) and other property in the port, and a prosperous community of Italian traders, protected by treaty, became established. During the Norman occupation the Maghrib was thrown wide open to Italian commerce, but in the anti-Christian reaction that followed the Norman withdrawal, the Almohads refused to trade with Europe, until Genoa won a concession to send ships once a year to the Maghrib ports. The profits and customs dues to be collected from trade were effective in eroding religious scruples on both sides of the Mediterranean and Pisa, too, was later granted commercial rights in several ports, including Tripoli. Trade relations with Europe improved under the Hafsids, and new treaties were signed with Venice, Pisa, Genoa, and several Sicilian cities. The Pisans, at that time the most active traders on the North African coast, won special privileges, which they consistently abused. Despite continual protests and representations by outraged rulers, Pisan and other Italian traders broke treaties and promises and pirated, rioted, robbed, and cheated along the North African coast to such a degree that the Muslims came heartily to dislike and mistrust all Christians. For centuries the Christian states complained of the evil of Muslim piracy in the Mediterranean, but the Christian pirates, of whom little was ever heard in Europe, were equally the scourge of Muslims.

Trade between Italy and the Maghrib was at its height in the thirteenth century but later, when Venice replaced Pisa as the leading Italian mercantile power, the Levant trade became the more important. In Roman times the local products exported from Tripolitania were oil (in great quantities) and a little corn and wine; the locally-produced exports shipped from Tripoli a thousand years later, greasy and washed wool for the growing Italian textile industry, skins and hides, and leather, reflected the change from settled agriculture to stockraising by nomads; indeed medieval Libya must have been at least as 'rich in flocks' as Pindar had described it in the fifth century B.C. A little oil was also exported, possibly from surviving Roman groves. The Venetians held the monopoly of the export of salt from the valuable deposits on the Tripolitanian and Tunisian coasts, and the Church was presumably unaware that by the thirteenth century many a Christian child was being baptised with holy water containing a solution of this 'infidel' mineral.

The great camel caravans, spending a year or more on the northward journey through the Tibesti or Ghat or Ghadames, brought the raw wealth of central West Africa across the Sahara. From about the twelfth century onwards Muslim traders and Islam penetrated the negro states of ancient Ghana, Mali, Songhai, and Kanem. The alluvial gold exported by these states from the upper tributaries of the Niger and Senegal earned them, and later the great trading cities of Timbuctu and Gao, a fabled reputation in the Maghrib and in Christendom. West African gold and ivory were re-exported to Europe through the Maghrib ports, while Christian ships, which by the late Middle Ages were carrying the Christian and Muslim trade of the Mediterranean, brought the exports of Asia to the Maghrib. Out of the Levant, where the trans-Asiatic caravan roads ended, the Venetians and others brought Chinese silks and Indian gems, Persian artifacts, and the spices of Arabia and the Indies to Tripoli and the neighbouring emporia. From Italy, from central and northern Europe, and from Muslim Spain, came the metals and the manufactured goods that North and Central Africa lacked. Sound timber, another North African rarity, was a valuable European export, without which the vessels that harried the coasts and shipping of Christendom could not have been built. From Venice came glassware, some of it finding its way to Fezzan and Central Africa; from the Italian cities came arms and textiles; and from England heavy woollen broadcloth.

Tripoli literally dazzled the visitor with the prosperity brought by trade with three continents. The Arab traveller Al-Tigiani, who spent a whole year, 1307–8, in Tripolitania, wrote: 'When we approached, we were blinded by the brilliant whiteness of the city from which the burning rays of the sun were reflected; I was convinced that rightly is Tripoli called the "White City".' He mentioned three bath-houses, and declared he had never seen cleaner streets anywhere (so perhaps the reputation the city now has for cleanliness is not entirely due to modern Italian influence, as is commonly thought) and most of them, he says, 'cross the city lengthways and crosswise, giving the appearance of a chessboard' – which seems exaggerated.

Medieval Cyrenaica derived a little prosperity from the passage of trade and pilgrim caravans between Egypt and the Maghrib.

Ibn Haukal described Barce before the Hilalian invasion as a 'medium city', the capital of a populous region and an important caravan centre. Idrisi, writing about 150 years later, after the invasion, said few people lived there and that its markets were little frequented, adding 'in other times this was not the state of things'. There was no other town near Barce, but he described Tolmeita (Tulmitha) as a well-inhabited stronghold that exported honey, butter, and tar to Alexandria. Benghazi seems to have been deserted before the year 1000. It was mentioned again around 1250 but, according to tradition, not until the fifteenth century was it refounded by Tripoli merchants. It took its present name from a holy man, Ibn Ghazi, whose tomb stood nearby.[1] The caravan route from Mecca, Medina, and Egypt to Kairouan, Fez, and Marrakesh arched south-westwards from Tobruk to Agedabia, by-passing Barce and the Gebel Akhdar. Agedabia, standing at the junction with the trail to the ancient trading oasis of Augila was, before the Hilalian invasion, a notable town with markets, bath-houses, and gardens, but by Idrisi's time it had declined to a mere 'two castles in the sand'. Genoa's medieval prosperity was partly due to the monopoly of the Cyrenaican trade, and in 1236 the republic won a concession to do business along the coast from Tripoli to Egypt. From Cyrenaica, wool, feathers, cosmetic oils, skins, leather, wax, and fruit were imported.

In the late Middle Ages Christian and Muslim privateers were making increasingly bold raids on the shipping and the coastlands of the opposing faith. In 1335 Tripoli, which had just undergone a series of *coups d'état*, was stormed by the fleet of a Genoese freebooter, Filippo Doria. Seven thousand men, women, and children were captured, together with a huge booty of 1,800,000 gold florins. The Genoese government, fearing reprisals on Genoese communities in Tunis and Egypt, joined other states in condemning this act of piracy. Doria sold the town to Ahmad Ibn Makki, the governor of Gabes in Tunisia, for 50,000 gold pieces, of which half were later found to be counterfeit.

In turn, North African warships plundered the coasts of Italy and ships from Tripoli, in particular, were notorious for their raids along the south coast of France. At the end of the fourteenth century these pirates were said to be ruining the trade of the lower Tyrrhenian

[1] The early Arab name 'Bernik', still in use in parts of Cyrenaica, was a corruption of the Greek Berenike.

Sea, and in 1393 they sacked Syracuse. Unlike the Genoese or the rowdy Pisans, the Venetians were tactful in their dealings with Muslims. Good manners and their growing economic power won Venetian merchants generous trading concessions in Tripoli, where they established a *fonduk* in 1350. They were allowed to pay cash guarantees on customs dues instead of surrendering the sails of their ships on arrival in port, as was the usual practice; they could organise, but not accompany, their own trading caravans into the interior, and even the minting of Venetian gold coins at Tripoli was allowed. Venetian galleys sailed regular routes in the summer, and called at Tripoli twice a year. Genoese ships came and went as was convenient, but Florence, after capturing Pisa and Livorno in 1421, adopted the Venetian system, and her ships sailed a regular service Gaeta–Naples–Salerno–Palermo–Trapani–Tunis–Tripoli. But the last call was later dropped from the route due to the city's declining trade in a period of chronic political instability. In 1460 the city declared its independence from the Hafsids, who had ruled intermittently for the past 250 years, and came under the oligarchic rule of an assembly of notables.

In the fifteenth century the Maghrib was invaded from the Iberian peninsula. The Portuguese, after freeing their country from Muslim rule, reversed the eighth-century invasion of the Arab–Berbers by attempting the conquest of Morocco. At the end of the century, crusading Spain captured Granada from the Muslims and carried the *reconquista* into North Africa. At the beginning of the sixteenth century Ferdinand the Catholic mounted an expedition under Cardinal Ximenes and Admiral Don Pedro of Navarre that extended Spanish power eastwards along the coast. In July 1510 an armada of ten galleys, thirty caravels, and fifty transports commanded by Don Pedro sailed from Syracuse and on 22 July landed 6,000 men at Tripoli. The fighting was soon over. After the walls had been breached, citizens armed with clubs and stones tried to defend the Great Mosque and the Castle. Artillery was turned on them and 5,000 were slaughtered in the streets. 'One could not put a foot down without stepping on a corpse', wrote Don Pedro after the fall of the town on 25 July. He found it bigger and finer than he had imagined, and declared it fit to be capital of an empire; the Spaniards were unable to make it one.

There had been much damage in the street fighting and the

Spaniards used the rubble and parts of the demolished city wall to fortify the Castle and build new defences. Tripoli was ruled from Sicily and was used purely as a naval base; most of it was deserted and in ruins, and trade ceased when the port was closed to merchant ships, even Venetian ones.

The Spaniards were not secure in Tripoli and they were too encircled by enemies and involved in European politics to extend the conquest inland. Many citizens had fled to Tagiura, a coastal oasis about 10 miles to the east of the city, and it became the centre of resistance to the occupation. But it was not the Africans who thwarted Spanish schemes for the conquest of Africa.

The Ottoman Turks had come to power in Anatolia in the fourteenth and fifteenth centuries and had taken Constantinople in 1453. By 1517 they had conquered Egypt and the semi-independent corsair captains were already seizing the Maghrib for the Sultan. In 1513 the Corsair Khair al-Din, one of the two brothers known to Europe as Barbarossa, took the island of Jerba, and in 1517 Algiers. From then onwards no remaining Spanish possession in North Africa, nor the coasts of Sicily and Italy, were safe from attack by Algerian galleys.

Tripoli was regarded by the emperor Charles V as one of the 'two eyes of Christendom'. It gave some protection to Spanish Sicily and to Christian shipping in the central Mediterranean, but it was more of a liability than an asset. In 1524 negotiations for its transfer to the Knights of the Order of the Hospital of St John of Jerusalem were started. The Knights, one of the great military Orders of the Church, dedicated to the defence of the Faith, had lost their stronghold of Rhodes to the forces of the Turkish Sultan, Sulaiman the Magnificent, in 1522, and had moved to a new base at Malta.

A delegation of eight Knights inspected Tripoli's defences in 1524. With their experience of the Turkish assault on Rhodes, they were not impressed by what they saw, and not until 1530 was Charles V able to hand the city over to the Order, which was under pressure from Pope Clement VII to accept responsibility for its defence. The emperor had needed no urging to rid himself of a troublesome possession which he knew the Knights would continue to hold as a Christian bastion against the Turk.

The Knights tried, with little success, to bring the city back to normal life. Their tiny force was kept busy completing the Castle and rebuilding the walls, and within a year of taking over they beat off an attack by Khair al-Din. Five years later there was an unsuccessful assault by Muslim forces from Tagiura, which was ruled by a Ragusan renegade, Murad Agha, the self-styled 'King of Tagiura'. Through Turkish aid, the oasis had become a little stronghold, with its own tiny port, and was considered the Muslim capital of Tripolitania. The Knights made several sallies and temporarily occupied Zanzur and Zavia, west of Tripoli, but their effective control did not extend beyond the city, which was called 'a Christian oasis in a barbaric desert'.

This outpost of Christendom fell in the summer of 1551. After the failure of a Turkish assault on Malta, led by Sinan Pasha, forces were joined for an expedition against the city with the great Anatolian admiral, Darghut Pasha. Although Sinan's fleet included 112 imperial galleys, two great galeasses, fifty brigantines, and transports carrying 12,000 soldiers and siege engineers, the Grand Master of the Order, Fra Giovanni D'Omedes, considered Tripoli could be defended from Malta. But, as a precaution, he sent the governor, Fra Gaspare de Valliers, 200 Calabrian recruits and twenty-five young Knights as reinforcements to a contingent probably numbering less than one thousand men. Turkish troops were landed at Zuara to attack overland from the west, the Turkish fleet anchored off the city, and Murad Agha brought up artillery from Tagiura. He opened fire on the Castle on 8 August. De Valliers, threatened with mutiny among the defenders, started negotiations with the Turks, and allowed them to occupy the town on 16 August. Murad Agha, in the name of the Sultan, was made king of Tagiura and Tripoli.

Europe was shocked by the fall of the 'Christian oasis' and, despite ineffectual attempts to recapture it, Tripoli was not to come again under European rule for 360 years.

Chapter 10

Turks and Karamanlis

THE DIVISION of the Mediterranean between the Christian states and the Turks in the mid-sixteenth century was little changed for the next 300 years. Turkish expansion was checked in 1565 when 50,000 men failed to capture Malta, and again in 1571 at the Battle of Lepanto. In the words of Cervantes, who lost an arm there, Lepanto 'broke the pride of the Osmans and undeceived the world, which had regarded the Turkish fleet as invincible.' Tripoli was assaulted from the sea and from the desert, but between the sixteenth and the twentieth centuries there were no conquests, only changes of régime.

In the meantime, the Mediterranean was becoming an economic backwater as the maritime states of western Europe, exploiting the new-found sea route to the Indies, by-passed the Muslim world and the Levantine and North African outlets of the ancient Asian and African caravan routes. As the trade that had brought Tripoli's medieval prosperity declined, a substitute was found in state-sponsored piracy, which for about two centuries gave an artificial wealth and prestige to a region of poor natural resources: by the 1560s 'God preserve you from the Tripoli galleys' was the farewell cry of Christian sailors in the central Mediterranean.

There were several Christian attempts to recapture Tripoli in the years following its fall to the Turks. One, by the Knights of Malta in 1552, failed and so did a great expedition sent eight years later. Murad Agha, after being deposed in 1552, had retired to Tagiura; Darghut Pasha became ruler of Tripoli and his galleys terrorised the central Mediterranean. It was to end this menace that Philip II of Spain in 1560 sent fifty-two Italian galleys, carrying 12,000 Spanish, German, and Italian troops, to North Africa. The island of Jerba, and not Tripoli, was captured, and most of the troops were massacred or enslaved when the fleet abandoned them. Although bishop Caracciolo of Catania, who was taken to Tripoli as a prisoner the following year, thought seventy ships and 10,000 men could have captured the city, the Jerba disaster had spoiled Christian enthusiasm and Darghut, the 'Terror of Tripoli', remained master of the sea. Before his death at the Great Siege of Malta in 1565, he had reopened trade relations with the great Sudanic kingdom of Bornu and had tried to pacify the *Gebel* and pre-desert tribes; but 'it is difficult to conquer people who carry their cities with them', he is supposed to have told the Sultan in explanation of the frequent revolts. The conquest of the desert and its people was sometimes the despair even of the Turks. But in 1577 Fezzan was invaded and tribute was imposed. The country nevertheless remained under the rule of the Ulad Mohammad Dynasty, which had been founded by a Moroccan *Sharif*, Mohammad al-Fazi, and which had brought law and order to the southern and central valleys after the nomads and the petty warlords had been subdued. Despite its population of only 5,000 to 6,000, Murzuk had become a great trading centre protected by the kingdoms of Bornu and Kanem.

In Darghut's time there were only thirty-five galleys in the Tripoli fleet yet, like the Algerians and the Tunisians, the Tripoli corsairs did as they pleased in the central Mediterranean and attacked the western coasts of Italy as far north as Genoa; many of the towers built as defence against the raiders still stand beside the Tyrrhenian and Ligurian Seas. The Italians rarely distinguished between the Barbary corsairs and vaguely referred to them, whether from Tripoli, Tunis, or Algiers, as 'Infidels' or 'Africans' or *Barbareschi*. Europeans at this time counted five rather vague North African races: the Turks; the Moriscos or Tangarins (Muslim refugees from Spain); Moors (mainly city-dwellers); wild or desert Moors; and Arabs (country people).

Although Tripoli lost five galleys, two galleots, and 1,200 men at Lepanto, her maritime power still increased and by about 1600 it was estimated 100 galleys, 100 ships, and 20,000 men would be needed to take the city: 130 vessels and 10,000 men more than bishop Caracciolo's estimate of forty years earlier.

Like Tunis and Algiers, the regency of Tripoli was closely ruled by the Turkish Sultans through a long succession of governors. But at the end of the sixteenth century a constitutional revolution that started in Algiers and then spread to the other regencies greatly limited the authority of the Sultan and his governors, the Pashas. The revolution went further in 1611 when a certain Sulaiman Safar made himself *Dey*,[1] with much personal power and purely nominal allegiance to the Sultan. For the next century Tripoli was ruled by a succession of adventurers and renegades who became *Dey* through force and skill. Nevertheless, payments of tribute to the Sultan and a show of allegiance were kept up.

Under the Greek renegade *Dey* Mohammad Sakisli (1631–49), the corsairs attacked and captured ships of all the Italian maritime states, as well as the Dutch and English merchantmen that were beginning to appear in the Mediterranean. They sacked Corsica, cut Venetian communications with Crete, terrorised the coasts of Sicily, Italy, and Provence, and when Mohammad extended his power to Benghazi, that also became a corsair base. Mohammad and his successor, Osman Sakisli (1649–72), were renegades and they surrounded themselves with renegades, who formed a ruling military oligarchy. The corsair ships had European captains: Murad the Fleming is one name that survives. Despite the papal ban on such exports, sails, swords, guns, powder, and shot were supplied from Europe. Ships were built by European slaves or renegades with timber imported from Anatolia and Egypt (where, presumably, it had arrived from more distant sources); the iron-work came from Salonika and the rigging from Smyrna. In the 1640s ten large ships were operating from Tripoli. The largest, carrying about forty guns, were manned by 300 *Janissaries* (professional soldiers) and about fifty Christian slaves, who acted as surgeons, carpenters, and technical specialists in general. The piracy that was the scourge and terror of seventeenth-century Christian sailors in the Mediterranean was largely the work of fellow-Europeans who had been forced, or who had chosen, to build, captain, maintain, arm, partly supply, and generally serve the ships of the corsair fleets.

In summer the corsairs roamed the seas between Malta, Calabria, Apulia, Sardinia, Corsica, and sometimes Liguria; in winter they went east to plunder the merchantmen sailing from southern Europe to Egypt and Syria. They rarely attacked warships and usually fled when one was sighted. Between 1668 and 1678, it is said, Tripoli alone took 104 Christian ships of which, despite treaties with France, thirty-three were French. An anonymous contemporary author complained: 'It is not possible to recall all the evil they [the corsairs]

[1] *Dey* was the title of the independent rulers of Tripoli and Algiers, *Bey* that of the rulers of Tunis (from the mid-seventeenth century) and the governors of Benghazi.

have done, and still do, to the Christians.' Yet the Christians actually encouraged the corsairs by readily buying their booty and by supplying them with strategic materials. The income from corsairing varied from year to year: in 1635 the Tripoli fleet showed a profit of 180,000 ducats and about 450 captured slaves, but in 1638 lost three ships, 200 men, and 100,000 scudi in one encounter with the Knights of Malta off Calabria.

Europeans called, and still call, the attacks on European shipping by Barbary corsairs 'piracy', but in North Africa these were, and still are, considered legitimate acts of undeclared war. A Libyan diplomat, Arif bin Musa, maintained in a recent article that 'Libya was, in fact... waging war against all European maritime powers operating on the Mediterranean Sea. And it was the Libyan Navy – not private individuals – which sank or seized European merchant ships....'[2]

European maritime powers frequently took reprisals for the attacks of the corsairs. The most common, and therefore presumably the most effective, method was to send a fleet to the offending corsair base to bombard the dockyard and the town. In 1638 a French fleet bombarded Tripoli as a reprisal for raids on the Provencal coast and afterwards France signed a treaty and established a consulate in Tripoli. A little later, other European states began accrediting consuls to the regency and buying safe passage for their merchant ships, at a considerable price. The main duties of the consuls were to ensure the safety of their countries' merchant shipping in Barbary waters and to redeem ships and crews taken in violation of treaties. Samuel Tucker, the first English consul, was accredited in 1658, four years after Admiral Blake had partially avenged the capture of English ships by bombarding the port. Diplomacy was frequently backed up by cannon: French squadrons appeared off Tripoli in 1660 and again in 1671; the Dutch, under their great seaman Admiral Michiel de Ruyter, were there in 1672.

Apart from the rewards of piracy and trade, on which a few ports and oases lived, the regency as a whole was desperately poor. Leo Africanus, a Spanish Muslim who in the mid-sixteenth century became a Christian scholar in the court of Pope Leo X, remarked in his *Description of Africa* on the scarcity and badness of the food all over Libya. Not enough was being grown and grain, in particular,

[2] 'Libya Was Sea Power in 18th Century' from *Modern Libya* (Spring 1965 supplement to *Afro-Mideast Economic Bulletin*).

was imported from Egypt and Sicily. Outside Tripoli, Leo says, the people were poor, badly housed, mean, ignorant, and thieving. Barca he calls 'a harsh and desert country' (although he was probably referring to the Sirtica), where there was no water and no land worth farming. The people subsisted on imported Sicilian grain, which they bought by selling their children into slavery. There was no reason for the economy to have improved after Leo's time; if anything, it probably worsened, especially towards the end of the seventeenth century when the European powers to some extent curbed corsair activity. The Englishman John Ogilby, writing in 1670, found: 'The Countrey is all Sandy, and so Barren, that no kind of Corn by the best Husbandmen be produced there; so that the Inhabitants would almost perish with Hunger if Corn were not Transported thither from other places to supply their defective Harvests.'[3]

As in the Middle Ages, the state of undeclared war between Tripoli and Europe did not greatly harm trade relations, and towards the end of the seventeenth century merchant captains could buy safe-conduct passes for a reasonable five scudi each. French ships brought textiles, wine, and paper; the Venetians silk and damask, glass and sulphur, iron, bronze, and copper; the English and the Dutch pitch and ropes, lead and manufactured goods. The main exports from the regency were senna, wool, leather, wax, dates, salt, and ivory, and there was a steady re-sale of goods taken by the corsairs. In 1693 the French were given permission to ship complete sets of marble columns from Leptis Magna for the building of Versailles and the church of St Germain des Prés in Paris.

To Bornu, a three-month caravan journey away, European-made wire, pins, needles, knives, and other metal goods were re-exported. In 1693 the French consul, de la Lande, said that the regency's most important commercial relations were with Fezzan and that twice a year the *Dey* sent a one hundred-camel caravan there with textiles and metal goods. From across the Sahara came gold dust, precious drugs, and slaves.

At the end of the seventeenth century between 500 and 600 negroes were arriving in Tripoli in chains every year. There was no telling how many more died from thirst, exhaustion, exposure, or ill-treatment on the journey; estimates vary between one in five and nine out of ten. In 1551 an English traveller, Nicholas Nicolay, had

[3] Ogilby, *Africa, etc.*, London, 1670.

recounted how negro slaves were sold in Tripoli after being walked up and down and having eyes and teeth examined, like horses. During the rule of Osman Sakisli, Christian slaves were being taken to Tripoli at the rate of 1,500 to 2,000 a year. The European slaves, most of them Italian, provided the state and private owners with cheap, but for the most part skilled, labour. The slaves' only real freedom was the practice of their religion; the Franciscans had started a mission in the city in 1630 (the Order has been there ever since) with the purpose not of converting Muslims, but of dissuading Christian slaves from bettering their lot by becoming converts to Islam. As slaves, all classes were treated equally, but a man was ransomed in proportion to his wealth. The slave artisans worked at their trades, but those with no skills were sent to the quarries at Gargaresh or Henshir, near Tripoli. Their daily ration was one pound of barley bread, barley soup, and fresh water. Some men were slaves for forty or fifty years, but those who accepted Islam were freed, and many of these converts in time became senior officials of the state.

After the death of Osman Dey in 1672, Tripoli went into a long decline. The Barbary corsairs were still the terror of the little Italian states, but were merely an unpleasant pest to English, Dutch, and French shipping. Reprisals became more drastic and more effective. In 1675 an English squadron under Admiral Sir John Narborough blockaded the port, bombarded the fortifications, burnt part of the corsair fleet, and freed all the English slaves. Ten years later the French bombarded the fortifications, burnt part of the corsair fleet, and freed slaves of all nationalities. In 1692 the French were back again.

Tripoli's state of political chaos was characterised by a succession of 24 *Deys* in the 39 years between 1672 and 1711. Writing in 1686, the Franciscan, Francesco da Capranica, commented sourly on the political scene: 'It is more a republic than a kingdom, and the butchers and the cobblers have risen to the highest ranks. The rule of the *Dey* is permanent, but usually it lasts no more than a year because, when it is no longer liked, any drunk can rouse the city and have the rulers' heads off.'[4] He had little praise for the judicial system either, and remarked that, without even consulting counsel, the courts 'straightaway, as it suits their fancy, order the striking off of arms, legs, ears, noses or chins, and think nothing more of the matter.'

[4] Quoted by Bergna, *Tripoli dal 1510 al 1850*, Tripoli, 1925.

Welcome revolution came in 1711. Since the Turkish occupation, the *Janissaries*, a class of professional soldiers, had married local Arab and Berber girls, and there had grown up a racially-mixed class of soldiers and senior administrators, the *Cologhli*. Unlike the European renegades, they were generally popular. A leading *Cologhli*, Ahmad Karamanli (his family was from Karamania in Anatolia), led the revolution of 1711 against the ruling *Dey*, Mohammad Halil Ibn al-Ginn. While 'Son of the Devil' Halil was out of the country, Karamanli, who was an outstanding cavalry commander, occupied Tripoli with his troops. He was both ambitious and energetic, and had one advantage every ruler of the past forty years had lacked, the full support of the army and the people. As his intention was to rule independently, with the minimum of allegiance to the Sultan, he had all the leading Turkish officials and sympathisers massacred at a banquet. But the goods confiscated from his 300 victims he sent to the Sultan: a clever bribe, for the Sultan was so mollified by it that he recognised Karamanli as Pasha of Tripoli by special decree.

Ahmad, who built Tripoli's handsome Karamanli Mosque, made himself protector of the corsairs, and they again became more active. At the same time, through skilful diplomacy, he kept up good relations with the European consuls. He brought Cyrenaica into Tripoli's orbit and started the practice of sending younger members of the family to govern the notoriously unruly province. He died in 1744 and was succeeded by his son, Mohammad. Early in his ten-year reign Mohammad kept the corsairs in check but later, as state revenues fell, attacks were again started on Neapolitan and Sicilian ships. The shipping of the great naval powers was rarely molested, for by the second half of the eighteenth century the corsairs were no longer masters of the Mediterranean and by 1765 only four ships were operating from Tripoli. But the corsairs were also being paid, or bribed, to remain inactive. Nearly every maritime power was insuring its shipping by buying safe-passage from the Karamanlis. Through a treaty with the Turkish Sultan, also recognised by Tripoli, Austria in 1726 bought 'protection' for all her subjects and ships, including those of some Italian states. The superb Venetians were too proud to buy immunity directly; instead they paid absurdly high fees for the right to exploit the Zuara salt deposits. Even Denmark and Sweden paid well for the safety of their shipping. The notoriety of the corsairs, and not their actual strength, brought in these annual subsidies, for the arsenal and the stores were empty and the fleet rotten and undermanned. When, in 1770, the Turkish Sultan asked for help against Russia, Tripoli could only send him two hulks with mutinous crews.

A description of Tripoli, written in 1783 by Miss Tully, the sister of the British consul, tells how:

> 'Previous to entering the Bay of Tripoli, a few miles from the land, the country is rendered picturesque by various tints of beautiful verdure: no object whatever seems to interrupt the evenness of the soil, which is of light colour, almost white, and interspersed with long avenues of trees; for such is the appearance of the numerous palms planted in regular rows, and kept in the finest order.... The whole town appears in a semicircle, some time before reaching the harbour's mouth. The extreme whiteness of square flat buildings covered with lime, which in this climate encounters the sun's fiercest rays, is very striking.... On entering the harbour, the town begins to discover dilapidations from the destructive hand of time, large hills of rubbish appearing in various parts of it. The castle, or royal palace, where the Bashaw resides, is at the east end of the town, within the walls.... This castle is very ancient and is enclosed by a strong high wall which appears impregnable.'

She also found that:

> 'They do not excel here in shops, the best of these being little better than booths, though their contents are sometimes valuable, consisting of pearls, gold, gems and precious drugs. There are two covered bazars, or market-places; one of which is very large. ... The other bazar is much smaller, and has no shops in it. Thither only black men and women are brought for sale!'[5]

Mohammad Karamanli had been succeeded in 1754 by his brother, Ali, during whose forty-year rule the regency continued to decline. Towards the end of Ali's life the French consul wrote: 'He rules, but is not obeyed. Shut up in his harem... he builds nothing, repairs nothing, lets all collapse.' In 1790 the youngest of his three sons, Yusuf, shot the eldest, Hassan. When Ali named his second son, Ahmad, his heir, Yusuf started a rebellion against them both. In the midst of this strife Tripoli was seized by a Turkish adventurer,

[5] Dearden (ed.), *Tully's Ten Years' Residence at the Court of Tripoli*, London, 1957, pp. 35–6, 40.

Ali Burghul, but in 1795 he was expelled by the reunited Karamanli family. Ali and Ahmad then abdicated in favour of Yusuf. Like the founder of the Karamanli Dynasty, Yusuf was ambitious, cunning, and popular, and he took advantage of the Napoleonic wars to regain some of Tripoli's lost prestige. The corsairs again started preying on Christian shipping, with Naples, Sardinia, and Corsica suffering the most losses. He successfully played off one European power against another, although his ties with France (despite the British blockade, he kept the French garrison of Malta supplied) brought him into conflict with Britain and the Turkish Sultan.

He also involved himself in a war with a new naval power, the United States of America. Between 1790 and 1800 the Americans had paid over 2 million dollars in safe conduct to the Barbary regencies. In 1801 Yusuf demanded increased payments and, when they were refused, seized American ships. President Thomas Jefferson retaliated in 1804 by sending a squadron of seven warships under the command of Commodore Edward Preble to demand satisfaction. One ship, the *Philadelphia*, ran aground, was captured by the corsairs, and refloated. The Americans then took a local ketch, which they renamed *Intrepid*, and sent it into the harbour under the command of Lieutenant Stephen Decatur. With five officers and seventy-two men, he boarded *Philadelphia*, overpowered the crew, and blew up the ship, a schoolboyish adventure that Lord Nelson is said to have called 'the most bold and daring act of the age'. *Intrepid*, loaded with gunpowder, was later sent into port to blow up the corsair fleet, but exploded prematurely with the loss of twelve volunteers on board. Meanwhile, an American consular official, William Eaton, had raised a motley force of 400 men, marched into Cyrenaica, and captured Derna. He was planning to advance on Tripoli and depose Yusuf, but peace was made before he could accomplish this bold assignment. Derna was evacuated and American cargoes and prisoners were released.

When the Napoleonic wars ended the corsairs, and the Karamanli Dynasty with them, were doomed. It was a sign of the times when, in 1816, the British consul, Colonel Hanmer Warrington, actually had a corsair captain hanged for attacking a Hanoverian ship sailing under British protection. Two years before, the Congress of Vienna had acknowledged that slavery and piracy should be abolished, and in 1816 Admiral Sir Edward Pellew (Lord Exmouth), the commander of a British naval expedition against the Barbary regencies, forced

Yusuf to honour treaties with Piedmont–Sardinia and Naples–Sicily. Nevertheless, the corsairs remained faintly active, although their only prizes were papal freighters and Sicilian fishing-smacks. In 1819 an Anglo-French squadron fairly effectively curbed even this activity, and by the 1820s Sardinia was in a position to dictate terms to Tripoli. The Greek war of Independence brought about the final collapse of the Tripoli corsairs. Under a treaty obligation, the regency sent what the Turkish admiral put in charge of them called a few badly-armed fishing boats, most of them originally Maltese or Italian. This pathetic little fleet was destroyed at the Battle of Navarino in October 1827, and by the 1830s French and British warships had cleared all corsairs from the Mediterranean, which had hardly been free from piracy since late Roman times.

For 300 years Tripoli had lived, unproductively and parasitically, by pirate wars on the divided states of Europe. The apparent wealth of the regency was quite artificial and, certainly from about 1670 onwards, its naval strength illusory. That no decisive action was taken to stop the capture of ships, the enslavement of crews and passengers, the looting of cargoes, and the extortion of safe conduct tribute was a standing reproach to every one of the major European naval powers. Even more senseless and selfish was the export of European arms and naval stores to the regencies, and the courting of the corsairs by the French and others as allies against common enemies.

Paolo Della Cella, who was surgeon to a military expedition sent to Cyrenaica by Yusuf Karamanli in 1819, found the regency in a beggarly state. The desert beyond Tripoli was 'infested with vagabond hordes, and to be robbed by them was the least of the risks to be run'. Saharan caravans, he learned, were still setting out from Misurata with loads of European textiles and Venetian coloured glass jewellery – 'for the belles of Timbuctu' – and were returning with gold, ivory, and slaves, but even this trade was falling off. At Benghazi he found a tumbledown, flyblown village with a population of about 5,000; even the *Bey*'s castle threatened to collapse every time its nine guns fired a salute.

Tripoli's economy was nearly ruined by the ending of corsairing, which was soon to be followed by the diversion of trans-Saharan trade westwards and southwards to the 'European' ports on the Atlantic coast. Tribal and dynastic troubles in both Tripolitania and Cyrenaica meant that a standing army of 45,000 men, in an estimated population of only 650,000, had to be maintained. In 1820 the main revenues of the state were the Tripolitanian land taxes and tribute from Cyrenaica and Fezzan, but about two-thirds of this income was spent on the Pasha's harem and court, or handed out in the form of political gifts and bribes.

Yusuf had to find more money. In 1807 he had raised the tax on every palm- and fruit-tree; later he debased the coinage and imposed a 'contribution' on his Jewish creditors. But in 1830 France demanded, and was given, his promise to abolish piracy and the enslavement of Christians. Through French diplomacy, most of the smaller Mediterranean powers were freed from paying safe-conduct tribute. (It is a measure of the terror inspired by the almost non-existent corsairs that such payments were still being made.)

By now, the Karamanlis had lost most of their popular support. In 1831 a revolt broke out in the Giofra oases and spread to Fezzan. The following year, when a British squadron threatened to bombard Tripoli for non-payment of debts, Yusuf tried to raise money by pawning the town's defensive guns and by an extraordinary levy of the people. This caused rebellion to break out in Tripoli itself in July 1832 and Yusuf was forced to abdicate in favour of his son, Ali. In 1834, after three years of virtual civil war, the Sultan Mohammad II confirmed Ali as Pasha. But it was expected, especially after the French occupation of Algiers in 1830, that the regency would soon be annexed by one or other of the great powers. The town of Tripoli was still in revolt when, in March 1835, the Ottoman government sent a fleet for the supposed purpose of supporting Ali and crushing the rebels. While Turkish troops occupied the town, Ali went on board the Turkish flagship to welcome the Sultan's representative. He was quietly arrested and the fall of the Karamanli Dynasty, after 120 years of independence, was immediately proclaimed from Tripoli Castle.

Chapter 11

Turks, Explorers and Sanussis

AFTER THE FALL of Algiers to the French and Mohammad Ali's achievement of near-independence for Egypt, Turkey reoccupied Tripoli to prevent further loss of nominally Ottoman North African territory. Apart from its dubious strategic value, the province was hardly a desirable possession. With the suppression of the corsairs, its main income was from the slave trade, and that was soon to be curtailed through diplomatic pressure brought by Britain. The Ottoman governors soon found that the Libyans, while prepared to pay homage to the Sultan, were not at all willing to pay his taxes, and well into the second half of the nineteenth century the army was fighting rebels in the interior of the country.

In 1835 there were two serious uprisings, one led by Abd-al-Jalil Saif al-Nasir in Fezzan, and the other by Jumah bin Khalifa, who was ruling from the hill town of Yefren as uncrowned 'King of the Western Gebel'. In 1836 Taher Pasha, the Admiral-in-Chief of the Turkish fleet, failed to penetrate Jumah's mountain defences, and was replaced in 1838 by Ali Askar Pasha. Both he and Mohammad Amin Pasha, appointed in 1842, mounted fairly successful campaigns against the rebels, but the task of subduing areas where central government, although sometimes acknowledged, had not been formally imposed since Roman times was almost too great even for the Turkish army. Jumah was captured and imprisoned in 1842, and there was peace until 1854 when he escaped, returned to the mountains, and renewed the revolt. Only when he was killed in 1856 was Turkish rule firmly established in the *Gebel*, although merely the submission and taxing of the people were involved.

Herodotus, Pliny, and Ptolemy were still Europe's main sources of African geography when Jonathan Swift wrote:

> So Geographers in Afric-Maps
> With Savage-Pictures fill their Gaps:
> And o'er unhabitable Downs,
> Place Elephants for want of Towns

or, rather, for want of knowledge. At the beginning of the nineteenth century, Europeans knew less of the interior of Africa than of the earthward face of the moon. But there was by then an incentive for opening up the continent as a market for cheap, factory-made goods, and with these commercial considerations were allied humanitarian, religious, scientific, and political ones.

In the eighteenth century a few Europeans had used Tripoli, on the shortest route from the Mediterranean to Central Africa, as a base for penetration of the interior. In 1710 two priests, Padre Carlo da Genova and Padre Severino da Salesia, left the town and crossed the Sahara to preach the Gospel in the kingdom of Masina on the Upper Niger. They died soon after reaching their destination, but that they went so far and survived for so long was a brave achievement.

Libya, apart from the coastal area and a sprinkling of classical place-names, was a blank on the maps, and throughout the nineteenth century Europeans could travel through unexplored country in Tripolitania, Cyrenaica, and Fezzan. Not until 1819 did Paolo Della Cella become the first European to give a first-hand account of the Sirtica. The English Beechey brothers, Frederick and Henry, followed him four years later and, like Della Cella, corrected many European misconceptions about Cyrenaica. Their descriptions of the Gebel Akhdar, the Green Mountain, contrasted with the popular idea of endless sands and desolation. They demolished myths, handed down from classical times, of the poisonous beasts and burning sands of the Sirtica. 'The Sirtis', they state with calm assurance, 'possesses, in fact, no terrors peculiar to itself. At least,' they add with half-fearful doubt, 'not that we are acquainted with.' Even when the English traveller and amateur archaeologist, H. S. Cowper, rode through the Tarhuna and Garian hills in 1895 and 1896, he was exploring country barely visited by Europeans since pre-Islamic times, and as a result came to some disastrous conclusions about the Roman stone olive-oil presses still standing. They were probably 'symbolic structures . . . nearly akin to the mysterious *Asherim* of the Baal worshippers' and erected 'with intense religious fervour'. Any archaeological puzzle can be all too easily attributed to religion.

Most European travellers on the southward route from Tripoli to Central Africa were at first British, or British-sponsored. In 1788 'An Association for promoting Discovery in the Inland parts of Africa' had been founded in London, and for the next twenty years it organised the exploration of the Sahara and the western Sudan, areas that, despite early British penetration, were later to become part of the French African empire. The western Sudan was first approached from the north when Frederick Hornemann, a German travelling on the instructions of the association, left Cairo in 1798 disguised as an Arab and accompanied by a German servant, Joseph Frendenburgh. They passed through the oases of Siwa and Augila and reached Murzuk – the first Europeans, apart from slaves, to do so. Frendenburgh died ('led astray by wine and women', Hornemann recorded) and his master, after spending seven months in the oasis, went on to Tripoli, which he reached in August 1799. The following year he started south again and died, reportedly of dysentery, in the Niger region.

In the early nineteenth century Tripoli was the best base for the penetration of the Sahara and the lands to the south. It was almost on the edge of the desert and, better still, Yusuf Karamanli not only had some control over Fezzan and the great caravan trail part of the way to Bornu, but was on terms with the Sultans of Bornu and Sokoto. He claimed he could guarantee the safety of any traveller from his capital to Bornu, and between 1819 and 1825 three British expeditions, taking advantage also of the cordial relations between the Pasha and consul Warrington, travelled into the interior. A specific promise from the Pasha to provide British travellers with an escort to Bornu resulted in a young surgeon and 'gentleman of great science', Joseph Ritchie, being appointed British vice-consul in Fezzan. Once there, he was to gather information on the country and later go on to Bornu and the Niger. Accompanied by Captain George Lyon, R.N., he left Tripoli in 1819 and travelled through Beni Ulid and Socna to Murzuk, where the party ran out of money and Ritchie died. Lyon returned to Tripoli.

The Pasha renewed his offer of safe conduct, this time for a fee of £5,000. Walter Oudney, a Royal Navy surgeon, Lieutenant Dixon Denham, and Lieutenant Hugh Clapperton, R.N., were selected by the British Colonial Office for 'the successful prosecution of the discoveries now attempting in the interior of Africa'. Oudney, like Ritchie, was appointed British vice-consul, and his duties were to include 'the extension of our commerce' in the interior. He was to take samples of British manufactures with him, study the market, and make Britain's name known; the main duty of Denham and Clapperton was to trace the course of the River Niger. Escorted by

200 of the Pasha's troops, the party left Tripoli in February 1822 and travelled to Bornu by way of Murzuk. Oudney died in January 1824, but Denham and Clapperton explored Bornu and Hausaland before returning to Tripoli a year later. The central Sahara and the important caravan oasis of Ghat, as well as Bornu and the shores of Lake Chad, had been charted, and the expedition had shown that the Tripoli–Bornu route could be safely travelled by Christian gentlemen in European dress.

The first European known to reach the fabled city of Timbuctu, the African Samarkand, was a Scotsman, Major Alexander Gordon Laing. He set out from Tripoli in 1825 and after two months' travel arrived at Ghadames where the people, he wrote, 'vie with each other in the continual performance of kind and hospitable acts'. In August 1826 he entered Timbuctu, but when he left the town a month later he was murdered, the British wrongly alleged on the order of the Pasha of Tripoli.

In the meantime an Italian, baron Enrico Minutoli, was exploring the Libyan Desert between Egypt and Cyrenaica and from 1824 to 1826 a Frenchman, Jean Pacho, travelled through Cyrenaica, the Marmarica, and the oases of Augila, Marada, Giarabub, and Siwa.

As a result of information compiled by the Ritchie, Lyon, and Oudney missions, the British government was trying for humanitarian and commercial reasons to persuade the Pasha of Tripoli to stop the trans-Saharan slave trade by offering him a 'pecuniary compensation'. The problem, as outlined by Denham, was that Moorish merchants in Bornu would only accept slaves in payment for their wares, and as long as they refused any other exchange the slave trade would continue. During the 1830s the anti-slavery campaign of Sir Thomas Fowell Buxton drew the attention of the British public for the first time to the horrors of the trans-Saharan slave caravans. Basing his figures on explorers' reports, he estimated that 20,000 slaves were being taken every year to Barbary and Egypt, with 42 per cent (an impossibly precise figure) dying on the way. In 1840, and again in 1843, the British and Foreign Anti-Slavery Society called on the Sultan of Turkey and the governor of Tripoli, among other interested parties, to abolish this traffic. At the insistence of Britain, the Sultan did in 1848 forbid the governor of Tripoli and Turkish civil servants there to deal in slaves. But in August the following year the British vice-consul in Murzuk reported the death from thirst of a whole caravan of 1,600 slaves travelling up from Bornu; six months later he reported another 800 deaths from thirst. Meanwhile, the vice-consul at Benghazi had learned of 400 slaves, out of a gang of 1,600, dying on the march from Wadai, and a check on Tripoli port returns in 1850 disclosed that the number of slaves being shipped from there to Albania, Rhodes, Cyprus, Constantinople, and the Levant was actually increasing. Again through British pressure, the Sultan in 1855 prohibited the transport of slaves from Tripoli, Benghazi, and Derna to Crete, where they were forwarded to other parts of the eastern Mediterranean. This was followed by a *firman* (decree) from the Sultan forbidding the sending of slaves by land or sea between Tripoli and Turkey and in 1857 by the abolition of slave dealing, but not slavery, in the Ottoman empire. Although the traffic was not to be ended for at least another half-century, Wilhelm Heine, a German artist who visited Tripoli in 1859, found that: 'Since the prohibition of the import of slaves into the Regency, caravans coming from the interior have diverted their traffic eastwards, to Egypt, or westwards, to the Moroccan coast, and as a result transport has lessened and imports have fallen off considerably.'[1] Slaves continued to be taken across the desert, not up to the coast, but only as far as Fezzan, where they tended and watered the gardens in the oases. At least until the First World War there was a steady traffic in slaves on the Wadai–Cyrenaica route and even in 1920–21, while on her incredible journey to Kufra, Rosita Forbes learned that caravans were carrying to Gialo 'smuggled slave boys and girls of eight to ten years ... solemn little beings with chubby black cheeks peering out of the pointed hoods of minute camels'-hair burnuses.' The last Saharan slave caravan is said to have reached Fezzan in 1929.

It was to report on the slave trade of the great commercial oasis that James Richardson went to Ghadames in 1845. He then travelled to Ghat, where he found slaving was the only commercial activity, and returned to Tripoli by way of Murzuk in 1846. The outcome of his journey was the Central African Mission of 1850. Its object was to open 'regular and secure' communications between the Mediterranean and the River Niger, something that even now only aircraft can provide. Accompanying Richardson was a young German professor, Dr Heinrich Barth, who had ridden and walked from Tangier to Alexandria between 1845 and 1847, and another German,

[1] Leva, 'Tripoli in una Descrizione di Cent'Anni Fa', *Africa*, March 1967, p. 78.

Dr Adolph Overweg, both of them travelling in the service of the British government. The party left Tripoli in March 1850, explored the Garian hills, crossed the Hammadah al-Hamra to Murzuk, and then went down to Ghat. After passing through the district of Air to Agades, the party split up. While Barth went on to Kano, Richardson marched eastwards, but died of fever before he could reach his destination. Barth and Overweg then explored the country to the north, west, and south of Lake Chad but in September 1852 Overweg died. Barth turned westwards and travelled through Sokoto to Timbuctu, which he reached in September the following year. He stayed there six months and returned to Tripoli in September 1855. His magnificent achievement is described in methodical detail in his monumental and fascinating five-volume *Travels and Discoveries in North and Central Africa* which covers the geography, ethnology, history, and languages of the countries he visited. He stands as probably the greatest explorer of the Sahara and the western Sudan. On his return from Timbuctu he had met another British mission led by Dr Edward Vogel, at Kukawa, west of Lake Chad. Vogel, also German, had left Tripoli in 1853 and had travelled via Murzuk, making botanical and zoological studies on the way. He was killed on the orders of the Sultan of Wadai in 1856.

Although the Central African Mission was followed up by expeditions inland from the Atlantic coast, British interest in the Sahara route faded; in 1860 the vice-consuls at Murzuk and Ghadames were recalled, and the exploration of the great desert was carried on mainly by Germans, French, and Italians. During the 1860s and '70s the Frenchmen Mircher, Polignac, Duveyrier, and others travelled in Fezzan and the Ghadames–Ghat area. In 1852 James Hamilton explored the oases of Gialo and Siwa. Krafft-Kraffshagen, disguised as a Muslim pilgrim, wandered through Tripolitania in 1860, at the same time that Smith, Murdock, and Porcher were carrying out some of the first excavations at Cyrene.

Then, in 1864, the German Gerhard Rohlfs, probably the boldest explorer of Libya itself, crossed the wild Ghibla area from Ghadames to Mizda and later travelled from Tripoli through Murzuk, Bornu, and Sokoto to Lagos. In 1869 he was back in Tripoli and marched from there to Egypt via Gialo and Siwa. Four years later, at the head of a German scientific expedition, he tried to reach the unexplored and almost legendary oasis chain of Kufra, but was forced back from this African Lhasa by the hostility of the inhabitants. In

1878, on a mission from the Kaiser to the Sultan of Wadai, he went down from Tripoli through the Giofra oases to Zillah, crossed to Gialo, penetrated the awful Calanscio Sand Sea, and reached the forbidden oasis. He was lucky to come out with his life and eventually reached Benghazi.

Another German, Moritz von Beurmann, left Benghazi in 1862 to search for the remains of Edward Vogel. After passing through parts of Fezzan never before visited by Europeans, he reached Wadai where, like Vogel, he was killed. Alexandrina Tinne, a young Dutch heiress, was brutally murdered on the Murzuk–Ghat trail; Gustav Nachtigal, on an epic journey from Tripoli to Wadai and then up to Cairo, explored the Tibesti Mountains; and in 1867 Erwin von Bary roamed the Gebel Garian studying megalithic monuments. He later went on to Ghat and Air and died in Ghat in 1877. The last wide-ranging expedition to, or through, Libya for many years was in 1881 when the *Società d'Esplorazione Commerciale* of Milan sent its president, Manfredo Camperio, to study trade and investment prospects. During the 1880s, after the French annexation of Tunis and the British occupation of Egypt, the Turkish authorities actively discouraged European travellers. Explorers, after the European partition of Africa, were anyway turning to more rewarding areas of the continent, and Tripoli never became the great gateway to Central Africa that the British had envisaged earlier in the century.

In the middle of the nineteenth century there arose in Cyrenaica the religious revivalist movement, the Sanussia, that was to be the making of modern independent Libya. Its founder, Mohammad bin Ali al-Sanussi al-Khattabi al-Idrisi al-Hassani, was born at Mustaganem in Algeria in the late 1780s of a family claiming descent from the Prophet's daughter, Fatima. Sayyid Mohammad was a pious intellectual and in 1821 he started eight years of study at the Karuwiyin University at Fez, where he came into contact with several of the mystic confraternities of Morocco. He returned to Algeria in 1829 with some fame as an ascetic. Accompanied by his first disciples (*ikhwan*) he then set out through the Sahara and Tunisia, Tripolitania and Cyrenaica, preaching greater Islamic unity and a return to the religion of the Prophet, stripped of later additions and irrelevant detail. He eventually arrived in Cairo, but had to abandon his plan to study at Al-Azhar University after offending the authorities by his uncompromising attitude. Instead, he went to the Hijaz and studied under various *shaikhs* at Mecca and Medina. At Mecca he met his most powerful supporter, Amir Mohammad Sharif, the future Sultan of Wadai, and in the famous theologian Ahmad Ibn Idris al-Fasi, head of the Moroccan Al-Khadria confraternity, he found a tutor with ideas in sympathy with his own. Together they went on a missionary journey to Yemen, and when Al-Fasi died there, he left instructions to his disciples to follow the teaching of his favourite pupil. As head of the new Order of the Sanussi, Sayyid Mohammad (known by his followers as the Grand Sanussi) established his first *zawiya*, or monastery-college, near Mecca. On a second journey to southern Arabia he made contact with the puritanical confraternity of the Wahabbis. About 1840 Sayyid Mohammad decided to return home, but was prevented from reaching Algeria by the French invasion. He had little choice but to settle in Cyrenaica and about 1843 he established his first African *zawiya* in the Gebel Akhdar, a few miles from the site of Cyrene. This *Zawiya al-Baida* (the White Monastery) became the Mother Lodge of the Order.

Within a few years, Sayyid Mohammad was able to return to Mecca, where he preached to pilgrims from all parts of the Islamic world. In the meantime the *ikhwan*, the brothers of the Order, were going out from Baida to teach Sanussi doctrine and to found new *zawiyas*. When Sayyid Mohammad returned to Cyrenaica in 1853, he decided to move the headquarters of the Order to the poor but healthy oasis of Giarabub, about 180 miles south of Tobruk. His main purpose for doing so was to isolate the Order from political or religious interference by Turks or Europeans. Giarabub was astride important trade and pilgrim routes, and was nearly in the centre of the growing sphere of Sanussi influence in Egypt, Libya, and Sudan. It was there that he built the Islamic University that was soon to become second in Africa only to Al-Azhar, and there he was buried in a great domed tomb after his death in 1859.

The Sanussi are a strictly orthodox order of Sufis, or Muslim mystics. They use no physical aids to mysticism and have never been either particularly puritanical or fanatical. They are not a sect, but an ascetic fraternity, originally with a strong proselytising mission. They preach greater devotion to, and deeper understanding of, Islam; the making of good Muslims is the first object, to which the making of good mystics is only secondary. To the Grand Sanussi, the faith and morals taught by the Prophet were as valid for nineteenth-century Saharan society as for seventh-century Arabian and, as could be expected, his greatest following was not among the townspeople but among the desert tribesmen and the oasis-dwellers.

By the time of the Grand Sanussi's death, the Order and its *zawiyas* were established among the nomadic and semi-nomadic tribes, and in the oases, of Libya and western Egypt. Religious and temporal power being allied in Islam, the Grand Sanussi was considered by those under his spiritual influence to be their ruler. To the simple people of the North African hinterland, accustomed to revere *marabuts*, or holy men, the Head of the Order was deeply respected for his dual leadership, and Rosita Forbes, writing in 1921, declared: 'I have never travelled in any country so united in devotion to its leader as Libya.'

The Order's wealth and temporal power resulted from its industrious exploitation of the meagre resources of the eastern Sahara and the collection of tithes from the faithful. The *zawiyas*, which were colleges, monasteries, and markets, were often built at watering places on the trade and pilgrim routes, and travellers who halted there to take advantage of the three days' free hospitality offered, were subjected to Sanussi doctrine. *Ikhwan*, travelling with the trade and pilgrim caravans, broadcast the Order's teaching across Africa, to Kanem and Borku, to Senegambia and northern Nigeria. The prosperity of the Benghazi–Wadai caravan route in the later nineteenth century was largely the result of Sanussi enterprise and protection, and the Sultan of Wadai used to put his north-bound caravans in the care of his 'brother and fellow-ruler', the Grand Sanussi. Individual *zawiyas*, supported by gifts of land by the faithful, and ruled by *shaikhs* of the Order, gained considerable local political influence by offering unbiased mediation in tribal, commercial, and religious disputes. In Cyrenaica the *zawiyas* became an integral part of the tribal system, in effect tribal institutions. Wherever Sanussi influence spread, security, justice, education, and trade tended to follow.

The Grand Sanussi was succeeded by his second son, Mohammad al-Mahdi, who fulfilled all the conditions of an ancient prophecy which told that the Mahdi who would conquer the world for Islam would be born of parents named Mohammad and Fatima, would spend several years in seclusion, and would reach his majority on the first day of the month of Moharram in 1300 A.H. (12 November 1882).

There were by then thirty-eight *zawiyas* in Cyrenaica and the Sirtica, a further seventeen in Egypt, and eighteen in Tripolitania. There were others in Fezzan, Algeria, Tunisia, and Asia, but the area of greatest influence was between Agedabia and Tobruk. Under Al-Mahdi the Order reached the height of its power and in the 1880s had between 1½ and 3 million *ikhwan*, each one of them a more or less active missionary agent. The Mahdi extended and consolidated Sanussi religious, political, and commercial influence, but this tide was to be halted, and then rolled back, by the French advance across Central Africa.

Yet Al-Mahdi wanted no war. When the Sudanese Mahdi Mohammad Ahmad, appealed to the Order for help against the British, his appeal went unanswered, and the Sanussis were in fact disgusted by the atrocities committed by his followers. Nevertheless, a very unjust image of the Order and its head was built up by foreigners. The French traveller Henri Duveyrier warned in 1863 that the Order must be watched 'and its development opposed wherever possible'. He noted that Giarabub, which he called 'a great fortified convent', was well supplied with arms and powder and, moreover, had fifteen cannon. He complained that the Order opposed the French in Algeria, Tunisia, and Senegal, and he suggested that the renewal of anti-European feeling among Muslims was in part due to Sanussi propaganda. He alleged: 'At a sign from his superior, any affiliate will, without hesitation, become a propaganda agent, a soldier, a bravo, or a sneaking poisoner for the greater glory of God.'[2]

The Grand Sanussi and, for the most part of his life, Al-Mahdi, were in fact on the defensive against their neighbours. In the north, the Turks were wary of the Sanussis, who wielded more power over large areas of the country than the Ottoman governors; according to Duveyrier, more than one governor considered himself first a Sanussi servant and second a Turkish official. In the south, Sanussi authority was threatened by the French advance from the Congo towards Wadai.

In 1894 the headquarters of the Order was moved to Kufra, the almost inaccessible group of oases some 400 miles south of Giarabub, and from which the great Wadai–Benghazi and other trade routes could be controlled. Before then, Kufra had been one of the Sahara's

[2] Duveyrier, *Le Confrérie Musulmane di Sidi Mohamed ben Ali es-Senousi, etc.*, Rome, 1918.

most notorious brigand strongholds; under Sanussi rule, traders were protected and customs dues levied, the villages of Jof and Taj were built, gardens were cultivated, and the oases, visited by *ikhwan* from many countries, became the home of a godly and respected community.

But even as the Order was reaching its greatest power, it was forced to retreat before the French. Al-Mahdi had to abandon his defensive policy and move his headquarters to Ghiru, north of Borku, to direct operations against the French advance from Lake Chad. He was determined to protect the trade system on which the Order lived and, although he had no regular army, he united the tribes and supplied them with arms and money. Having failed to prevent the French occupation of Kanem, he died suddenly in June 1902. As his sons were then minors, he was succeeded by his nephew, Sayyid Ahmad al-Sharif, who moved the headquarters of the Order back to Kufra. Sayyid Ahmad fought the French advance from Central Africa into Kanem spasmodically from 1904 to 1911, but he was unable to halt their penetration. In every district they occupied Sanussi influence waned and when, in 1910, Turkish troops marched into the Tibesti, Sanussi influence was virtually limited to the country north of the 20th parallel.

The trans-Saharan trade system, which had been in existence even before the Phoenicians went to Tripolitania or the Greeks to Cyrenaica, was still active in the 1870s, but thirty years later had virtually collapsed. The penetration of the Senegal and the Niger–Benue river basins by the French and the British diverted commerce from the Sahara to the Atlantic. Then the railways came, and in 1905 the great trading city of Kano in northern Nigeria was linked by train and steamer with Liverpool via Lagos, and no longer by camel and galley with Venice via Tripoli. From Britain came cheaper goods, more quickly delivered. When the railway had been built, a ton of merchandise could be sent from Liverpool to Kano for a little over £3; from Tripoli alone the cost of delivery to Kano was between £6 and £6 10*s*. At the same time, there was less to export across the Sahara. Alluvial gold was not as plentiful in western Sudan in the nineteenth as in earlier centuries; the slave trade was illegal and slaves were not easily taken from territories coming under British and French rule. Other, cheaper, sources of raw material were being exploited; the development of South African ostrich farms to meet the demands of European fashions, for instance, ruined the Sudanese feather industry.

Of the four great trails that crossed the Sahara in the nineteenth century, one started in Morocco and the other three in Libya. The greatest went from Tripoli to Ghadames, whose merchants monopolised its traffic, and then on to Ghat, Air, Zinder, and Kano. Although it was the longest and the most dangerous route, it gave the best returns. The Bornu route, the ancient Garamantean road, from Tripoli to Murzuk, Bilma, and so south of Lake Chad, was fast and relatively safe until it was ruined, first by political instability in the Chad region, then by the Turks' inability to protect the caravans from Tebu and Tuareg raiders, and finally by the coming of the railways. The easternmost route, from Benghazi to Gialo, Kufra, and the Tibesti to Wadai, developed rapidly after the rise of Wadai in the early nineteenth century, and flourished under Sanussi protection.

From Tripoli and Benghazi the south-bound caravans carried European arms and ammunition, glass and mirrors, *baraccans*, tarbushes, Tripoli silk brocade, English cottons, drugs, and Venetian writing paper, and returned with cured goat skins, worked leather, ivory, kola nuts, ostrich feathers, Kano cottons, a little gold dust, and a few smuggled slaves. The decline of Saharan trade between the 1870s and the First World War was reflected by the fall in the value of Sudanese goods sent to Europe via Tripoli. Ivory exports, which were worth about £36,000 in 1880, were down to £4,000 in 1910; over the same period, exports of ostrich feathers fell from £120,000 a year to £4,000. In the decade 1882–92 exports to Europe from Sudan were worth about £15 million annually; in 1911 they amounted to a bare £1,800,000. This dwindling trade was almost completely halted by the French occupation of Wadai, Tibesti, and Borku in 1906–14, and by the Italian invasion of Libya in 1911.

In the second half of the nineteenth century, Libya was allowed to be itself. Turkish rule was not harsh, but indifferent. So long as they paid their taxes and remained loyal, the Libyans were left to their own ways and their poverty. They rarely suffered, or gained, from being Ottoman subjects. Tripoli, no longer a corsair base and capital of an independent state, took on the more natural role of provincial capital and chief port and market town of Tripolitania.

Deprived of its best sources of income, corsairing and slaving, the country existed on its own resources of fishing, farming, and stock-raising. The unexploited agricultural potential was tremendous, although perhaps overestimated by visiting Europeans, who were too ready to agree with the old Oriental proverb that: 'Grass never grows where the Turkish hoof has trod.' Just about enough was grown to feed the population or at least to prevent mass starvation. In trying to provide for the effect of the notoriously fickle climate, the government assumed that there would be four good harvests, with a surplus for export, every ten years, four fair harvests, with little or no export surplus, and two bad or very bad years when imports would be needed to prevent famine. In good years up to 40,000 head of cattle could be exported; in a year of drought, such as the 'year of the slaughtering' of 1871, great numbers of sheep and cattle died for lack of water and fodder. The main wealth of the peasant farmer was the palm-tree which, according to an ancient Arab proverb, needs only to stand with its feet in the water and its head in the sun to yield a harvest. From 1868 onwards the esparto grass that grew on the Gefara Plain was exported to Europe, and particularly to Britain, for paper-making. But the method of collecting, by pulling up with the roots, meant that there was no second growth and that supplies had to be found further and further inland, and wood pulp soon became a serious competitor anyway.

In 1856 the Dutch consul estimated that Tripoli, with its port, could become the first town of North Africa. The country might be, if not the granary of Rome, then at least that of Malta, Marseilles, and Paris; but before this could happen, firm, co-ordinated, and efficient government was needed. No good could come of the country so long as it was governed by men whose only concern was to enrich themselves during their two- or three-year tours of duty. The consul also pointed out that there was little use in sending honest governors to Tripoli so long as their staff was dishonest or too big; he cited the Bearer of the *Narghile* (Water-Pipe) as a supernumary member of the Pasha's entourage.

The Turks were not colonisers. Apart from their religion, they had nothing in common with their Libyan subjects and they lived and ruled as foreigners in a foreign land. In Tripoli and Benghazi, Turkish influence was strong, among the tribes it was weak, and in the far south almost non-existent. The explorer Rohlfs commented: 'In Tripolitania, more than anywhere else, the work of Turkey is really the negation of any civil government.'

Foreigners have never easily governed Libya and its people. The Turks, with their beggarly revenues, inefficiency, and corruption, were able to do little for the country, and any attempt at improvement was likely to meet passive resistance from the tribes. In 1870 Ali Rida Pasha was dismissed from the governorship because his well-meant attempts to improve the economy were opposed by those who believed their vested interests were being threatened. Unpopular measures were likely to lead to trouble: a series of insurrections, culminating in an attack on Tripoli itself, resulted from the attempt to introduce compulsory military service, and in 1906 tax increases were violently resisted by the tribes. The Young Turk movement of 1908 was disliked in Libya, and its new social and religious programme so scandalised a nation of conservatives that all Young Turk civil servants were recalled to Constantinople.

In Cyrenaica, the tribes were in effect ruled by the Sanussis on behalf of the Turks. Besides providing education, security, and justice, the Order insisted that the tribes, notorious tax-evaders, paid their dues to the government, and so long as this was done and there were no major disturbances the Turks were content to allow the Sanussis to wield very considerable power in the interior. Evans-Pritchard has in fact described the government of Cyrenaica at this time as a 'Turco-Sanussi condominium'.

A tax on men, animals, trees, crops, and wells met the simple expenses of the Turkish administration and paid the civil service, the army, state pensions, and the allowances of the small, bored community of Turkish political exiles in Tripoli. Up to 1887 the only schools, apart from the Italian ones and the Sanussi *zawiyas*, were the *katatib*, the traditional Koranic schools. By 1890 seven mosque schools, teaching elementary subjects, had been opened in Tripolitania. A military school was started in Tripoli in 1888, and in 1897 the city's famous Arts and Crafts School was founded. The Jews had their own schools and one, at Tigrinna near Garian, was said to date from Roman times. By 1911 there were almost 3,000 Libyan and European children at Italian schools in Tripoli, Homs, Benghazi, and Derna, but in the country as a whole very few children ever received any formal education.

The *Vilayat* of Tripoli, roughly comprising Tripolitania and Fezzan, was governed by a *Wali* nominated by the Sultan. From 1879 onwards Benghazi was a separate *Mutassarif*, more or less comprising Cyrenaica, under the direct control of Constantinople.

Not even the size of the country was known, and the frontiers were ill-defined. Confusingly, 'Tripoli' was the town, Tripolitania proper, and all Turkish North Africa. The census of 1911 gave 576,000 people in Tripolitania and Fezzan, while Cyrenaica probably had about 250,000 inhabitants. Tripoli at that time had a population of 29,869, of whom 19,409 were Muslims, 6,460 Jews, and about 4,000 Europeans, mostly Greeks, Maltese, and Italians; some of them, it has been suggested, were the descendants of the Christian slaves of earlier centuries. There were two cinemas and two churches, one Roman Catholic and one Greek.

The country had neither roads nor railways, and even the coastal shipping services were Italian-run. Traditional industries were dying out as Saharan trade declined and no new ones were being started. In 1911 the main exports to Britain, Turkey, and France were 'the products of primitive husbandry', as an Italian writer put it: livestock, skins, dates, and a little grain. Textiles, food, and a few manufactured goods were imported from Europe and Turkey.

Turkish Tripoli had a picturesque charm for European and American visitors who, in their accounts of their visits, illustrated with bad photographs and worse water colours, habitually forecast its occupation by one or other of the European powers, with Italy the most likely. This would happen 'when sufficient excuse arises, or untoward events take place to lead to the dismemberment of the unfortunate Empire which for so long seemed inevitable.' Thus H. S. Cowper in 1897. He said of the country:

> 'Waterless, treeless, except for its waving palms and olives on the coast, nearly tradeless, and it may almost be said harbourless, it lies, rather a desert than a country – a buffer state of sand as it were – between fertile Tunisia and fecund Egypt....
>
> 'Tripoli is, for an Oriental state, moderately well governed, and her people are fairly satisfied. Trade may indeed be bad, and money may be scarce, but the climate is genial, the sun shines and the good folks are content to dream life away, heedless of the anxieties of nineteenth century civilisation. Why should they be disturbed?'[3]

But they were, fourteen years later.

[3] Cowper, *The Hill of the Graces*, London, 1897, pp. 304, 309.

Chapter 12

A 'Historic Destiny'

ON 1 OCTOBER 1911 a great iron battlefleet steamed southwards across the Mediterranean, carrying the three-days-old war between the Italian kingdom and the Turkish empire to the coast of North Africa. Leading the fleet, officially the Italian Combined Naval Force, were the battleships *Vittorio Emanuele*, *Regina Elena*, *Roma*, and *Napoli*. In an age when there was no arm more powerful than the ponderous iron battleship, they were among the greatest weapons in the Italian arsenal. Around them sailed a screen of cruisers, destroyers, and torpedo boats. The nearest Turkish warships were four torpedo boats on the Albanian coast, two ironclads and lesser craft in the Dardanelles, and a broken-down fleet reportedly sailing westwards from Beirut. The Italians were confident of their command of the sea and anyway, their objective was not the ragged Turkish navy but the little ports of Turkish Tripolitania and Cyrenaica. For the intention of the brave southward-sailing fleet was to realise the thirty-year-old ambition of an Italian Libya and the older dream of an Italian North African empire.

The fleet anchored on 2 October off the town of Tripoli that a French traveller had recently called 'the only Mediterranean port that has preserved all its medieval originality'. After a 24-hour delay, the guns of the Italian ships were swung round and at 1515 hours on 3 October bombardment of the three outlying Turkish forts began. Shelling ceased at dusk, but started again at dawn next day. On 5 October 900 marines went ashore and captured the badly damaged forts and their batteries of short-range Krupp guns.

The Turkish commandant, who had few troops, decided to withdraw to save the town from bombardment. Another 1,700 Italian seamen were landed, and by the night of 5 October they had occupied the town and the area immediately outside the walls.

There the advance halted. Instead of attempting to destroy the Turkish forces of under 5,000 men, who escaped inland and joined up with Libyan tribesmen, the Italians chose to await the arrival of their main expeditionary force, which sailed in from Naples and Palermo seven full days after the first landing at Tripoli. It was hoped that a diplomatic settlement with Turkey could be reached by showing 'peaceful intentions' in Libya. But the Turks, in Libya at least, had no such intentions, and they rallied so many Libyans to their side that they were soon ready to counter-attack. The Italians were very nearly overwhelmed by strong Turco-Libyan assaults at Henni-Sharia Shatt, a mile or two east of Tripoli, on 23 October, and again at Henni, Sidi Mesri, and other points east of the town on 26 October.

Meanwhile, more landings had been made on the coasts of Tripolitania and Cyrenaica. The navy had occupied Tobruk roadstead on 4 October; Derna was taken on 18 October after heavy shelling, and troops went ashore at Homs the same day, although the town was not taken until the 21st. On the 18th another fleet anchored off Benghazi, which the Turks had started to defend in the face of hopeless odds: against the guns of seven cruisers and troops packed into twenty transports there were 200 infantrymen, eighty horsemen, and eighteen small guns. On expiry of a 24-hour ultimatum, shelling of the town began. The Great Mosque, the Franciscan Mission, and the British and Italian consulates, filled with refugees, were all hit. The Turks surrendered late on 19 October. Rough seas delayed landings and although, once they got ashore, troops quickly occupied the centre of the town, they met unexpected resistance from the inhabitants of the suburbs. The Turco-Libyan forces withdrew and set up a great camp at Benina, about 12 miles to the east.

By the end of October, the Italians had five small bridgeheads on the Libyan coast. Their forces had been increased to 34,000 men, 6,300 horses, 1,050 wagons, 48 field- and 24 mountain-guns, but European observers of the campaign judged the troops 'excitable and unstable'. Supporting the campaign were 145 warships and 114 other vessels. The newest tools of war, including machine-guns, radio-telegraph, and motor transport, were being used, and even the aeroplane was making its first battle trials. A dozen Farman and Blériot machines, as well as two airships, had been brought to Tripoli for reconnaissance purposes and before long the possibilities of the new air arm were being exploited. On 1 November 1911 an aeroplane was used as a weapon for the first time in war when Lieutenant Gavotti, flying over the Gefara Plain at 2,000 feet, tossed a hand-grenade at Libyan irregulars below. The effects of this aerial bombardment were not recorded.

After a mild insurrection in Tripoli itself at the end of October, harsh reprisals were taken on the civilian population, and *The Times* reported that 'the flood-gates of blood and lust had been opened'. On 5 November 1911, exactly one month after the fall of Tripoli, king Victor Emmanuel issued a royal decree bringing Tripolitania and Cyrenaica under the Italian Crown, although international law recognised no sovereignty over unconquered territory. It was not guessed that between the decreeing and the doing there were to be twenty years of almost continual fighting in Libya. For the Libyans, far from hailing the Italians as liberators, had done the unexpected by joining the Turks in the war against the invaders. After that, Italy could no longer treat the Libyan campaign as, in the words of the London *Standard*, 'a sort of holiday parade'.

Forty-eight years before, in August 1863, when the two-year-old Italian kingdom still lacked Venice and Rome, the *Opinione* of Turin was warning with some foresight: 'If Egypt, and with it the Suez Canal, falls to the British, if Tunis falls to the French, and if Austria expands from Dalmatia into Albania, etc., we will soon find ourselves without a breathing space in the dead centre of the Mediterranean.' Italy was even then beginning to resent restriction in her 'home' sea by the Mediterranean activities of Britain and, particularly, of France. The need for a 'breathing space' and the control of the narrow seas off Sicily was felt even as the third war of Independence was bringing the Venetian territories into the kingdom. As early as 1838 Mazzini had said that 'North Africa must belong to Italy', and as her intended prize in the Mediterranean lottery played out by the great powers in the 1860s and 1870s, Italy chose Tunisia. The tip of Africa nearest to Sicily, and not only geographically, Tunisia had been Rome's first African colony and was in the second half of the nineteenth century again being settled by an active community of Italians that by 1881 numbered about 25,000. Although the French were also active in Tunisia, Italian interests seemed assured by the signing of a twenty-year agreement with the Bey in 1868, and national pride was duly humiliated when, in May 1881, the Bey recognised the protectorate of France.

It was largely the loss of Tunis that made Italy join Britain, France, Belgium, Germany, and Spain in the great 'scramble' for

Africa in the 1880s. A latecomer in Africa, Italy was also a newly-united, newly-independent, and relatively poor country, and as such had to be content with rather meagre pickings from the division of the continent, the barren but strategically useful territories of Somalia and Eritrea. By 1900 Turkish Libya was one of the mere half dozen African territories still not under European claim, and it was there that Italy had been looking for a Mediterranean 'breathing space' and a consolation prize ever since losing Tunisia. As far back as the 1880s the 'imperialist' Prime Minister Francesco Crispi was talking of making the seas between Sicily and the two Sirtic Gulfs 'almost an Italian strait'. It was he who drew attention to the strategic importance of Libya and warned of the danger of another power occupying it. Crispi believed that if his country was to have an empire, better a Mediterranean one. 'Mare Nostrum' was a phrase again heard in Rome during his ministry, particularly after the French started calling the Mediterranean a 'French Lake'. Indeed, in later years the Italians were to justify their invasion of Libya by claiming that they had been forced into it to counter the expansion of France and other powers in the Mediterranean.

By the 1880s it was realised that Italian fleets operating from Tripolitania and Cyrenaica could guard the central Mediterranean, which the opening of the Suez Canal had made a great international waterway, while the port of Tobruk, a German traveller noted, was the key to the eastern Mediterranean. Tobruk, in fact, lies in a nearly straight line with the ports of Benghazi, Tripoli, and Zuara, and this line forms the base of a triangle whose second side, starting from Zuara, passes along the south-east coast of Sicily and the 'sole' and the 'heel' of the Italian 'boot' to the Albanian port of Valona. The triangle's third side extends from Libya's eastern frontier, up the west coast of Greece, to Valona. Occupation of Libya would give Italy the control of two sides of this central Mediterranean triangle, apart from British Malta just within its north-west boundary. Mussolini, who said 'for others the Mediterranean is just a route, for us it is life itself', hoped to have the third side in his grasp when he invaded Albania and Greece at the beginning of the Second World War. In addition, Libya was always considered a potential base for the Italian penetration of Africa to Lake Chad and beyond.

Italy waited thirty years for Libya, having decided that it must be taken with the least trouble at home and abroad. A vague policy of 'peaceful penetration' was started in the 1880s; for the territory was to be bought, not conquered. 'Peaceful penetration' was a half-hearted project that went slowly forward for many years. Popular enthusiasm for this, and every other Italian imperial policy, cooled for several years after 1896, when the shattering Ethiopian victory at Adowa brought down the Crispi government. Still more harmful was the positively hostile attitude of the Turks, particularly after the 'Young Turk' revolution of 1908. To Constantinople, Tripoli's only real value was as a strategic buffer between British Egypt and French Tunisia, and while the Turks themselves made no attempt to develop the country, they did not encourage attempts by others, and particularly Italians, to do so. Nevertheless, Italian and other businessmen, explorers, and scientists did manage to penetrate Libya in the last years of the nineteenth century and study what was then an almost unknown country.

Travellers were impressed, perhaps over-impressed, by the potential wealth of the neglected countryside. In 1879 the German explorer Rohlfs noted that the country north of Tocra in Cyrenaica was so green that it reminded him of Italy. He thought it was a land the Italians should reconquer and he was unable to understand why their claims to Tripoli were not being harder pressed. 'To me,' he said, 'the possession of Tunis is not worth one-tenth that of Tripoli.' Five years later, the Italian explorer and patriot Manfredo Camperio seriously proposed the settling of Italian farming colonies in Cyrenaica. He also judged the country between Tripoli and Homs to be ideal for European farmers. Other late nineteenth-century travellers agreed that there was a splendid future for energetic Italian colonists, farmers, and traders in Libya. In 1911 a writer was optimistically estimating that one-quarter of the country could be cultivated by irrigating it with underground water raised through artesian wells. A complaint current in Italy long before the invasion of Libya was that the work of hundreds of thousands of emigrants to the Americas was being lost. How much better, it was argued, if emigrants could go to an Italian Mediterranean colony where their work would benefit both themselves and the mother country. 'To emigrate is servile,' Italians were told, 'but to conquer colonies is a worthy task for a free and noble people.'

Italian shipping lines were calling regularly at all the main Libyan ports at the end of the 1880s. Schools were opened to spread Italian language and culture, and by the early twentieth century Italian was widely spoken. In 1905 the great Banco di Roma was ordered to make an 'economic penetration' of the country. The first office was opened at Tripoli in 1907 and within three years there were branches in Benghazi and twelve other towns. The bank not only financed new businesses, but bought controlling interests in shipping lines serving Libyan ports and in the export trade in esparto grass, cereals, ostrich feathers, ivory, wool, and sponges. It even organised the first mineral-prospecting expedition in Tripolitania. Despite Turkish attempts to hinder its activities, the bank by 1910 controlled much of the modest internal and foreign trade. The bank was unable to buy land. While there were no official restrictions on its sale to foreigners, the Turkish authorities, by dropping an occasional hint to landowners, ensured that little was bought either by Italian individuals or organisations. So long as land could not be bought, there was little chance that the policy of 'peaceful penetration' would transform Libya into the hoped-for 'extension of the Sicilians and the southern Italians'.

Hope and fear, hope that the policy of 'peaceful penetration' would eventually succeed, fear that war with Turkey in North Africa would lead to a European war, were the emotions of a generation of Italian statesmen and diplomats who dithered over the Tripoli question at the international conference tables. Italy was not ready to fight Turkey for the possession of Tripoli until a fistful of assurances had been gained, most of them several times repeated, of the disinterestedness of every power that could have any possible interest in the territory. The attitude and actions of France, in particular, were a continual cause for upset. It was feared, and rightly as events later showed, that the French would sooner or later push the vague frontier between Tunisia and Tripoli eastward. Then there was a suspicion, also justified, that France was nibbling at the remoter borders of Turkish Africa, for after the main European 'scramble' for Africa in the 1880s, France in the 1890s was still slowly extending her claims from Central Africa towards the shadowy southern frontiers of Tripoli. Britain was a lesser bogy and it was assumed that her moral backing for any Italian move in North Africa had already been bought by Italy's non-interference in Egypt. So when, in August 1890, Britain and France announced agreement of zones of influence in the territories south of Tripoli, it was French intentions, rather than British ones, that disturbed Rome. Turkey was the first to denounce the Anglo-French accord, but by

January 1891, Italy was also complaining, and Rome demanded clearer definition of Franco-Turkish zones of influence in Africa. The hinterland of Tripoli, it was angrily pointed out, was 'an essential element in the stability of the Mediterranean'. Italy was concerned that the *status quo* in and around Tripoli be maintained for, as no more than the self-appointed heir to Turkish North Africa, she could only make bitter verbal protests when Turkey allowed the legacy to be frittered away.

Britain and France came to wider agreement on spheres of influence in Africa in 1898–9, and although both Constantinople and Rome were assured that there were no French claims on Tripoli, France let it be known that she was not yet ready to recognise Italy as Turkey's heir in Africa. In fact, the French seemed to have had no intention of taking Tripoli, but used the possibility of their doing so as a bargaining point in their relations with Italy. A French writer also expressed the view that: 'The Turks are the best neighbours we could have on our Tunisian frontiers. We will gain nothing from another power installing itself in Tripolitania.'

It was not until 1902 that a promise of French acquiescence, or at least indifference, to any Italian action in Tripoli was finally won in exchange for recognition of French claims in Morocco. The year 1902 was crucial for Italian hopes in North Africa. In May, after confirming British rights in Egypt, Italy was given assurances of reciprocal recognition of rights in Turkish Africa. When, in the same year, the Triple Alliance with Germany and Austria came up for renewal for the fourth time, Italy won from both allies a guarantee of freedom of action in Tripoli. Even Tsar Nicholas II, during a state visit to Rome, was persuaded to 'consider with benevolence' Italian interests in North Africa.

International opinion had seemingly been won over and an early invasion was expected. In April 1902 a left-wing deputy told parliament in Rome that Tripoli was 'necessary to the existence of Italy'. Another deputy claimed that the occupation would raise the value of Eritrea by making possible the opening of an overland trade route between the Mediterranean and the Red Seas. While most Italians agreed that not to take Tripoli would be a 'national disaster', there were also lugubrious warnings that an invasion of a country not worth having at any price would be a useless expense. But it was international tension, and the real danger of starting a European war by hasty action, that persuaded the government to postpone the invasion. Indeed, the Banco di Roma was ordered to start its work in Tripoli only after the 1904 agreements between Britain, France, and Spain on the future of all North Africa had partly slackened the tension.

At the Algeciras Conference of 1906 Italy collected further assurances. Yet other powers, among them Germany and even the United States, were obviously interested in Libya, and an Italian writer at the time complained that it would soon become an international claim, as Morocco was to be. In 1908 the Jewish Territorial Organisation sent a commission to Cyrenaica to study a plan for founding a Jewish homeland there under Turkish protection. The scheme was soon dropped, but it had shown that the Italians were not the only ones thinking of a promised land in North Africa.

France was still a considerable menace. For years Italy had been complaining that the French advance into Central Africa and Sudan was ruining the Saharan caravan trade, and with it the economy of Tripoli, by diverting commerce westwards along the new railways to the Atlantic ports of West Africa. Then, with growing unease, Rome watched the advance of the red, white, and blue tricolour towards Bilma, Borku, Djanet, and the Tibesti. Suspicion of French motives was confirmed when, in May 1910, Turkish and Franco-Tunisian commissions agreed on a new frontier that gave Tunisia a large area of coastal belt that might have been assumed to belong to Tripoli.

In 1911 Italy acted. It was just thirty years since Tunis had been lost and 'peaceful penetration' had proved a failure. In April Arabic-Italian manuals began appearing on civil servants' desks in Rome. Then, in the summer, came the Agadir crisis; Italy stood aside while France took Morocco by placating Germany with a slice of Congo territory. Italy would move now or never in North Africa to restore the equilibrium lost by this latest French expansion in the western Mediterranean.

For many years the Turks had opposed the 'peaceful penetration' of Tripoli, and it was this 'hostility' that Italy built up into a *casus belli*. When two Italians, one of them a priest, had been murdered in Libya in 1908 and the Turkish authorities failed to make a satisfactory investigation, the Italian press had been able to shriek that Italian lives and property in Turkish Africa were in danger. The press continued to campaign for occupation, and by the summer of 1911 Rome was reported to be facing the crudely engineered crisis 'with resolution'.

International relations were more than usually strained and complex in 1911, and the new Giolitti government had to direct the crisis warily if a major war was not to break out. Autumn was chosen as the best season, both climatically and politically, for action in North Africa. Giolitti's stated intention was to 'isolate the Libyan action as much as possible so as to avoid, above all, those repercussions in the Balkans that experience has shown to be wellnigh impossible in winter'. In the summer of that tense year the crisis reached the stage of Turkey being warned that 'unless her attitude to Italian interests in Tripoli changed, the results would be far graver than adverse articles in the press and speeches in parliament'.

A diplomatic campaign had meanwhile been started to ensure that the crisis was strictly confined to Tripoli. Sir Edward Grey, the British Foreign Secretary, when approached in July, assured Italy of Britain's 'sympathy' in the crisis, and in September he flatly refused a Turkish appeal to Britain to mediate. France gave 'explicit and categorical' assurances that she would stand by earlier agreements with Italy, thereby giving what amounted to a guarantee of non-interference. From St Petersburg came friendly words from Neratov, the Russian Foreign Minister. Italy's Triple Alliance partner, Austria, put aside misgivings about likely repercussions in the Balkans and promised not to put 'any difficulty' in Italy's way. Giolitti's main embarrassment then was the carefully cultivated friendship between Turkey and Germany, the third Triple Alliance partner. The Germans did, in fact, at the last minute try to mediate in the crisis, seeing in Italy's intended action a grave threat to Turco-German relations. Rome informed Berlin that mediation was useless; Italian patience was exhausted and the 'stability of the Mediterranean' was about to be ensured; and the general feeling in Italy was that the time had come to forestall possible German action in North Africa.

By the end of August, Giolitti and General Pollio, Chief of the General Staff, had finished planning the Libyan campaign, and early in September the Turkish governor of Tripoli, Ibrahim Pasha, went to Constantinople to report on Italian war preparations. There was very little Turkey could do, for troops had recently been withdrawn from Tripoli to put down a revolt in Yemen. But a cargo ship, the *Derna*, carrying in her hold 20,000 rifles, 2 million rounds of ammunition, and some mountain guns for distribution to trustworthy Libyan tribesmen, sailed from Turkey. On 24 September, while *Derna* was still crossing the Mediterranean, Turkey was warned that the Italian government considered the sending of war material to Tripoli 'an obvious threat to the *status quo* in North Africa'. Two days later, *Derna* started unloading her cargo in Tripoli roadstead and, on 28 September, Italy issued an ultimatum. It complained that for many years Italian interests in Tripoli had suffered on account of the deplorable Turkish administration. It called the shipping of arms to Tripoli 'a manifestly hostile act' and claimed that the Italian community in Tripoli was in danger. Italy's intention, the ultimatum announced, was the military occupation of Tripolitania and Cyrenaica. Turkey was to declare within twenty-four hours that there would be no objection to such a move.

On 29 September, having received an 'unsatisfactory' reply (it was in fact reasonable and conciliatory), Italy declared war and Giolitti was able to announce that the nation was about to fulfil *una fatalità storica* – a historic destiny – by invading Libya.

International reaction to the war was more hostile than had been expected, not on account of the invasion as such, but because the fighting between Italy and Turkey was seen as a threat to the delicate balance of power in the Balkans, and therefore to European peace. In Britain *The Times* considered that Italian grievances against Turkey 'hardly offered an adequate explanation of such drastic action'. It was feared that the occupation of the Libyan ports might provoke strong Muslim reaction in India and elsewhere and that Malta's strategic importance had been neutralised. Some months after the invasion the British ambassador in Rome, Sir J. Rennell Rodd, was expressing a fear that was to come very much closer to reality a generation later. Italian Libya, he warned, might be used as a base by an 'anti-British German or pan-German alliance' to 'obtain possession or control of Egypt, and with it, of the great trade to the east....'

French opinion was more hostile than British, especially when the Italian warship *Agordat* arrested two French cargo ships, the *Carthage* and the *Manouba*, on partly justified suspicion of carrying troops and equipment to the Turks in Libya. Further friction was caused by the smuggling of Turkish war material into Tripolitania from Tunisia. Most Italians, and most of their political parties, apart from a few doom-prophesying voices on the far left, were deliriously enthusiastic about the invasion, at least until the novelty wore off and the casualty lists began to lengthen. A twenty-eight-year-old revolutionary, Benito Mussolini, denounced the invasion and called for class wars, not imperialistic ones. 'Every honest socialist must disapprove of this Libyan adventure,' he said, 'it means only useless and stupid bloodshed.' It was a criticism echoed by Lenin the following year.

Libya was invaded under a disastrously false impression. As a result of some clumsy contacts with a few affable, self-seeking dignitaries before the invasion, it was assumed in Rome that even if the Libyans did not actually join the war against the Turks, they would at least remain neutral. It is said that Italy was so sure of future Libyan support that arms were actually sent to some of the tribes in the summer of 1911; red, white, and green bunting was certainly delivered to Benghazi before the invasion.

The Libyans were not, as it happened, in the least impressed by the Italian propaganda that hailed the invasion as liberation from rulers who had sunk the country into a state of 'squalid abandon' during eighty years of mismanagement. European-style political propaganda was in 1911 a pointless weapon in a country where religion and politics were so close and where, moreover, the Turkish Sultan, as Caliph of Islam, was seen as the godfather of the new anti-European Islamic nationalism. It was a situation as paradoxical to European Christians as it was logical to Libyan Muslims. Italian political reconnaissance had almost entirely overlooked the significance of the common religion of Turks and Libyans; for it was in the name of Islam, and not of Ottoman imperialism, that Asiatic and African Muslims fought side by side against the invasion of one of the 'lands of Islam' by Christian armies. As the fighting developed, bands of rugged tribesmen rode in from the desert and the pre-desert to join the war. They were a far tougher enemy than the relatively easy-living people of the coast and, although Ottoman subjects in name, they in fact acknowledged no authority but their own leaders. They fought alongside the Turkish regulars to keep the independence they had always known, and expected to lose if the Italians were victorious.

The Turks were surprised, but grateful, for this popular support. Without it, their poorly equipped regular forces of less than 5,000 men might not have held out against the invasion for long. A few able officers were sent from Constantinople via Egypt and Cyrenaica to direct the war effort. Among them were Enver Pasha, one of

Turkey's new young rulers, and Mustafa Kemal (Kemal Ataturk, later the first President of the Turkish republic). Into the Turkish camp at Benina, beyond the range of the great naval guns off Benghazi, rode tribesmen from all over western Cyrenaica, rallied and led by the *shaikhs* of Sanussi *zawiyas*. Similarly led, the tribesmen of eastern Cyrenaica assembled outside Tobruk and at Enver Pasha's camp overlooking Derna.

The Libyan irregulars, the majority of them armed with old, single-shot Greek rifles, learned the rules of modern war the hard way. They soon recognised, for instance, the foolhardiness of mounting a wild, wide-shooting, free-for-all cavalry charge against fixed positions manned by disciplined, dug-in troops protected by barbed wire and machine-guns, that deadly combination that was soon to destroy whole armies in Flanders. Caution, but never patience, was learned by the picturesque horsemen who rode to battle in a cloud of dust and a flurry of whirling robes. The Turks did their best to discipline these highly impetuous irregulars, many of whom were in the field only when there was actual fighting to be done.

At the beginning of November 1911 the Italians started a new offensive from Tripoli. By the 6th the front had been pushed about 3 miles to the east of the town walls. A month later, Ain Zara was taken, Tagiura oasis was captured in mid-December, and Gargaresh (now a western suburb of Tripoli) was occupied on 20 January 1912, by which time the front line was extended in a semi-circle of about 6 miles' radius around the town. Meanwhile, the Homs bridgehead was slowly deepened, and in February the dominating Monte Mergheb strongpoint was captured. Misurata Marina and Misurata town were taken in June. Between April and August landings were made on the coast near the Tunisian frontier to stop the smuggling of supplies to the Turco-Libyan forces from French territory. Troops went ashore at Zuara at the beginning of August and the town fell on the 6th. But by the beginning of September the westward advance from Tripoli had only reached Zanzur, 10 miles away, and eleven months after the first landings not one of the bridgeheads had been linked up. There had been little advance in Cyrenaica, where the land rises more steeply from the sea than in Tripolitania. After several brisk engagements in March, Italian lines had been extended in a fortified perimeter about 5 miles around Benghazi. Throughout the summer of 1912 the invaders sat behind their elaborate defensive works at Derna, solidly besieged by about 10,000 men, while the action at heavily fortified Tobruk was limited to minor skirmishes.

The war was reaching stalemate. The Italians, with their command of the sea, could not be driven from the coastal enclaves covered by the heavy guns of the warships, yet any advance inland broke down under haphazard but overwhelming Turco-Libyan attacks. The war was demoralising for Italy, but it was far worse for a Turkish government beset with troubles in the Balkans and at home, and unable to send reinforcements to Libya.

Peace talks had opened quietly at Lausanne in July. Giolitti hoped to influence the negotiations by being able to announce a big Italian advance in Tripolitania, but none took place. Peace was declared rather suddenly at Ouchy, near Lausanne, on 17 October 1912. The Libyans seem to have been unaware of the negotiations, and the news that a treaty had been signed deeply shocked them; according to an Italian officer who was on the front at the time, the news left them 'stupefied and disillusioned'.

The terms of the peace treaty, probably drafted in haste, were vague and ambiguous. On 15 October the Sultan issued a decree, approved by Italy, granting full independence to Tripolitania and Cyrenaica. It was agreed that Ottoman interests in both territories were to be looked after by the Sultan's representative whose status, and the conditions of independence under Italian sovereignty, the king of Italy would later define. These arrangements became part of the peace treaty signed two days later. Turkey was to withdraw her troops from Libya and Italy was to return to the Dodecanese Islands taken during the war. Simultaneously, the king issued a royal decree reminding Libyans that they were now Italian subjects and the great powers speedily recognised Italian sovereignty in Libya.

The Italians had apparently won a cheap and fairly easy victory, and so it would have been had the Turks not tucked a rather nasty booby-trap between the lines of one of the most important of the treaty terms. The Sultan-Caliph, whose diplomatic and religious interests in Libya were to be looked after by a representative, also kept the right of appointing the Grand Qadi of Tripoli, and so still effectively controlled religion over much of the country, an arrangement agreed by Italy as a gesture of goodwill to her new Muslim subjects. But the Italian negotiators at Lausanne had failed to realise that the nature of the authority they had agreed to allow the

Sultan was, to Muslims, political as well as religious, and that the Sultan's secular influence would be felt in Libya for as long as he exercised his spiritual authority there. As a result, most Libyans still considered the Sultan their rightful ruler and the Italians as unlawful invaders to be driven back to the sea. Few Libyans accepted the European idea of division of political and religious authority between Italy and the Sultan respectively. Yet it was a division the Italians sincerely intended, and the Turks pretended to intend, when the peace treaty was signed. These ambiguities were not cleared up until Italy signed the other Treaty of Lausanne with Turkey in 1923.

While Turkey officially had no further quarrel with Italy after October 1912, many Libyans were determined to continue the fight on behalf of the Sultan and few of them obeyed the Italian order to disarm. Hardly forty years had passed since the Italians had won their own independence; indeed, the fourth war of Independence, as Italy's efforts in the First World War are sometimes called, had still to be fought. Yet in Libya in 1912 they started fighting one of the last and one of the hardest of the classic colonial wars, memories of their own recent history apparently forgotten.

Tribal leaders from all parts of Tripolitania, who met at Azizia to discuss the action to be taken now that Turkey had 'deserted' them, fell into two parties. Mohammad Farhad of Zavia emerged as the leader of a 'peace' party that was ready to submit to the Italians, trusting that the independence granted by the Sultan would be recognised. Most of the chiefs sharing this view were more pro-Italian than they cared to admit in public, and it was through their co-operation that much of northern Tripolitania was peacefully occupied in the autumn and early winter of 1912. The opposing 'war' party was convinced that real independence was only to be won by force. The leader of this group of 'rebels', as the Italians called all hostile Libyans, was Sulaiman Baruni, a forty-two-year-old Ibadite Berber from the Gebel Nefusah. Bearded and dapper, a poet and a student of Arabic literature, he had sat for Tripolitania in the first Turkish parliament elected after the 1908 revolution, and had recently returned home to fight the invasion. When the Azizia meeting broke up, he slipped away to the *Gebel* where, after rallying several thousand men of the hills to his side, he called upon Italy to recognise him as head of an independent Berber state with its capital at the picturesque hill-town of Yefren.

The call was well timed, for the possibility of allowing the *Gebel* tribes limited rule was just then being seriously considered in Rome. Baruni might have won his case had he been cautious, but when he allowed Italian troops to be attacked, General Lequio, whose First Division had climbed the *Gebel* escarpment and taken Garian unopposed at the beginning of December, was ordered to advance on Yefren. Lequio met and attacked about 4,000 of Baruni's men at Asabaa, between Garian and Yefren, on 23 March 1913. The tribesmen were routed and lost most of their equipment before they could load up their camels and escape. Baruni fled; on 9 April he crossed the Tunisian frontier and eventually reached Constantinople.

The Battle of Asabaa opened most of the western *Gebel* to the Italian advance. Yefren fell on 27 March, Giado and Jawsh were occupied within the next fortnight, and on 12 April the tricolour was hoisted over Nalut. The occupation of the 'imposing *Gebel* front' had been completed in just three weeks. At the end of April a small column reached the oasis of Ghadames, some 200 miles south-west of Nalut. Earlier in the month, 150 tribal leaders and notables from as far off as the Sirtica and Fezzan, had assembled at Tripoli to take part in a mass ceremonial act of submission.

In Cyrenaica the front lines were still within shell-shot of the coast, and the Sanussi Order was organising the united resistance that Tripolitania was unable to offer. Numbers of Turkish troops who should have left the country under the terms of the peace treaty, were still fighting alongside the irregulars. Enver Pasha continued to organise operations and before being transferred to Turkey's Balkan front late in 1912, he visited the head of the Sanussi Order, Sayyid Ahmad al-Sharif, at Giarabub. During the meeting, Sayyid Ahmad confirmed his readiness to continue the war as the Sultan's representative, and thenceforth the Order considered itself the rightful government of the territory it had undertaken to defend.

In the spring of 1913 the Italians opened a big Cyrenaican offensive, broke out of the Benghazi bridgehead, and on 13 April stormed and captured the sprawling Turco-Libyan camp at Benina. The Second Division then pressed on north-eastwards through the hills to Jardas al-Abid, where it met up with the Fourth Division which after landing at Tolmayta had advanced southwards through Barce. By mid-May the columns had crossed the hills around Cyrene and had reached the coast at Marsa Susa. But an attempt to break out of Derna behind a curtain of heavy artillery-fire ended in disaster and the Italian advance on the town from the west was held up until the autumn. Meanwhile, there was a successful southward advance from Benghazi, and Suluq and Qaminis were taken.

By the end of the year large-scale resistance in the Gebel Akhdar was failing as forces under the personal leadership of Sayyid Ahmad were pushed eastwards off the mountains and into the desolate Marmarica region south of Tobruk. The main Turco-Libyan camps were broken up. The Turkish troops had no more heart for a fight that was not even theirs, and it was not long before their commander, Colonel Aziz al-Masri, unable to co-operate further with Sayyid Ahmad, withdrew most of his troops and artillery into Egypt. A strong rearguard of tribesmen on the Gebel Akhdar started the type of guerrilla warfare so well suited to their temperament and the terrain, but the Italians soon learned to match these tactics. The Cyrenaicans lost heavily during tough fighting in the spring of 1914, and by the summer of that year the life had almost been choked out of the resistance in northern Cyrenaica.

The Tripolitanian war, meanwhile, had been carried to the edge of the desert. Mizda, the first of the real oases, was occupied in July 1913. The swift southward advance, that by the following summer was to take the tricolour as far as Ghat, had been ordered by the politicians against the advice of the military. Pietro Bertolini, whose Ministry of Colonies had been formed in October 1912, was haunted by the old French bogy. In 1913 French columns were advancing on Djanet, only 50 miles from Ghat, and into the Tibesti. Bertolini judged that a lively Italian advance into Fezzan was needed if the red, white, and green tricolour, and not the red, white, and blue one was to fly over the southern oases. Once again, it seemed, Italy was being forced into an African adventure by French expansion.

Sirte, the anchorage nearest to Fezzan, was made the base for a southward advance through the Giofra, the plan being to skirt round the hostile tribes of the barren Hammadah al-Hamra plateau. Sokna Oasis in the Giofra was duly occupied as an advance base in July 1913, while a great expeditionary force, known as the Fezzan Column, paraded at Sirte under the command of Lt-Colonel Antonio Miani, a staff officer of mixed abilities. The column left the coast on 9 August and, after dallying at Sokna for many weeks, crossed the Gebel Soda in December. It then wound down into the great Wadi Shatti where tribesmen inspired by Sanussi propaganda had rallied. They were dispersed in three engagements in December, leaving all western Fezzan exposed. Sebha fell to Miani's troops on 17 February 1914 and Murzuk was taken two weeks later. Another column of troops, composed mainly of Eritreans (*Askaris* from the Italian East African colony served in Libya from 1912 onwards) and Libyan auxiliaries, marched across the *Hammadah* from Mizda to Brak. During that long trek the column met hardly a living thing; all the *Hammadah* people, with their flocks and herds, had moved quietly away eastwards to join the sinister concentration of tribesmen building up in the Sirtica. For, despite their miseries, the Libyans had not lost their will to resist. There was smallpox, typhus, and even plague in the sprawling camps; there was little food, little help from outside, and much death, and many thousands of good men had already been killed.

Miani occupied certain Fezzanese oases, but so long as the tribes were at large and unsubdued in the vast spaces of the desert he had no more hope of properly conquering Fezzan than had the Roman general Balbus 2,000 years before. Nowhere in Libya was the Italian hold on the country as sure as it seemed, and least of all in Fezzan, where huge distances isolated the few garrisoned oases, and where lines of communication were dangerously long. Sayyid Ahmad soon realised that Fezzan had become the key to the war: if the Italians could be driven from the southern oases, there was no saying where in the desert they might be able to hold a new front. And he saw that the Fezzanese garrisons could only survive so long as the lumbering camel caravans continued to bring them regular supplies from the coast.

So it was that the great camp at Zillah, deep in the desert to the east of Uaddan, became the base for raids on the Fezzan supply columns. Men from the Sirtica and the Giofra assembled there under the command of Sayyid Ahmad's youngest brother, Sayyid Safi al-Din. The first attack came on 26 August 1914, when a column marching across the *Hammadah* was wiped out. That was the beginning of the end of the brief occupation of Fezzan. From then onwards no caravan was safe and Fezzanese garrisons, their supplies cut off, were surrounded by Sanussi forces supported by men of the Wadi Shatti and even by Tebu and Tuareg from the furthest corners of the desert.

The garrisons at Edri and Ubari were overrun and massacred, the fort at Sebha was captured, Murzuk fell, and troops who had hoisted the tricolour over Ghat only four months before were forced to retreat into southern Algeria and seek French protection. Just before Christmas Miani fell back to Sokna and on 26 December his column, by now barely numbering 1,000 men, was in sight of the sea at Misurata. Gheriat and Ghadames were also abandoned in December, by which time the government in Tripoli was sufficiently alarmed to declare a state of emergency. But Miani was not sent the Eritrean reinforcements he requested, and he had to recruit more local troops.

One of the greatest Fezzanese leaders, the aged Saif al-Nasir, now openly joined the offensive. At one time the supposed friend of the Italians, he had later been imprisoned by them, but in the autumn of 1914 had been sent back to the desert so that he could pacify his followers, something that the 'Old Robber', as the Italians called him, had no intention of doing. Instead, in January 1915, he sent his son Ahmad to take the Giofra oases of Uaddan, Hon, and Sokna. The garrisons retreated, first to Bu Najim and then, still pressed by Ahmad's men, to Beni Ulid. By February 1915 the Italians were barely holding the line Mizda–Nalut.

The counter-attack ordered by Tripoli in March turned to disaster. A column sent against Sanussi forces south of Mizda was nearly wiped out, and on 29 April fell the greatest blow of the war. Colonel Miani had marched out of Misurata to attack the Sanussi camp at Gasr Bu Hadi, south of Sirte. His column of 4,000 Italians was supported and covered by 3,500 Libyans under the command of Ramadan Shutaywi (Sceteui to the Italians, and also known as Suwayhili), chief of the Misuratino region of north-east Tripolitania. After fighting the Italians in 1911–12, Shutaywi had co-operated with them for a while, but was later gaoled for Sanussi leanings. Miani wrongly thought that he could now be trusted. Just as the attack on Gasr Bu Hadi began, Shutaywi ordered his men to turn and fire on the Italians. It was never known how many were killed; only Miani and a handful of men escaped the massacre. Through his treachery Shutaywi captured 5,000 reserve rifles, millions of rounds of ammunition, several machine-guns, six sections of artillery with abundant ammunition, and all the supplies, including the funds, of the column. The well-armed Libyans pushed home their victory and Shutaywi, with 12,000 riflemen and a dozen pieces of artillery, was soon marching on Misurata.

The tribesmen grew bolder as the withdrawal became a rout. Garrisons simply abandoned their strongholds without staying to defend them and fell back as best they could across the hot, waterless hills and plains to the coast. There was no proper organisation, and relief columns sent up-country from Tripoli were usually too small and too late to be of use. Sinawan, Mizda, and Qusabat fell in June, and the Libyans were soon at Ben Gashir, only 15 miles from Tripoli.

A general withdrawal to the coast was ordered on 5 July. The Tarhuna garrison was all but massacred during its break-out to the sea; a thousand men at Beni Ulid surrendered helplessly before they had tested their strength; the Garian garrison retired to Azizia and was then forced to withdraw hastily to Tripoli; 4,500 men abandoned Misurata for Misurata Marina; and even Zuara was evacuated from the sea. By 1 August the only Tripolitanian towns still held by the Italians were Homs, Misurata Marina, Tagiura, and Tripoli itself, where there were 40,000 troops to man the machine-gun nests and the stout new wall circling the outer suburbs.

Italy had suffered the worst defeat since Adowa and the Tripolitanian campaign was almost back to its starting point. Since the previous August the Italians had lost an estimated 3,000 men killed, as well as 2,400 prisoners, thirty pieces of artillery, 15,000 rifles, and huge quantities of ammunition and stores. The effect on Libyan morale of what even the Italians themselves admitted to have been a 'shameful retreat' was tremendous and harmed the Italian cause far more than the loss of men and equipment. The fact that in May 1915 Italy had joined the European war against Austria was offered as an excuse for a disaster that had by that time become almost complete.

Although the whole of the northern shoulder of Cyrenaica had been claimed as conquered in 1914, in reality the enemy still roamed freely across most territory not actually within range of the garrison forts. When the Tripolitanian campaign collapsed and troops were also transferred to the European front, withdrawal northwards was ordered in Cyrenaica, where there was soon no Italian garrison more than 20 miles from the coast.

On 5 August Misurata Marina was evacuated. It was a foolish move, not least because the port could easily have been held. No sooner had the garrison been taken off in ships than Ramadan Shutaywi rode in, and the little harbour was soon sheltering Turkish and Austrian submarines, and later German ones, that ran the British blockade of the coast to bring in supplies. This underwater traffic continued until the end of the fighting in Europe. Even before Italy joined the European war, Turkey was helping the rebellion in Cyrenaica and when, in 1915, the two countries were again formally at war, Turkish aid to both Tripolitania and Cyrenaica was increased.

The Italian withdrawal from inland Tripolitania had left a power vacuum that several great rival chiefs attempted to fill, and in doing so they dragged the country into tribal warfare and chaos. By early 1916 the two main parties in the struggle were the Sanussis, who were active throughout the Sirtica and had much influence with the *Gebel* tribes, and Ramadan Shutaywi, lord of Misurata and the nearby coastlands, who could never again be called a Sanussi supporter. War broke out between Shutaywi and the Sanussis when Sayyid Safi al-Din tried to extend Sanussi influence over all 'free' Tripolitania. Shutaywi, who had his own plans for Tripolitania, defeated the Sanussis in a battle near Beni Ulid, and their influence outside Cyrenaica was thereafter limited to parts of Fezzan.

Then Sulaiman Baruni suddenly reappeared, bearing the Sultan's title of governor of Tripolitania. He had come from Cyrenaica, where he had been put ashore by the Austrian submarine that had brought him out of exile in Turkey. He won the support of Ramadan Shutaywi, Abd-al-Nabi Bilkhayr (Abdenebbi Belcher to the Italians), chief of the Orfella, Ahmad Marayid of Tarhuna, and even of the *Gebel* tribes, and from this unlikely and uneasy alliance was formed an independent republic with its capital at Misurata. The central powers supplied it with arms, cash, and other needs by submarine. Local produce was also exported by submarines, which were soon running to a fortnightly schedule. Turkish and German officers were smuggled into Tripolitania, and they not only helped with the administration of the republic, but also trained a small regular army, and even set up a munitions factory and a meat-processing plant with equipment brought in by the underwater supply route.

Submarines were also supplying equipment through the port of Bardia on the Egyptian frontier to Sayyid Ahmad, for the British blockade of the Egyptian port of Sollum had cut off supplies from abroad. Sayyid Ahmad, too, had Turkish and German officers among his helpers and advisers. As early as the summer of 1915 they were pressing him to attack the British in Egypt – their enemy, but not necessarily his. The Sanussi leader was in a difficult position. If he ignored the advice of his helpers he risked losing the foreign supplies on which his people depended. But his men were already fighting the Italians in northern Cyrenaica and the French in Sudan, and were in no state to open a third front. Finally, and against his better judgement, he allowed the Turks to lead his men in an attack on British posts in western Egypt in November 1915. The following January, when the Turco-Libyan invasion had reached El Daba, a few miles west of El Alamein, the British counter-attacked. The invaders were quickly routed and were driven back into Cyrenaica, although the Sanussi threat to Egypt was not ended until early in 1917. The hard-fought campaign achieved something the Italians had failed to do in five years: it broke the Sanussi will to resist. There was black famine across the land and Sayyid Ahmad realised that his long-suffering, half-starved people could fight no more.

To his cousin, Sayyid Mohammad Idris, he not only transferred all religious, political, and military control in Cyrenaica, but also agreed to his opening peace talks with the British. Then, after failing to carry his cause into Tripolitania, he sailed from Sirte in a German submarine bound for Istanbul. He never saw Libya again and he died, still in exile, in 1933.

Chapter 13

The Years of Accord

SAYYID IDRIS was only twelve years old when his father, Mahdi, died in 1902. He was too young to become Head of the Order and it was Sayyid Ahmad, his cousin of twenty-nine, who took over the leadership for the next fourteen years. Before succeeding to the leadership in 1916, Sayyid Idris had made a favourable impression on the British, and not only because the Sanussis had attacked Egypt wholly against his advice.

When Sayyid Ahmad went into exile, Britain and Italy agreed between themselves to recognise Sayyid Idris as Head of the Order, but to sign no pact with him without the consent of the other. Both countries were ready to discuss terms with him because he was the only man who could properly claim to speak for Cyrenaica. Because Britain wanted the Sanussi threat on the Egyptian frontier ended and Italy wanted peace in Libya while the Alpine front was bolstered up, an Anglo-Italian mission opened negotiations with him at Zuetina in July 1916.

From the outset the British negotiator, Colonel Milo Talbot, was on good terms both with his Italian colleagues and with Sayyid Idris, but between the Sayyid and the Italians there was mutual dislike and distrust. Talks broke down but, because all the parties needed peace, were reopened at Acroma, near Tobruk, in the spring of 1917. Turkey, whose influence had by then fallen very low in Libya, was barely discussed, and there was no Turkish pressure on Sayyid Idris during the negotiations.

Colonel Talbot successfully steered the Italians and the Sayyid into an armed truce. They agreed to stop fighting; there was to be free movement and trade between the Italian and the Sanussi zones of Cyrenaica; each party was to maintain law and order in its own zone; the tribes were eventually to be disarmed; and Muslim religion, law, and teaching were to be practised in the Italian zone. But neither the Italians nor the Sayyid were prepared to make further concessions beyond these superficial agreements.

The British and the Sayyid soon reached an understanding. Peace was made, prisoners were exchanged, limited trade between Egypt and Cyrenaica was re-started, and Sanussi rights in Egypt were defined. Both parties were satisfied, the British because Egypt's western frontier was secure again and the large forces guarding it could be deployed elsewhere, and the Sayyid because he was now in fact, if not in name, recognised as the ruler of all Cyrenaica beyond the Italian-occupied coastal belt. The dissatisfied party was Italy. The parts of Cyrenaica she had conquered she kept, and she had won a badly needed peace, but that was all. She had hoped to negotiate better terms, but had failed to do so. In fact, it was plain that neither she, nor the Sanussis, expected the exhausted peace of Acroma to last for long.

The reconquest of Tripolitania was made the first objective of the Italian armies that the armistice of November 1918 had freed for duty outside Europe. The military situation in western Libya had changed little since 1915. The Italians were still virtually under siege in their coastal enclaves, and the bombing of Misurata by Italian and Malta-based British aircraft in 1918 had not prevented the formal proclamation of the Tripolitanian republic by the rebel government there. But Turks and Germans still in the country when the armistice was announced had crossed into Tunisia, where they had been promptly rounded up by the French authorities and handed over to the Italians.

General Garioni was sent to Tripoli with reinforcements of troops from the Alpine front to prepare for reconquest. By March 1919 about 70,000 fighting men had been concentrated in and around the town. Ships were delivering quantities of equipment, including tanks, heavy artillery, aeroplanes, and flame-throwers, and Garioni had announced that reconquest would be completed 'within two months'.

Had the Italians moved quickly and decisively, Garioni's boast might well have been fulfilled, for the Tripolitanians were disorganised and disunited. But the only military activity was the occupation of the coastal strip between Tripoli and Zavia, and that was done because the locals wanted it. (The port of Zuara had been reoccupied in 1917 following a request by a pro-Italian faction there.) The Italians hung around Tripoli, trusting that the build-up of men and equipment would alone be enough to persuade the country to submit peacefully. It was to hasten the submission of the tribal leaders that Major-General Giuseppe Tarditi was detailed to open negotiations with them, after first warning that there would be military action if they were unco-operative. This was an empty threat, and the Libyans knew it. They had already guessed the truth that the Italians themselves were only pretending to ignore: that no government would dare ask a shell-shocked nation reeling towards chaos, as Italy was in 1919, to fight even a colonial war.

Tarditi began negotiating with the tribal leaders at a camp near Tripoli. Among those present were Ramadan Shutaywi, Sulaiman Baruni, and an Egyptian pan-Islamic agent, Abd-al-Rahman Azzam (later to become the first secretary of the Arab League). Tarditi adopted a pose of condescension towards the Libyans, but they simply ignored it and treated him as an equal. They called the bluff about military action and, turning the tables, promised to start a guerrilla war from the western Gebel strongholds if the negotiations were unsuccessful. They then offered to stop fighting, but not to disarm, if the Italians would recognise the Tripolitanian republic and allow self-determination on the lines recently laid down by President Wilson of the United States; Italy would keep garrisons at Tripoli, Homs, and Zuara.

Under the circumstances, these demands were not unrealistic, and the outcome was partial Italian surrender in the form of the Fundamental Law of June 1919. This was followed in October by the issue of a statute giving Tripolitanians the right to a parliament, Italian citizenship, and other benefits. The Italians were to exercise control through governing and local councils, and there was to be general disarmament of the tribes.

Many Italians were disgusted with what they considered a humiliating settlement, particularly when most of the 70,000 men who had been sent to Tripoli to reconquer the country 'in two months' were brought home, having fired not a shot in anger. Marshal Pietro Badoglio, commenting later on events in Libya in 1919, remarked: 'We got ourselves mixed up in some real black comedy'. Farce might have been a better word. Both Italians and Libyans soon found themselves reduced to political and military stalemate. The Italians were left almost militarily impotent when Garioni's troops were posted home, but the Libyans were, as ever, disunited and warring among themselves. Genuine efforts to put into effect the delicate constitutional arrangements of the October Statute failed, for there was no collaboration between the various chiefs under Italian influence; not one was leader enough to unite the others behind him, and there were, besides, many who wanted more independence than the milk-and-water freedom the Italians proposed giving.

Leading the independence movement were the four members of the Reform Committee that theoretically ruled the country on behalf of the Tripolitanian republic; the main activity of this state seemed to be the fighting of tribal wars against Ramadan Shutaywi's many personal enemies. The committee, founded by Abd-al-Rahman Azzam, proposed allowing the Italians no more than trading rights in Tripolitania. Its policy, inspired by Azzam's notions of Arab nationalism, was promoted in the Tripoli news-sheet *Al-Liwa al-Tarablasi* (The Tripolitanian Banner) but was far too advanced for a country where tribal loyalties were still all-important; few heeded the call to the 'Tripolitanian Nation' to rise 'in the defence of liberty'.

Early in 1920 Ramadan Shutaywi saw a chance of conquering all Tripolitania, and the *Gebel* tribes joined him in an attack on his old enemies, the Orfella tribe. The Italians, unable to oppose him, managed to rally some tribes against him. Fears that this 'ferocious adventurer', as the Italians called him, would overrun the country ended in August when he was killed in battle and his body was literally thrown to the dogs. But governor Menzinger was called home for his inept handling of the crisis.

Menzinger's replacement, governor Mercatelli, was not only badly briefed, but was also hamstrung by his superiors in Rome. After Shutaywi's death, there was hope that Tripolitania would be brought to peaceful, constitutional order, if the Italians took the initiative. But Italy was in chaos, and when Mercatelli asked permission to reoccupy Misurata Marina, the first step in the proposed pacification of the country, he was told by a harassed cabinet in Rome that 'every warlike act, even an insignificant one, would have unfortunate repercussions' – in Italy, not Tripolitania. Instead, he had to be content with ordering the recall from the interior, on the grounds of economy, of his few political officers, and with them his best means of influencing the tribes.

Tripolitanian chiefs who met at Azizia at the end of September 1920 agreed to assemble in congress elsewhere to decide the action to be taken, since none was being taken by the Italians. The 'National

Congress', claiming to represent the 'Tripolitanian Nation', despite the absence of many great chiefs, duly met at Garian in November. Sulaiman Baruni, who seemed bent on a course of his own, announced that as an Ottoman senator he was unable to attend, but among those present were leaders from Italian-occupied territory who hoped to put the Italian case to the assembly.

Azzam opened the meeting by declaring that Italy was on the verge of revolution and incapable of fighting an offensive war. Although he proposed the lobbying of opposition parties in Rome for recognition of a completely independent Tripolitanian principality (Amirate), neither an Amir nor an Amirate were mentioned in the declaration of the National Congress, signed by forty-seven delegates on 18 November 1920, calling for a Tripolitanian government accepted by the majority and 'constituted on the principles of Muslim law, under the authority of a Muslim'. The proposed government was to wield 'every civil and religious power within the statutory limits to be determined by the Tripolitanian Nation', and its authority was to extend 'over all the country within the accepted frontiers'. All ideas of Italian sovereignty had been rejected outright.

The declaration was carried to Rome by a five-man delegation led by Mohammad Khalid al-Gargani, who later attended the Muslim Revolutionary Congress in Moscow. Mercatelli, whose refusal to issue passports had not prevented the delegation leaving Tripolitania, followed it to Rome, where he intended at least to safeguard his personal interests, for he was aware that it was partly through Libyan pressure that his predecessor, Menzinger, had lost his job. The delegation had actually started talks with the Minister of Colonies when it was discredited, not by Mercatelli, but by another Libyan delegation that had come to put its own case. Led by Hassuna Pasha Karamanli, the aged mayor of Tripoli and the long-standing friend of Italy, the second delegation represented the pro-Italian faction in Tripoli and the coastal belt, as well as the Berbers of the western Gebel. It was honourably received after Karamanli had denounced Gargani and his colleagues as revolutionary troublemakers. Official recognition was withdrawn from the Garian delegation on the grounds that its members did not, as they claimed to do, represent all Tripolitania, but Gargani won much sympathetic support from Italian communists, socialists, and other opposition parties.

The official slighting of the Garian delegation started another round of troubles in Tripolitania, where the 'rebels' hoped that a renewed threat of war might yet panic Rome into agreeing to their terms. When, in addition, the old Arab–Berber quarrel broke out again in the western Gebel, Mercatelli saw a chance of making useful allies of the Berbers. He was unable to support them militarily, but he asked Sulaiman Baruni, who still had great influence in the Yefren area, to organise an 'anti-rebel front' among his Berber followers. Baruni did as he was asked, probably in the hope of somehow re-establishing his short-lived Berber state of 1911–12. He was again unlucky, for the orthodox Muslims were determined to crush the Berber members of the Ibadite sect. Yefren was attacked by overwhelming 'rebel' forces and fell in July 1921. Mercatelli had sent a relief column, but logistic problems and shortage of water had halted it at Bir Ghanem, only 50 miles from Tripoli and thirty short of Yefren. Tired of fighting both the Libyans and his superiors in Rome, Mercatelli resigned. There was a short interval before the appointment in July of his successor, count Giuseppe Volpi, the first governor with the strength and initiative to break the Tripolitanian deadlock.

In October 1919, Cyrenaica, like Tripolitania, had been granted a statute providing for a parliament, governing councils, Italian citizenship for all, and other benefits. The Italians believed that these liberal arrangements, which did give considerable freedom, could bring lasting peace to the country. But the Cyrenaicans were no more pleased with the prospects of indirect Italian rule than the Tripolitanians were. Sanussi followers flatly rejected the statute on the grounds that to accept its terms would imply recognition of Italian sovereignty, recognition that Sayyid Idris had specifically refused to give during the Acroma negotiations three years earlier. One hundred Cyrenaican chiefs met at Agedabia and issued a declaration that the people of Cyrenaica, with the statute or without it, would only tolerate the Italians as traders on the coast. It was a blunter answer even than the Tripolitanians were later to give at Garian, and although the Italians called it 'an act of open rebellion', they were incapable of dealing with it as such. Instead, they reopened negotiations. The outcome was the agreement of Regima: signed on 25 October 1920, it replaced the unworkable terms of the Acroma accord.

The new agreement gave to Sayyid Idris the hereditary title of

1. A Fezzanese rock-drawing of the long-horned, backward-grazing cattle described by Herodotus

2. The site of Germa, the Garamantean capital in the Wadi Ajal

3. Cyrene, the Roman Forum

4. Sabratha, the Roman Theatre

5. Leptis Magna, the Severan Basilica

6. A Roman dam in the hills near Tarhuna, south-east from Tripoli

7. Tripoli, the Arch of Marcus Aurelius and the Gurgi Mosque

8. Nalut, the 'Castle'. The doors give access to family storage vaults

9. The remains of a slave who died on the desert crossing. Several slaves were shackled to the iron bar

10. Graziani's barbed-wire fence on the Libo–Egyptian frontier

11. The Duce reviews his Libyan subjects

12. Marshal Balbo hands over the key of a colonial farm to a newly-arrived Italian family

13. An Italian colonial village—Battisti in Cyrenaica

14. An Italian colonial farmhouse in Cyrenaica, now occupied by Libyans

15. Murzuk, former capital of Fezzan

16. The results of Italian colonisation. A recent view of olive groves on the Gefara Plain near Tripoli

17. The Libyan oil industry. Moving a drilling rig across the desert

18. An oil-rig in Esso's Zelten field

19. Lines bring oil from individual wells to the gathering centre at Zelten

20. A new mosque in Tripoli

21. A street in the Old City of Tripoli. Men wear the traditional, all-purpose garment—the *baraccan*

22. The new administrative capital of Baida in the Gebel Akhdar

23. H.M. King Idris I at the official opening of the Marsa al Hariga oil terminal, February 1967

'Amir' and recognition as the independent ruler of the oases of Giarabub, Augila-Gialo, and Kufra, with Agedabia as his administrative centre. The Italians paid him and his family monthly allowances, contributed to his general expenses, and subsidised his army and police force, as well as tribal and *zawiya shaikhs*, members of parliament, and a crowd of petty officials and hangers-on. They consulted him when appointing officials in his territory; he was allowed freedom of movement (the use of an official steamer was one of his perquisites); and his people were well represented in the Cyrenaican parliament. He in turn agreed to put the new constitutional arrangements into effect, to limit his army, and to break up the armed Sanussi camps within eight months.

The Cyrenaican parliament met for the first time in Benghazi in April 1921. Most of its sixty members were tribal *shaikhs* elected by their followers, and there were few urban members. The Italian community had only three representatives.

Italy had made concessions and was spending freely; it has been said that the subsidies were merely bribes to keep troublemakers quiet. But at least there were renewed prospects of peace, and it was not entirely the Amir's fault that his side of the agreement was not kept in full. Eight months after the agreement, the armed camps were still working as local government centres and the Amir was claiming that attempts to disband them had brought snarls of protest from the tribes. A compromise was reached when another accord, signed at Bu Mariam on 11 November 1921, put the camps under Italo-Sanussi control until they could be broken up. There were five of these 'mixed camps' and from them Italian and Sanussi troops, all on the Italian payroll and ration strength, jointly policed the tribal lands. But underhand attempts to make the camps centres of Italian influence in the interior of the country were a failure.

At the end of 1921 events were moving towards a climax. The Italians were at last becoming disillusioned with 'reasonable' settlements and appeasement. After the Bu Mariam accord and the fantastic arrangement of the 'mixed camps', it was plain that peaceful policies were doing Italy no good; in Cyrenaica, as in Tripolitania, the stage of 'get on, or get out' had been reached.

Early in 1922 count Volpi had started the reconquest of Tripolitania that the Fascists were to continue after coming to power at the end of the year. The Tripolitanians, alarmed by Volpi's new 'hard line', turned to Cyrenaica and the Sanussis for help. At a meeting with Sanussi representatives at Sirte, they agreed to the extension of the Sanussi Amirate into Tripolitania, where no chief capable of uniting the country behind him had yet come forward. Although the Italians had intended the title of 'Amir' as an honorary one when they conferred it on Sayyid Idris, he was to the Libyans Amir both in fact and in name. For this reason, and because he had apparently won handsome concessions for his own people, his prestige was high throughout Libya.

It was nevertheless an awkward choice that Sayyid Idris had to make when Tripolitanian representatives offered him the Amirate of all Libya at Agedabia in April 1922. To accept would certainly have snapped his already strained relations with the Italians, and he was not yet ready for that, but to refuse this call to patriotic duty would have greatly offended the Tripolitanians, who had already swallowed enough pride in their negotiations with the Sanussis. Idris played for time, first by asking leave of the Italian government to go to Egypt for rest and medical treatment, and then by offering to mediate in the Tripolitanian war. The request was refused, and in reply to the offer he was told that any interference in Tripolitanian affairs would be considered a breach of Italo-Sanussi pacts.

By the summer of 1922 Italians and Sanussis were preparing for another round of war. In August Sayyid Idris learned that he had been formally proclaimed Amir of Tripolitania, but not until November was he persuaded to accept the honour that, as his advisers pointed out, would at least ensure the friendship and moral support of the Tripolitanians during the fighting to come.

Then Idris suddenly left the country. Pleading ill-health, he went in December with a small retinue first to Giarabub, and afterwards to Cairo, where he was to live in exile for more than twenty years.

Six years earlier Sayyid Ahmad, the soldier, had sailed into exile when his war had failed. His successor, Idris, the scholar, the diplomat, and the man of peace, also chose exile when the failure of the peace he had negotiated was certain. He left behind him soldiers, his brother, Sayyid Mohammad al-Rida, and his cousin, Sayyid Safi al-Din, to lead his people in the next inevitable round of war.

Chapter 14

La Riconquista

GIUSEPPE VOLPI, the Venetian who was to start the reconquest of Tripolitania, arrived in Tripoli in August 1921. As the colony's eleventh governor in ten years, he needed all his past experience as businessman, diplomat, politician, and colonial administrator to end Tripolitania's post-war crisis. He admitted some years later that the situation as he found it was far worse than he had imagined it would be.

Protected by their barbed-wire entanglements, the Italians ruled Tripoli and the coast up to Zuara; they held Tagiura, Homs, and Azizia, but little else. Beyond the wire defences, and sometimes even within them, the Reform Committee issued edicts, collected taxes, and raised its own levies. In Rome, the Garian delegation was still winning left-wing support for an independent Tripolitanian Amirate. The would-be Amir-maker was the Reform Committee secretary, Abd-al-Rahman Azzam. His first choice for Amir had been Ramadan Shutaywi and, after Shutaywi's death, Ahmad Marayid, the unimpressive Reform Committee chairman.

Volpi never took Azzam very seriously and considered the rebellion and the call for an Amirate as the work of a few troublemakers. But others saw the rebellion, and especially Azzam's part in it, as the first stage of a dangerous pan-Islamic plot to drive Italy out of Tripolitania, which would then become the base for an international anti-colonialist movement. Egypt's achievement of independence in 1922 added to these fears.

Even before arriving in Tripoli, Volpi must have known that the stalemate could not be ended by the peaceful means, already proven as worthless, that he was supposed to use. Nevertheless, he followed Rome's brief until the end of 1921 and, like Mercatelli, laid aside plans for the reoccupation of Misurata Marina when ordered to do so. (That the Italian Senate believed a report that 100,000 armed tribesmen were ready to defend Misurata and its port shows just how out of touch Rome was.)

Volpi toured the country, interviewing chiefs friendly and hostile. He made it clear that he was willing to uphold the traditional authority of the chiefs over their own people, but would recognise no paramount chief or Amir claiming to represent the whole country; power was to pass through the parliament and other constitutional channels promised two years before. To scotch claims that Tripolitania's troubles were due to the failure to put the terms of the Fundamental Law of 1919 into effect, he ordered preparations to be made for parliamentary and other elections in January 1922.

But late in 1921 he began to hear disturbing reports of the first tentative approach to Sayyid Idris by Tripolitanian envoys, and of the meeting of Tripolitanian and Sanussi representatives at Sirte. Volpi, who had gone to Libya with few illusions, by now had none at all. He saw that the situation would steadily worsen so long as the Italians refused to use force. A strong blow aimed at the very centre of the rebellion was needed to end the years of stalemate, and to make the chiefs of uncertain loyalties declare for or against Italy before they could achieve their dangerous alliance with the Sanussis. The centre where the blow was to be struck was Misurata and the port of Misurata Marina.

With Italy itself in an ugly, mutinous mood, Rome was more reluctant than ever to send troops to fight an uncertain campaign in Libya. Volpi therefore decided to mount the assault himself, using only the troops already in Tripolitania. Well may he have felt the 'tormenting unease' he later admitted to, for he was staking the last of Italian prestige, and his own career, on this attempt to show that the sword, if properly used, may prove mightier than the pen, and the better tool for cutting this particular Gordian Knot.

His forces were ready on 18 January 1922, and on the following day the Minister of Colonies approved the reoccupation of Misurata as an 'internal action' of the colony, which meant that Volpi took the blame for any failure. A week later a makeshift little fleet, with the Syracuse mailboat *Brasile* as its flagship, sailed from Tripoli with 1,500 troops. After a successful dawn landing near Misurata Marina on the 26th, the assault on the little port faltered, although there were only an estimated 200 defenders. While watching the fighting Volpi made up his mind that Libya could never be conquered by peaceful means, and he later observed to his second-in-command that 'Italy is forever destined to bathe the assertion of her rights in blood!' The attack very nearly failed. Naval and air reinforcements had to be sent from Italy before Misurata Marina was taken, seventeen days after the first landing; seventeen hours should have sufficed for the operation.

Within a week of the assault the Reform Committee had called for an attack on all Italian posts. The Eritrean garrison at Azizia was besieged after the railway line from Tripoli had been cut, and there were many minor incidents and skirmishes. At the end of February a truce was arranged, coinciding with another cabinet crisis in Rome and the appointment of a new Minister of Colonies, Amendola. Rome was, as ever, unclear about events in Tripolitania, but early in March Volpi went to Rome and had his plans approved after discussing them with the new Minister. Then, with the cease-fire extended until 10 April, negotiations were started at Fonduk al-Sharif with all the main tribal leaders. The Italians asked for a return to normal and peaceful conditions. (Quite what was meant by 'normal conditions' was uncertain, for there had been none since 1911.) The chiefs, who had been warned that they would be punished if they failed to co-operate, would only repeat their demand for self-rule under a Muslim leader. Talks stumbled on for a few days and then, on 1 April, Ahmad Marayid, probably at Azzam's dictation, wrote to Volpi that chiefs had decided to meet again at Garian, and that Volpi would be told of their decisions in due course. Marayid's note also revealed that the Sirte conference of Tripolitanian and Sanussi representatives had agreed to a united Tripolitania and Cyrenaica under an elected Muslim leader with supreme religious and civil powers.

The very same day the Minister of Colonies was telling parliament in Rome that although the 'rebels' could not be talked to on equal terms, the government was ready to listen to Libyan demands through the constitutional channels provided. If the chiefs wanted peace, he said, Italy would collaborate; otherwise she would assert her rights by force. Marayid's note and the Minister's speech, delivered simultaneously, showed that both sides were utterly at cross purposes and were hardly arguing common points any more.

Volpi, after making a last unsuccessful appeal for more negotiations, announced his intention to abolish the traditional authority of the tribal leaders. 'Neither with the chiefs, nor against the chiefs, but without the chiefs' is how he described the new policy of direct rule by Italy.

The Tripolitanians still had two hopes, one false, the other exaggerated. The false hope was that the Italians would not fight the serious war that, even in 1919, when there had been 70,000 troops in Tripoli, had been carefully side-stepped, and that had been elaborately avoided ever since. The exaggerated hope was of early agreement with Amir Idris. That he took another eight months to make up his mind to accept the offered Amirate of all Libya in fact made little difference to the situation in Tripolitania, where too much was expected from the accord with the Sanussis. Moral support, greater political and bargaining power, these the alliance could bring; what it could not bring was the military aid and the threat of a new Sanussi war in Cyrenaica that Tripolitania needed desperately that April when Idris was formally offered the Libyan Amirate. (Although the Italians believed Idris was ready to send half his forces to support the Tripolitanians.)

The accord with the Sanussis, had it come a few months earlier, might have saved Tripolitania by giving its leaders a stronger voice at the conference table. But after Misurata Marina, it was too late. The seventeen-day minor operation had broken the deadlock and had returned the military initiative to the Italians. For this the Tripolitanians had themselves to blame. The Italians, and Volpi among them, had been as unreasonably apprehensive of the possible results of a Tripolitanian pact with Amir Idris as the chiefs had been expectant. When word of the negotiations with the Sanussis reached Tripoli, Volpi decided to lose no more time, and attacked Misurata Marina. He, at least, realised the value of his achievement there, but the 'rebels' did not, and they continued to misjudge the man and his ability. The Misurata operation had been successfully, if slowly, completed with embarrassment to Rome. It had not started an unpopular, government-toppling colonial war that the fainthearts had long forecast would result from such action. At Misurata Marina, Volpi had shown that reconquest need only depend on the Italian army's ability to carry it through and he had, as a result, gained something few Italian governors of Tripolitania had had up to that time: the full support of the central government.

When the cease-fire ended on 10 April 1922, Volpi was ready to start the 're-establishment of normalcy', the pre-Fascist name for reconquest. He had about 15,000 men under his command, against perhaps seven thousand. The 'rebels' attacked Zavia, but within ten days a young colonel, Rodolfo Graziani, and other competent officers whom Volpi had drawn around him, had reoccupied the whole of the Tripoli–Zuara coastal strip.

Azizia, where the Eritrean garrison had been under siege since early February, was then relieved. With the Tripoli railway cut, the little town had been supplied from the air. Aircraft had flown in stores, munitions, and troops, and had evacuated civilians, a remarkably bold use of air transport for 1922. The relief of Azizia was supervised by the hero of Vittorio Veneto, Pietro Badoglio, newly arrived in Tripolitania, and Graziani marched into the town on 30 April. He and other commanders, at the head of fast-moving columns, then pushed on through heat and sandstorms, smashing all opposition. By mid-May most of the Gefara was reoccupied. At the end of the month Graziani was given the task of pacifying the western end of the Gebel Nefusah. He took Jawsh on 12 June and by 5 July the tricolour was again flying over Nalut.

By then, Volpi had decided that no more pacts could be made with the Libyans and he proclaimed a state of siege. Martial law became effective 'wherever there are acts of rebellion, or wherever rebels are found'. It was the formal declaration of war.

In April Amir Idris had been formally offered the Amirate of all Libya. In August, although he was not yet ready to accept it, he was invested with the title by the Tripolitanians who still looked to him to save them from the Italian advance by threatening a new war in Cyrenaica. The hope that he would join Tripolitania with Cyrenaica in a solid anti-Italian front was never realised. But Volpi was not to know that at the time, and in the summer of 1922 he only saw the need to smash the Tripolitanian rebellion before the seemingly fatal union could take place.

Mussolini, in spats, marched on Rome on 28 October 1922 and Italy started the twenty-year adventure of Fascist dictatorship. For some months the change of régime had little effect on the course of events in Libya. The ten-month-old campaign in Tripolitania continued, Graziani taking Yefren three days after the march on Rome. But Volpi, writing some years afterwards, hailed the coming of Fascism, since for him it had meant: 'The absolute identity of policy and intention and the end for ever of the tormenting unease which up to then had increased the difficulties of action.'[1] There was, after all, no need for such qualms in the service of a leader who declared himself to be 'always right'. Mussolini's appointment of

[1] *La Rinascita della Tripolitania*, Milan, 1926.

Volpi's old friend Luigi Federzoni as Minister of Colonies, was a great service to Volpi, for an old friend in Rome was a useful asset in Fascist Italy. Federzoni's plan for Tripolitania, which Mussolini personally made known to Volpi, was the conquest and agricultural development of all the territory that could be usefully occupied.

Graziani, meanwhile, had become the hero of the reconquest. In June he had stated his objective when he had written to a chief defending the *Gebel* escarpment: 'The sovereignty of Italy extends from the sea to Tummo [in the Tibesti foothills] and whoever opposes its movements, or its officials, or its troops in any part of the territory is, in fact, a rebel against the great and powerful Italian Government.'[2]

At the end of 1922 the Italians held the hills from Nalut to Garian (which Graziani had taken in November) and most of the Gefara west of Azizia. In January 1923 the navy supported an advance eastwards along the coast from Tripoli to Homs. Qusabat fell on 4 February and two days later the tricolour was raised over the Castle at Tarhuna; all Ahmad Marayid's personal documents, including his correspondence with Amir Idris, were found in his house in the village.

Graziani continued his advance in the spring of 1923; nomads and their flocks were bombed from the air as they fled eastwards and southwards before the oncoming columns. The large coastal oasis of Zliten was taken on 23 February and on the 26th Misurata town fell. All the coast from the Tunisian frontier to the Gulf of Sirte had been reoccupied and Volpi cabled to Rome: 'This, in a word, is the catastrophe of the rebellion ... and the completion of a wonderful page in colonial military history.'

General Luigi Bongiovanni became, in January 1923, the first Fascist governor of Cyrenaica. He had a personal directive from Mussolini to 'stamp hard' there, for the state of the country was, to the new Fascist way of thinking, 'unseemly'. In March, with the Tripolitanian rebellion safely contained, Bongiovanni invited Mohammad Rida al-Sanussi, Amir Idris's brother and now, after Idris's departure for Egypt, acting Head of the Sanussi Order, to break up the 'mixed camps' and other armed posts. When this was not done the Italians suddenly occupied the camps and arrested the Sanussi forces in them; on 6 March Bongiovanni explained to the Cyren-

[2] Balardinelli, *La Ghibla, Tripoli,* 1935.

aican parliament in Benghazi 'the new line of conduct the Government has been forced to adopt'.

Rome's demands were then made known: the terms of the Regima accord were to be put into effect, there was to be 'direct and absolute' control over the Gebel Akhdar, and the recognition of Italian sovereignty throughout Cyrenaica. But Sayyid Mohammad claimed to have no power to negotiate while Idris was in Egypt, and it was not until Bongiovanni announced plans for the occupation of the coastal and *Gebel* zones that the Sanussi leader offered to ask Idris to come home, or at least to approve the opening of talks. The sudden occupation of Sayyid Mohammad's administrative centre at Agedabia on 21 April was, said Bongiovanni later, 'a worthy reply'. It had, Fascists pointed out, been given on the anniversary of Rome's foundation. At the same time, all pacts with the Sanussis were declared null and void.

The second Italo-Sanussi war had actually started in March with the Italians advancing into and occupying certain areas south of Benghazi. In the same month the Cyrenaican parliament was disbanded after five not particularly constructive sessions.

By the time the Fascists came to power, it was plain that bribes and intrigues would not make Libya a province of the New Roman empire. Volpi had shown in Tripolitania that a war of conquest was demanded of a régime that had gained power and intended to keep it by violence and that exalted ruthlessness, discipline, and aggression. The conquest of all Libya was almost a sacred duty if Fascism was really to be the 'education for combat' that Mussolini intended. The Libyan war of 1922–32 was good propaganda material for militant Fascism both in Italy and abroad, but only in the last stages of the war were there signs of the flaunted ruthlessness, and even of the desire to shock international opinion, that later characterised the conquest of Ethiopia.

In 1923 the Italians had much prestige to regain. They had collapsed at Caporetto on the Alpine front in 1917, but had redeemed themselves at Vittorio Veneto the following year. There had been a dozen minor Caporettos in Libya since 1911 but, as yet, no victories of redemption. The Libyans had no reason to respect the Italian as a soldier nor, with his post-war political record in Libya, as a ruler. Fascism stressed many characteristics wholly un-Italian, but it did at least put into the reconquest some of the purpose and spirit that had been lacking before.

The war of reconquest was long, petty, and spiteful. It was fought by small numbers over vast areas. At the start of the fighting the Italians had in Cyrenaica eleven battalions, artillery in plenty, and two squadrons of aircraft. The Sanussis could perhaps have mustered 2,000 more or less regular riflemen, between 3,000 and 4,000 irregulars, half a dozen machine-guns, and a few pieces of artillery. The Italians held about twenty posts, including all the main towns, around the arc Qaminis–Derna; Tobruk was an isolated stronghold. No Italian garrison was more than 20 miles from the sea.

The occupation of the Sanussi headquarters at Agedabia had not caused the expected collapse of resistance, although over 20,000 nomads had 'submitted' in the spring of 1923. The main objective that year was merely the pacification of the areas between Qaminis and Agedabia. This was done by making surprise attacks with armoured cars and motorised infantry on nomad camps. Between May and September 800 nomads were killed and 12,000 sheep were killed or captured, for it was Italian policy to slaughter or confiscate flocks of nomads who failed to surrender. During 1924 mechanised raids on the camps continued, but resistance was hardening; in the Gebel Akhdar, in particular, the war began to take on the form it was to have for the next eight years.

By 1924–5 the Italians found themselves directly or indirectly at war with most of the nomads of Cyrenaica. The people of the towns and villages did little fighting, but gave more material aid to the rebellion than the Italians realised. A few tribes near the coast were neutral and submissive. But the people of the hills, where there had been no formal rule by a central government since late Roman times, and the people of the desert, who had always ruled themselves, fought boldly to keep their independence. Although the fighters were labelled 'rebels' and the non-combatants *sottomessi*, those who had 'submitted', there was no clear-cut distinction between them. The *sottomessi*, and even many of the Libyans in Italian service, were on the side of the rebellion and quietly but actively supported it. Pay, rations, information, and even arms and ammunition found their way to the 'rebels'; during skirmishes Libyans serving in the Italian army dropped much live ammunition on the ground to be picked up by the guerrillas later.

Sottomessi supported the rebellion by paying a compulsory tax to Sanussi agents and by gifts of arms, clothes, foodstuffs (much of them supplied by the Italians in the first place), and horses. In the camps of the *sottomessi* the fighters found help and shelter. A supposed *sottomesso* might be spending half his time riding with the guerrillas, a guerrilla might spend weeks resting in a community of *sottomessi*, to all intents and purposes a peaceful shepherd. It was a ridiculous situation, for the Italians were both fighting the rebellion and indirectly supplying it with the greater part of its material needs. The guerrillas bought additional supplies in Egypt and paid for them with the 'taxes' or religious dues collected by the Sanussis from guerrillas, *sottomessi*, and townspeople alike.

The Cyrenaican nomads fought for the freedom to wander the hills and deserts with their flocks and herds; they had a pathetic fear that the Italians meant to massacre them all to make way for mass settlement of colonists. They fought for their religion against the Christian armies, and the Eritreans were fanatically Christian, at least when shooting Muslims. The Sanussis kept up the fighting spirit of the people far more effectively than the Fascists did of the Italians. There was, despite a high casualty rate, no shortage of volunteers for the guerrilla bands.

From about 1924 onwards the main guerrilla stronghold was the vast natural fortress of the Gebel Akhdar. The limestone tableland of northern Cyrenaica, covered with maquis and woods, cut by ravines and caves, is ideal guerrilla country, and there it was that Fascist Italy was defied for eight years by forces that at no time numbered more than one thousand active fighting men.

The leader of the resistance, and indeed of all Cyrenaica, was Omar Mukhtar, a Sanussi *shaikh* who was already more than sixty years old, white-bearded, and bespectacled, when he took command of the Gebel Akhdar bands in 1923. With the Sanussis he had fought the French in Sudan and then the Italians in 1911–16. He was a model of the soldier-patriot and his attributes were those of the traditional National Hero; he was a simple, holy, brave, and stubborn old man, a fine tactician and leader who made the most of his tiny forces. As official representative-general of the Sanussis, Omar Mukhtar was commander-in-chief of all the mobile guerrilla bands (*adwar*) ranging in size from one hundred to 300 men, but always operating in groups small enough to hide their arms and disperse for a while into the camps of the *sottomessi* if too hard-pressed. Each band was usually manned and supplied by the tribe after which it was named, and it was Omar Mukhtar who kept the peace between these traditionally rival groups. He also planned and co-ordinated all operations, organised the collection of taxes and their spending on supplies in Egypt, and, in addition, commanded his own fighting band.

His men were continually on the offensive. There was a constant bubbling of minor engagements and skirmishes: a raid here, a killing there, an ambush elsewhere. Like naughty boys, the bands roamed the countryside, dodging the lumbering columns sent against them. The Italians, who dared not split their forces into small, mobile groups for fear of attack by greater numbers, hit out powerfully at an enemy that rarely waited to take the blow. Territory that had supposedly been 'pacified' always harboured 'submitted' guerrillas ready to join the fight again; indeed, throughout the war the Sanussi and Italian governments were known respectively by the people as the Night and Day governments. It was, for the Italians, a frustrating campaign, and they did not learn readily from their mistakes. The army lacked self-confidence and was, at least until Graziani took over, commanded by men with little imagination or initiative who preferred to send optimistic but misleading reports to Rome rather than propose new ways of fighting the enemy.

At the end of 1924 the western end of the Gebel Akhdar was conquered, although not really pacified, and in April the following year columns pushed across the hills, forcing Omar Mukhtar and his followers eastwards into the forests and gorges of the central plateau. But in that year, 1925, the pacification of little northern territory was claimed. Governor Mombelli, who had replaced Bongiovanni in 1924, preferred to take Giarabub, the 'home' of the Sanussi Order, mistakenly believing that its fall would destroy the prestige of the Order and so, perhaps, end the rebellion. An attack on Giarabub had been considered several times since 1911, but it was only in 1925 that Egypt formally recognised the oasis and an adjoining strip of frontier territory as Italian. A new campaign was started to prevent Omar Mukhtar riding to the defence of the holy oasis and it was planned to make propaganda among the tribes out of his failure to do so.

A mechanised column of 2,500 men started in January 1926 to march against the tiny blind-walled village of Giarabub, dominated by the dome of the Grand Sanussi's tomb. Photographs of this and other marches by Italian columns across the desert show a crowd of trudging men, most of them be-fezzed Eritreans, mixed up with the baggage camels, the motor transport, and the armoured cars (like two tin cans on wheels), all straggling far and wide across the plain with apparently less order than workers going home at the end of the day.

On 5 February aircraft circled Giarabub and dropped leaflets calling for surrender and promising respect for the Holy Places. Two columns then advanced cautiously on the village and, as an anti-climax to the whole operation, met no opposition. Giarabub was taken on 7 February. The operation was a triumph of logistics (to supply 2,500 men across 125 miles of waterless desert requires good organisation) but had little effect on the course of the war.

Governor Mombelli, whose failure to crush the rebellion resulted in his recall to Rome, was replaced at the end of 1926 by General Attilio Teruzzi. On his arrival in Cyrenaica he promised to bring 'the full force of Roman law' down on the rebellion, but had not yet done so when, three months later, an Eritrean column was ambushed south of Barce and 300 *Askaris* were killed in the panic-stricken retreat that followed.

To clear the guerrillas from their strongholds in the caves and crannies of the wooded gorge of the Wadi Kuf, Teruzzi sent out self-supporting columns to follow, harry, and, if possible, surround the enemy. Air support was given where and when it was of use. The bands were duly driven from the Wadi Kuf and the land route from Benghazi to Derna was opened, speeding the flow of men and supplies into the hills. The guerrillas lost an estimated 1,100 men between April and September 1927, the year that marked half-time in the battle for the Gebel Akhdar and Cyrenaica.

The reconquest of Tripolitania south of the 31st parallel was cautious but sure, for the opposition was weaker than in Cyrenaica. The Tripolitanians and Fezzanese were not united, and there was no Omar Mukhtar to lead them, nor a Gebel Akhdar to shelter them.

In December 1923 Volpi's troops were marching into Beni Ulid; two months later Ghadames fell, and with the reoccupation of Mizda in June 1924 the most desirable parts of Tripolitania had been overrun.

The 1924 census counted an estimated 500,000 people in Tripolitania and Fezzan, of whom all but 100,000 nomads and oasis-dwellers were under Italian rule. The north of the country was at peace again and Volpi was starting to direct the development of the Fascist colony that was to continue for the next sixteen years. But all travel was still strictly controlled and men found guilty of rebellion were still being hanged in rows from the goal-post gallows in town squares, there to be photographed by Italians for the family picture albums. The army planners knew that all Tripolitania and Fezzan had to be occupied sooner or later for the sake of security, for unconquered tribes were rebellious ones. Volpi and his lieutenants, studying Miani's mistakes of ten years before, agreed that the Ghibla would have to be conquered, and not by-passed, before a further southward advance could be made; indeed, the long-term security of much already conquered territory depended on the eventual pacification of that unstable area which Colonel Graziani, whose special responsibility the Ghibla was, called 'the combustion chamber of Tripolitania'.

He spent three years conquering it. Italy had friends, or allies at least, among the half-dozen main tribes of the area. By exploiting the traditional rivalry between them, Graziani's political officers soon had them fighting what was virtually a civil war which the Sanussis condemned as 'fratricide'. The Berbers, the Mishasha, the Riaina, and some of the Ulad Busaif were allies of the Italians; opposed to them were the Zintan, other branches of the Ulad Busaif, and the Rogiban: very roughly, the northern Ghibla against the south. The allied tribes, the *aderenti* as they were called, were allowed to keep their arms and their freedom of movement, and were rather grudgingly subsidised. They had a steadying influence in the Ghibla and were a buffer against the fiercer tribes of the Hammadah al-Hamra. From time to time the army, supported by the *aderenti*, raided the 'rebel' camps as a reminder that the enemy was Italian as well as tribal. Occasionally, the air force made a raid, and in 1925 many of the Zintan were temporarily scared into submission when Caproni bombers dropped gas-bombs on their main camp at Al-Tabunia. (This was the only occasion the Italians admitted to using gas in Tripolitania.) The state of the Ghibla in 1924–7 was chaotic, although by 1925 there was a rough balance of power between the tribes, whose traditional rivalry prevented the area becoming a centre of popular revolt like the Gebel Akhdar. Italian penetration, although slow and tedious, did go on.

By the autumn of 1927 the army was preparing to link up the occupied zones of Tripolitania and Cyrenaica by conquering all the territory down to the 29th parallel. A great double pincer movement was planned to squeeze the Libyans simultaneously out of the Giofra oases and Augila-Gialo, and to mop up resistance in the Sirtica, where the Mogarba and Ulad Sulaiman tribes were a constant threat to the penetration of the Ghibla and the territory to the south of it. Miani's mistake of marching into Fezzan with unconquered tribes on his flanks was not to be repeated. The start of the campaign was delayed by renewed guerrilla activity in the Gebel Akhdar and on the Cyrenaican coast, and not until 1 January 1928 did Graziani lead his great Tripolitanian column out of Buerat al-Hsun, about 50 miles west of Sirte, just as a Cyrenaican column was leaving Agedabia.

The campaign's first success was scored the following day when Sayyid Mohammad Rida, who had been directing operations from his headquarters at Gialo, presented himself to the Italians at Agedabia and offered his unconditional submission. He was worn out by five years of war, and he believed that the new Italian offensive would end the rebellion. His surrender was in fact of little political or military value because the tribes realised it was a purely personal act that none were expected to copy. He was sent into exile in Sicily.

Bombed and strafed by the air force, chased across the desert by armoured cars and cavalry, and continually threatened by the steady advance of the infantry, the tribes were forced to clear a path for the oncoming columns, which met up south of Ras Lanuf on 13 January. Protected by a rearguard of riflemen and cavalry, the Libyans gave ground but not battle; they were not mopped up, but swept aside, still in good fighting order. Their greatest losses were in livestock (20,000 sheep and 8,000 camels were taken in the first three weeks of the campaign) and in baggage and food. But mobility was greatly increased by the loss of these impedimenta.

Early in February Graziani occupied the Giofra oases. The complimentary occupation of Augila-Gialo was completed two weeks later and the Sirtica was thus boxed in along its western and eastern flanks. Within the box, which was bottomless, was a mass of armed Libyans, ready always to attack outposts and supply-columns, and equally ready to disperse into the desert when attacked by superior numbers.

Eventually, a column of 1,500 men, led by Graziani and encumbered by a baggage train of 3,000 camels (for the army liked to live well, even in the desert), was cut off in the heart of the Sirtica.

At Bir Tigrift, 60 miles north of Zillah, Graziani on 25 February found himself opposed by about 1,500 tribesmen. In a seven-hour engagement the Libyans lost about 250 killed and many hundred wounded; the Italians claimed a great victory.

By mid-March eight bases had been set up in and around the Sirtica. Armoured cars and motorised infantry, directed by aircraft, were sent out from these strongholds to hunt down groups of nomads. Resistance was countered with great sweeps to and fro across the open desert, and even the remote Sanussi fastnesses in the far south of Cyrenaica, Tazerbo and Kufra, were bombed from the air. In the first five months of 1928, some 150,000 square kilometres of territory, covering six degrees of longitude and two of latitude, were occupied in a series of operations that, in the words of an Italian commentator, 'were worthy of entry in the most glowing pages of colonial-military history of the world'. In fact, the conquest of the Sirtica was a nice exercise in logistics, but not a particularly remarkable feat of arms. The rebellion had by no means been ended, although the guerrillas in southern Tripolitania and Fezzan had been virtually cut off from their comrades in Cyrenaica by the Italian thrust between them.

The military planners had meanwhile been pondering over an old adage to the effect that the southern Ghibla and the Hammadah al-Hamra were held from the Wadi Shatti, the Shatti from Sebha and Murzuk, and they from Ghat and Tummo. The implication was that all Tripolitania and Fezzan had to be conquered and pacified to their furthest limits if the occupation was to be secure; renewed attacks from the south by the turncoat Mishasha chief, Mohammad bin al-Haj Hassan, and the Saif al-Nasir family, were taken as proof of the theory. In the summer of 1928 a cautious advance through the Ghibla was started; Gheriat al-Scerghia was taken in July, the big re-entrant northward in the 'frontier' towards Mizda was eliminated, and by the end of the year a one thousand-mile front from Ghadames in the west, through Sokna, Zillah, and Augila to Giarabub in the east, was being held.

In January 1929, the marshal of Italy, Pietro Badoglio, was appointed governor of Tripolitania and Cyrenaica, which had been united for better co-ordination of military operations. One of his first actions was to issue a proclamation promising 'peace, clemency, and generosity' to those who submitted, 'whether big or small, individual or *kabila*' and war without quarter against 'the evil-intentioned and the rebels'. The proclamation was made known far and wide, and aircraft dropped thousands of copies on the Wadi Shatti area, where the followers of Ahmad Saif al-Nasir and Mohammad bin al-Haj Hassan were reportedly planning a mighty counter-attack that was to repeat the adventures of 1914 and drive the Italians back to the Gebel Nefusah. But Graziani had not spent three years securing the Ghibla in vain. In the summer of 1929 its occupation was consolidated by the planting of garrisons, complete tribal disarmament, and the blocking and poisoning of wells on the southern migration routes across the Hammadah al-Hamra to prevent tribesmen joining guerrilla concentrations in Fezzan. The myth of the 'unconquerable' *Hammadah* was ended. While Mohammad bin al-Haj Hassan was slowly forced southwards across the hot, barren tableland, Ahmad Saif al-Nasir was routed at Al-Shuwayrif, south-west of Bu Najim, on 26 May, at which Graziani crowed: 'Thus, in miserable fashion, the rebel plan failed once again.'

A stream of directives poured from Badoglio's office. 'All the population must acquire this conviction: that we are here, and here we will stay forever.' Italian officials were, without being offensive about it, to make their 'intellectual superiority' felt; they were to be 'just, scrupulously just', and to remember that 'under every *baraccan*' there was 'a heart capable of love and hate'. At the same time, the machine-gun was recommended as a more effective weapon against 'rebels' than artillery....

During the final stages of the reconquest, the Italians were fighting the Sahara itself, as well as its people. Badoglio found that: 'The armed adversary was the lesser evil. The more terrible enemy, and the truly inexorable one, was the distance and the absolute lack of resources.'[3] Yet he also realised that: 'The country cannot be said to be properly pacified so long as a single unit can flee beyond our effective control.'[4] Unconquered tribes were rebellious tribes.

The conquest of Fezzan was planned as a three-pronged, three-phase operation. Columns setting out from Al-Shuwayrif, Derj, and Gateifa had as their first objective the Wadi Shatti where Zintan tribesmen had concentrated. Then they were to break through Mohammad bin al-Haj Hassan's Mishasha to the Wadi Ajal, where Abd-al-Nabi Bilkhayr's 'Orfellini' tribesmen were grouping. The final operation would be to close in on Murzuk and attack Ahmad

[3] *L'Occupazione del Fezzan*, Tripoli, 1930.
[4] Ibid.

Saif al-Nasir and the Ulad Sulaiman. About 2,500 men, Italians, Eritreans, and Libyans, were to advance 500 or 600 miles into the desert, and long before the campaign started there was a great build-up of equipment and supplies. More Romeo and Caproni aircraft were assembled at the main air base at Hon and, their fuel supplies organised with meticulous detail, hundreds of heavy lorries rolled down the desert trails to the three main assembly areas, where great herds of baggage-animals were being marshalled.

When the campaign started at the end of November 1929, there were perhaps 1,500 weary Libyans in the field, and opposition to the Italian advance was light. The Al-Shuwayrif column occupied Brak on 5 December, and on the 14th reached Sebha. By 9 January 1930 Graziani was at Umm al-Aranib and a 150-mile dash across the desert with a light column to Waw al-Kabir enabled him to meet up with and rout the Ulad Sulaiman on 13 January. A week later Murzuk, the capital of Fezzan, was taken. The Derj column, meanwhile, had crossed the Hammadah al-Hamra and, after taking Edri on 21 January, crossed the sand sea to Ubari, which fell on 2 February. From Murzuk and Ubari two columns then marched on Ghat, which was occupied on 15 February.

During March the Harruj area of central Libya was mopped up and at the end of the month the tricolour was hoisted over the wells of Tummo, the most southerly Italian claim in Fezzan, some 600 miles from the coast. Libyans who refused to take advantage of the general amnesty declared by Badoglio slipped across the border into exile in Algeria or southern Tunisia.

An area of a quarter of a million square miles, twice that of metropolitan Italy, had been occupied in four months, but also eighteen years and six months after the first landing at Tripoli.

After Sayyid Mohammad Rida's surrender in 1928, Omar Mukhtar was officially appointed Sanussi representative in Cyrenaica. The operations in the Sirtica in the spring of 1928 had not changed the situation in the Gebel Akhdar, where Omar Mukhtar was still fighting with, as the Italians admitted, 'truly exceptional tenacity'. To counter the fairly successful Italian circling tactics, and to escape observation from the air, he shifted his operations to the wooded Shenshen zone and the Wadi Mehaggia. A carefully-laid plan to surround him failed because of the broken terrain, and he slipped through the net. But he was kept so continuously on the move that no large groups of guerrillas were able to form. Great sweeps up and down and back and forth across the *Gebel* mopped up some bands, but many more took refuge in the camps of the *sottomessi*, or slipped away into the Marmarica, where there had been little fighting.

When Badoglio, with Domenico Siciliani as his vice-governor, took command in Cyrenaica in 1929 he had reason to hope that the end of the rebellion was near. The bands had been driven hither and thither across the hills for so long that they were losing strength and cohesion. They had been pushed into the corners and fastnesses of the country and, in a state of mobile siege, they could no longer sow or reap their crops, or pasture their animals. They were exhausted, as were all the people of Cyrenaica, but the Italians always had fresh reserves of Eritreans to call on. Badoglio promised total war against the rebellion, and threatened: 'No rebel will be given quarter, neither he, nor his family, nor his livestock, nor his heirs. I will destroy everything, men and goods.'[5]

The Italians liked to think that it was Badoglio's threats that frightened Omar Mukhtar into opening negotiations in June 1929. In fact, he knew that the rebellion was failing, as much through Libyan exhaustion as Italian strength, and that to continue the fight would only bring more misery and ruin to the country. A truce was agreed and in talks with Siciliani, Omar Mukhtar promised peace and recognition of Italian sovereignty over all Cyrenaica. On 19 June he was forced to meet Badoglio, make an act of submission, and report: 'There are no more rebels.' Negotiations for a permanent settlement dragged on until the autumn but broke down, apparently because of disagreement over the future status of Sayyid Idris. By the beginning of November, Cyrenaica was again at war, and early in 1930 the great sweeps across the *Gebel* were restarted. The bands were losing heavily in every engagement; on 28 January, Omar Mukhtar escaped after being hurt in a fight in which 150 of his men were killed or wounded. In March alone, an estimated 800 guerrillas were killed.

In January 1930 the man with the ruthlessness and the ability to put down the seven-year-old Cyrenaican rebellion was appointed vice-governor. Rodolfo Graziani, whose recent conquest of southern Tripolitania and Fezzan had made him a national hero, had at thirty-six been the youngest colonel in the Italian army; he was a general at forty-two. Graziani was a big man, an impulsive

[5] Piccioli, *La Nuova Italia d'Oltremare*, Milan, 1934.

extrovert, and rather hysterical. He has been accused of waging a personal vendetta against Omar Mukhtar; his wife has claimed that he was 'incapable of hating'; yet after four years of service in Cyrenaica he was to be known as 'Butcher Graziani'.

He simplified the army's inefficient command system, substituting one command for the three he found in the *Gebel* zone. He grabbed the initiative from Omar Mukhtar by sending out fast-moving patrols to penetrate guerrilla territory and attack the bands ceaselessly. He realised that so long as the bands could move freely, they gave the impression of controlling the country, although out-numbered twenty to one. Graziani ordered the patrols 'to dominate the country by continual movement', and declared: 'We must always be on the move, even in empty country, to create the continual impression that we are masters of the territory.'[6] Not trusting his Libyan troops, he disbanded many of their units and replaced them with the very loyal, Christian Eritreans, who were loathed by the Libyans.

As the *sottomessi* were still the main source of the bands' supplies and recruits, Graziani had them systematically disarmed in the spring of 1930. At the same time, contact with the guerrillas was made a capital offence, and in two months twenty-seven Libyans were sentenced for this crime by a special military tribunal which flew round the country administering summary justice. The Sanussi *zawiyas* were closed, their *shaikhs* were arrested on charges of supporting the rebellion and were exiled, and Sanussi estates were confiscated. Graziani took drastic measures, at enormous cost and trouble, to control the *sottomessi*: almost the entire nomad population of northern Cyrenaica, with their flocks and herds, was forcibly moved away from the battle zones to bleak concentration camps on the coast and in the Sirtica. By the end of July 1930 they occupied 12,000 government tents. The camps, protected or cowed by machine-gun posts, were barbed-wire enclosures over one kilometre square in which hundreds of tents were pitched in straight rows. The nomads were kept alive with hand-outs of government tinned food, but the flocks diminished rapidly after the sparse grazing near the camps gave out. The official attitude was that the roaming Beduin were better off in their enforced state of sedentary and listless idleness because they could fully enjoy the state welfare services. Graziani's statement to the press in June 1931 that 'no radical

[6] Ibid.

change in life has been imposed on the people' was simply not true, for a 'concentration' camp, in its very purpose, was the absolute negation of nomadic freedom to wander. The *sottomessi* became caged beggars, living at bare subsistence level on begrudged government charity, and ashamed at having submitted while others were still fighting. Knud Holmboe, the remarkable Arabic-speaking Danish Muslim who travelled from Morocco to Derna in the spring of 1930, described in his book *Desert Encounter* a concentration camp he visited near Barce:

> 'The camp was immense. It contained at least fifteen hundred tents and had a population of six to eight thousand people. It was fenced in with barbed wire, and there were guards with machine guns at every entrance. As we drove up among the tents children came running towards us. They were in rags and hungry, half-starved, but evidently they were accustomed to getting money from the Commandant on his visits, for they stretched out their hands and shouted in Italian: "*Un soldo, Signore, un soldo*!"
>
> 'The Beduins gathered around us. They looked incredibly ragged. On their feet were hides tied with string; their burnouses were a patchwork of all kinds of multi-coloured pieces. Many of them seemed ill and wretched, limping along with crooked backs, or with arms and legs that were terribly deformed.'

– not that the deformities could be blamed on the war, or the Italians.

Cut off from the *sottomessi*, Omar Mukhtar shifted some of his operations to the Marmarica and sought more help from Egypt. To prevent arms and supplies reaching the bands from the Egyptian port of Sollum (the Egyptian authorities apparently turned a blind eye to the traffic) Graziani conceived one of the more ridiculous works of Fascism. He ordered the building of a barbed-wire fence, 10 yards wide and 5 feet high, along the 200 miles of Egyptian frontier from the sea to Giarabub. It was patrolled by armoured cars and aircraft, and there were standing orders that anyone trying to get through it was to be shot. Typically, Graziani compared his fence to the Great Wall of China; Alan Moorehead, the war correspondent, who first saw it in 1940, judged its conception 'absurd, its uses nil'.

Hundreds of miles to the south the oases of Kufra had been ruled since 1917 by Sayyid Mohammad al-Abid, a cousin of Sayyid Idris. News of Italian operations in the north, together with occasional air raids on the oases, decided him to open negotiations to save Kufra from the war, but after making preliminary contact, he was overthrown by an anti-Italian faction. Kufra was the last stronghold of the Sanussis in Libya and, if for that reason alone, was destined for occupation. The Italian offensive against the oases opened in July 1930 with air raids. For four months preparations were made for a three-pronged advance into this, one of the remotest corners of the Sahara. As with the Giarabub and Fezzan expeditions, logistics posed more problems than the enemy, and the 600 defenders of Kufra had some justification for hoping that the sand seas cutting off the oases from the outside world would defeat the invaders. The main Italian column of 3,000 troops, half of them camel-mounted, and 300 motor vehicles, left Agedabia in December 1930 and met up outside Kufra in January with motorised columns from Zillah and Waw al-Kabir. It was another magnificent exercise in logistics that Graziani frequently flew down from Benghazi to supervise. The defenders were routed at Al-Hawari on 19 January and by the 20th, with the occupation of Taj completed, the population was fleeing in mad panic. Men, women, and children were needlessly bombed and strafed from the air as they fled towards Egypt, the Anglo-Egyptian Sudan, and the Tibesti; others died in the desert from thirst, starvation, and exhaustion. The occupation of Kufra carried the flag to the frontiers of Sudan and the French colony of Chad, but had no effect on the course of events in the Gebel Akhdar.

In an engagement in October 1930 Omar Mukhtar lost his gold spectacles and their silver chain (odd wear for a guerrilla leader) and, when they were found by an Italian patrol, Graziani declared: 'Now we have the spectacles; the head will follow one day.' For another year Omar Mukhtar continued his operations while the non-combatant Libyans, destitute, frightened, and bewildered, cringed under a reign of terror. Graziani, with literal interpretation of the Fascist slogans on the walls ('Those who are not for us are against us') scourged the country into sullen submission. He saw pacification in terms of 'Romans' subduing 'barbarians'. Many of the so-called 'Romans' were Eritreans whose greatest virtue seems to have been their loyalty to the Italians. Their habit of exposing the large crucifixes hung from their necks, or sewn onto the breasts of their baggy uniforms, emphasised the Christian solidarity of the Eritreans and the Italians in the war against Muslims. Holmboe quoted Sayyid Idris as saying to him: 'Do you know why the Italians are using

Eritrean troops? Because the Eritreans are Christians. The Italians have created a religious war in Cyrenaica.'

By executions (shooting in the back or hanging), by sending men to slow deaths in the salt pans, by forbidding Sanussi practices, and by closing Sanussi mosques and *zawiyas*, by blocking the desert wells with concrete or poisoning the water to restrict the movement of tribes, and by arrests, deportations, and confiscations, the Italians gradually strangled the rebellion in all but Omar Mukhtar's last strongholds. If Holmboe's information was correct, the guerrillas were being bombed with mustard gas at least by the spring of 1930. Atrocity stories of captured guerrilla leaders being dropped alive from aeroplanes onto their own villages, or being run over by tanks, were circulated but seem to have been greatly exaggerated.

Holmboe, who was arrested and imprisoned by the Italians, and was highly critical of their methods, calculated: 'During the time I was in Cyrenaica thirty executions took place daily, which means that about twelve thousand Arabs were executed yearly, not counting those killed in the war or the imported Eritrean troops on the Italian side. The land swam in blood.'[7]

At the beginning of September 1931 Omar Mukhtar was reported to be in the Ain Lafa area, south of Baida, with about one hundred men. On 13 September he was ambushed, his horse was shot from under him, and, wounded in the arm, he was captured. Graziani, who was on holiday in Europe, flew back to Cyrenaica to interview him. After a summary court martial, the old patriot was hanged at Suluq before a silent crowd of 20,000 forcibly assembled Libyans.

In the words of an Italian commentator, Omar Mukhtar was 'the faithful and intelligent servant of Idris and the mind and heart of the Cyrenaican rebellion.' Idris has himself called him 'a supreme example of chivalry and godliness'. Main streets in Tripoli, Benghazi, and Baida are named after him, his mausoleum stands in Benghazi, and, after Idris himself, he was to become the greatest national hero of independent Libya.

His achievement was singular. In defying Fascist Italy for nine years he affirmed the maxim of a modern Middle Eastern general that 'Guerrilla warfare is war of the weak, but is not in itself weak.' The defiance and self-sacrifice of Omar Mukhtar and his followers were noble, but there is a suspicion that in its final years the fighting was prolonged for its own sake. Asked by Graziani his purpose in

[7] *Desert Encounter*, London, 1936, p. 203.

waging war, Omar Mukhtar is quoted as saying: 'I am a fighter, neither more nor less. The end rests with God alone.' Yet he might have spared Cyrenaica much misery had he surrendered when defeat was inevitable.

His death virtually ended the rebellion. Many patriots were captured or shot while trying to escape to Egypt, and Cyrenaica was turned into an armed camp. Everywhere, coils and fences of barbed wire restricted movement. With most of the nomad population shut up in the concentration camps, the Italians at last mastered the country with fixed forts festooned with wire, with patrols, armoured cars, tanks, machine-guns, searchlights, and aircraft. In December 1931 Graziani estimated that less than one hundred guerrillas were still holding out in the Gebel Akhdar, and on 24 January 1932 Badoglio thought the time had come to proclaim: 'The rebellion is completely and definitely extinguished. For the first time in the twenty years since the landing in this country the two colonies are completely occupied and pacified.'[8]

Graziani called the peace a *Pax Romana.*

[8] Piccioli, op. cit.

Chapter 15

Fourth Shore

THE CONQUEST was complete, and maps showing all Libya as Italian no longer lied. The workers and peasants, the 'Legionaries of Labour' and the 'Soldiers of the Soil', the Fascist slogan-writers called them, could now move into and develop the colony on Italy's 'Fourth Shore'. During the years of peace, Italian labour turned Libya into a remarkable showplace of Fascist achievement. There, as in Italy, wrote a propagandist, 'The Party is the soul of all, and everyone must unite to achieve that dynamic and creative harmony that alone can carry the colony towards the future destined for it by the Duce.'[1] Mussolini himself declared in 1934: 'Civilisation, in fact, is what Italy is creating on the Fourth Shore of our sea; western civilisation in general and Fascist civilisation in particular.'

It was less for Fascist ideals than in expectation of a worthwhile return on their investments that Volpi and other capitalists started the large-scale agricultural development of Tripolitania in the 1920s, at a time when many were still mocking at the costly reconquest of *uno scatolone di sabbia*, 'a crate of sand'. Volpi himself acquired a big estate near Misurata and encouraged others to follow his example. Land was sold, mortgaged, or rented in large concessions by the state and was worked, under Italian supervision and with Italian capital, by hired Libyan labour and by some Italian peasant families. The colonial government acquired land either by confiscating it from 'rebels' or, following a decree of July 1922, by taking over uncultivated ground 'for public use'. The government invoked Turkish and Muslim land-tenure laws which, broadly speaking, recognised as its owner anyone who settled on and cultivated previously untilled and ownerless ground. According to the rather flexible Italian interpretation of these laws, the mere intention to settle and develop the land was enough to justify its appropriation by the state. Tracts of land were declared state property on two

[1] Lischi, *Tripolitania Felix*, Pisa, 1937.

months' notice; objectors had the right to be heard by a commission and compensation was payable at 1912 values. Between 1922 and 1925 about 75,000 acres near Tripoli were appropriated and sold off cheaply as large estates or one-family holdings.

It was easy enough for Italians to acquire land, but to turn the scorched, dusty plains of northern Tripolitania into prosperous farms was not. At its best, the light, sandy soil had a mediocre potential, and the weather was heartbreakingly fickle. Olives and some orchard fruits did well under the dry conditions, but needed from five to fifteen unproductive years to mature, and the irrigation essential for most field crops was expensive. Nothing soaks up money like the desert and, for this reason, farming in Libya needed generous financial backing; it was the big concessions in which large sums had been invested that made the best progress in the early days.

The big concession system was not part of official Fascist colonial policy. Mussolini wanted Italy's landless peasants and unemployed to settle in Libya with their families and establish their own farms; he did not approve of scarce Italian capital being used to pay Libyans to work rich men's estates. The settlement of individual families in Tripolitania was encouraged under the governorship of Emilio de Bono (1925–9) and, although some large concessions were still granted, the concessionnaires were obliged to employ and settle Italian families on the land under long-term contracts. Between 1926 and 1929 a further 160,000 acres were set aside for sale on ten-year mortgages, and long-term credits for colonists were arranged. At the same time, the discovery (at a depth of about 1,300 feet) of a second water table beneath the Gefara Plain promised better irrigation from artesian wells.

In the early days, many of the little colonial farms were a failure. Some colonists were quite unsuitable and few of them had enough money to carry them through the first unproductive years. Others were too optimistic or, due to lack of technical and practical advice, knew nothing of local conditions (like the farmer who continued to plant the crops he had always successfully raised in his native Piedmont). There were those who were lazy or stupid (several settlers started their essentially pioneering mission by spending their time and money on building luxurious farmhouses), and others who were unlucky. But Italian colonists from the plains of Tunisia who settled in Tripolitania were more successful than those who came straight from Italy. In 1929–30 both the large estates and the smallholdings were hit by the international economic crisis just as they were becoming economically viable and there were many bankruptcies. As late as 1935 a French expert, Jean Despois, commented that 'colonisation in Tripolitania will never be anything but an unhappy affair', but added that settlers needed only to look across the frontier to the *Région Sfaxienne* of Tunisia, with its 2½ million flourishing olive-trees, to see what could be achieved, given time and hard work, under conditions very similar to Tripolitania's.

In Cyrenaica there had been some colonisation on the Benghazi–Tocra and Barce–Abiar plains even during the Sanussi war. The pioneer Cyrenaican colonists had an even harder time than those in Tripolitania and many of the first fields and orchards were laid out inside protective barbed-wire pallisades. At Abiar the early colonial farmhouses were fortified, like the farms on the Roman frontier 1,800 years before, and were protected against guerrilla raids with watch-towers, searchlights, and machine-guns. When peace did come in 1932, the colonisation programme was held up by two years of drought.

At the end of the Cyrenaican war, Rome began to pay more attention to Libyan colonisation. The state-financed and guided settlements at Tigrinna and Suani ben Adem in Tripolitania, Luigi Razza's *Ente di Colonizzazione per la Cirenaica* which started work in 1932 and later became a controlled public utility corporation, and the *Ente per la Colonizzazione della Libia*, were taken as models for large-scale state schemes. In Cyrenaica the *Ente* built four model villages and laid out 50-acre farms for 150 selected families from Puglia, very nearly the poorest region of southern Italy. These people, who were settled in the winter of 1933–4, were the forerunners of many thousands of state-aided peasant colonists.

The mass settlement of Italian families on the sandy plains of Tripolitania and the rocky wind-swept hills of Cyrenaica was not started until the late 1930s, after fifteen years of experiments with varyingly successful colonisation schemes. 'Demographic colonisation', as it was called, was largely the brainchild of Italo Balbo, the organising genius who in 1934 became governor of Tripolitania and Cyrenaica, united as the one colony of Libya.

He planned the settling of peasants, not by the dozen or the hundred, but in thousands at a time. Methods used and lessons learned in the Pontine Marshes and other Fascist land settlement and reclamation schemes in Italy were to be applied on an even grander scale. No longer were penniless peasants to be left unaided and unsupervised to fight the ungenerous Libyan soil and climate. The Fascist state would do everything possible to make colonial farming a success from the outset. All that would be required of the colonist and his family, who were to be selected 'for their fitness for the tasks the State intends them to fulfil', were faith, obedience, and service: 'Credere, Obbedire, Combattere' – Believe, Obey, Fight, as the banners said.

Although the costs would be enormous, Rome was prepared to spend lavishly on the scheme and accepted that for at least a generation to come Libya would be an even greater financial liability than it already was. In 1937 there were only 1,300 Italian peasant families farming in the colony, and many of them were wage labourers on the big concessions, the seven largest of which averaged 10,000 acres each. This was not what Rome wanted. It was considered necessary to settle peasants in Libya to reduce, or at least stabilise, Italy's population, which was rapidly increasing through official Fascist encouragement of fecundity and the closing of the United States to Italian immigration. Emigration, other than to Italian colonies, had anyway been discouraged since 1927 for fear that the nation's 'demographic energy' would be dispersed. Once established, the colonial farms would supply food, and grain and oil in particular, to Italy, where a policy of 'self-sufficiency' had been followed since the imposition of sanctions by League of Nations members after the invasion of Abyssinia. In 1928 the Minister of Colonies, Luigi Federzoni, had called for the settlement of 300,000 colonists 'to counterbalance the native population'. Ten years later, colonists were still needed on the Fourth Shore to make Libya an 'Italian country' and to consolidate Italian strategic control of both sides of the central Mediterranean basin. The colony was to be the Fascist Algeria, Malta, and Gibraltar combined. It was also believed that the successful colonisation of Libya would improve Italy's case for the annexation of more colonial territories, so much so that the French were highly suspicious of Balbo's colonisation plans and regarded settlers as potential recruits for an army of invasion.

Balbo's programme was approved by the Duce in March 1938. Some 20,000 colonists were due to arrive *en masse* the following October, which left a little over 200 days in which to make everything ready for them. The scheme was administered and carried out by three para-state organisations, the *Ente per la Colonizzazione della Libia*, the *Istituto Nazionale Fascista* (the Fascist social insurance organisation), and the *Azienda Tabacchi Italiani.* One and a quarter million acres had been appropriated for settlement and L. It. 60 million had been set aside for compensation of Libyan landowners. About 30,000 Italian and Libyan labourers were recruited to build eight new colonial villages (Crispi, Gioda, Giordani, and Oliveti in Tripolitania; Baracca, Battisti, D'Annunzio, and Oberdan in Cyrenaica), five agricultural centres, and to extend seven earlier colonial villages. The land for 1,800 farms was cleared and planted, wells were drilled and irrigation channels dug, access roads and tracks were laid out, and farmhouses and farm buildings, all nearly identical in their brilliant white concrete, were built. The immense task, which Balbo closely supervised in all its stages and details, was completed with 'Fascist speed'.

Meanwhile, selection committees in Italy were interviewing thousands of applicant families. To be chosen for colonisation a family had to be large (eight was considered the minimum number of people who could work one of the farms), healthy, literate, and, if not party members, politically sound. Colonists were selected from all parts of the country, but the majority came from Emilia and Veneto in the north-east. To desperately poor, and mainly landless, peasants the offer of a new life in Libya, no matter how hard, seemed to be another of the Duce's miracles.

Following precise directives, the 20,000 chosen people sold up and packed their personal belongings. (Baggage allowances were generous and the dismantled family bicycle could be taken, but playing cards were strictly forbidden.) In October 1938, still following the instructions of paternal officials, they put on their best clothes for the journey by special trains to Genoa, Naples, or Syracuse, where, with full international publicity, they were given a cheering, brass-band, and flag-waving send-off as they sailed away in fleets of liners. At Tripoli and Benghazi, which were hung with street banners proclaiming 'Mussolini redeems the soil and founds cities', they received a heroic welcome before being driven in army lorry convoys to their respective villages. Never was a mass movement of people better or more thoughtfully organised. A jovial, beaming Balbo had supervised the embarkation at Genoa (where, typically, he had stood godfather to a colonist's new-born baby), had sailed with the families, had welcomed them to Libya, and had personally seen many of them into their new homes.

Each family was allotted a house and farm ready for occupation. The fields had already been planted, there was a cow and a mule in the stable, tools, seeds, and fodder in the barn, a rubber-tyred cart and cut firewood in the yard. The house was roomy but austere (£600 was the average building cost), furnishings cheap but adequate. There was food for a week in the larder and on the kitchen table were a bundle of candles and *five* boxes of matches, which were provided whether electricity had been laid on or not. Martin Moore, the *Daily Telegraph* correspondent who accompanied the colonists on what Balbo called their 'humanised migration', wrote how: 'Twenty thousand peasants sat down at the same hours to identical meals spread on identical wooden tables in identical concrete houses.'[2]

The farms ranged in size from 37 to 124 acres, the smaller ones being those with the better soil and water, and were widely but regularly spaced across the treeless plains and hillsides. At the centre of the communities were the villages, where the dominating building was always the church, which usually had a plain, triple-arched portico. Grouped round a *piazza* were the co-operative shop and artisans' workshops, the *Casa del Fascio*, the post office, and the market, all built in dazzling white-painted concrete in the new, many-arched, and extremely attractive Fascist 'colonial style'.

'Demographic colonisation' was a costly operation and the state was estimated to have spent over £4 million (pre-war) on the 1938 migration even before the arrival of the colonists. Moore commented: 'It will be several decades before any of these immigrants begin to contribute their quota as taxpayers... everything depends upon the State continuing to pour money into Libya for many years to come... there is no foreseeable revenue which could balance the cost of garrisoning the coast and policing the desert.'[3]

For the first year, until the land became productive, the farmer was paid wages as an employee either of the *Ente per la Colonizzazione* or of the social insurance institute. Then followed a period of crop-sharing, half the value of his produce going to the farmer and half to the *Ente*, which also provided everything the farmer could not himself grow. After five years the colonist became a mortgagee with a debt to the *Ente* or the institute of about £1,000 at 2 per cent interest; 30 per cent of the original cost of the farm was an

[2] *Fourth Shore*, London, 1940, p. 132.
[3] Ibid., pp. 216–17, p. 221.

outright gift of the government. How soon the debt was paid off depended entirely on the farmer. Some holdings were inevitably rather better than others (although pains were taken to ensure that there were no great inequalities) and there was, particularly because this was Libyan farming, a great element of chance. But a hard-working settler, given reasonable fortune, could expect to own his farm within a minimum of twenty-one years of taking it over, and every family of 1938 was virtually certain to be free of its debt within twenty-seven years, or by 1964–5 at the latest.

In October 1939 a further 12,000 colonists in 1,600 family groups were brought in, with far less publicity than the previous year's contingent. They were settled under similar conditions in eight new villages in Tripolitania and Cyrenaica. That year work was also started on an aqueduct designed to carry water for thousands of future settlers nearly 100 miles from Ain Mara to the dry, western end of the Gebel Akhdar.

Had 'demographic colonisation' not been entirely ruined in Cyrenaica by the Second World War, and seriously disrupted in Tripolitania, there would have been 100,000 settlers in the country by 1942, and the settlement of half a million by the early 1960s was planned. That some colonists in Tripolitania successfully completed the twenty-year programme and duly became owners of their holdings shows that the scheme, at least as an agricultural and financial proposition, was basically a sound one. It would never have been a realistic solution to Italy's pre-war population problems, for the natural increase in population was greater than the greatest possible flow of migrants to the Fourth Shore. The scheme's long-term value was in providing Tripolitania, at least, with many farms that were quite well established by the late 1940s and were able to make some contribution to Libya's post-war economy. In 1950 the United Nations Commissioner in Libya reported: 'The Italian farms, both private concessions and para-statal settlements, represent a remarkable feat of pioneering and land reclamation which . . . has recently begun to demonstrate its full productive value.'[4]

The colony of Libya was almost entirely a Fascist creation. Volpi had started the development of the town of Tripoli in 1922 and by 1940 it was one of the most attractive cities on the Mediterranean.

[4] Pelt: First Annual Report. (For full titles of Pelt's reports see Bibliography.)

The economic development of Tripolitania did not effectively start until the mid-1920s, and that of Cyrenaica until the early 1930s. For twenty years, but particularly in the years after 1932, Fascist Italy poured wealth she could ill afford into Libya; while Italian housewives contributed their wedding rings to the national gold reserves, public buildings in Tripoli and Benghazi were being trimmed with imported marble and travertine. Even before 'demographic colonisation' began, Rome was supplying two-thirds of Tripolitania's revenue and three-quarters of Cyrenaica's. Years of backbreaking, and sometimes heartbreaking, physical labour were put into the country by thousands of Italians working with the enjoyment of people who customarily wish each other 'Buon lavoro!' before starting the day's work.

It was largely during the six-year governorship of Italo Balbo that the colony reached its state of genuinely impressive material development. Air Marshal Balbo was not quite thirty-eight when Mussolini appointed him governor-general. His broad shoulders and bull-neck made him look shorter than he was; a pointed chestnut beard gave him the appearance of a cheery Mephistopheles. He was tough, hugely enthusiastic, and dazzlingly successful in most things, a bold initiator and organiser, and an immensely likeable person. He had been one of Mussolini's right-hand men of the *Quadrumvirate* in 1922. Later, as Air Minister, he had built up the *Regia Aeronautica*, and it was he who had led squadrons of Savoia-Marchetti flying boats on their non-stop propaganda flights across the North and South Atlantic in the early 1930s. He ruled Libya with the pride of a prince and even the Libyans grudgingly admired him; to them he was the 'Father of Flying Men' because he flew himself on tours of inspection throughout Libya in his personal aircraft. To the Italians of Libya he was second only to Mussolini and once, for a few embarrassing moments during a parade in Tripoli, the crowd began chanting his name instead of the Duce's.

The Italians had been excessively severe in the closing, victorious stages of the Cyrenaican war, and one of Balbo's earliest and most delicate tasks was to try to win the confidence of the Cyrenaicans, whose country was still sad, ruinous, and depopulated. Villages and markets were dead, and the flocks and herds that represented the main wealth of the people had been decimated by war and drought; there were 800,000 sheep in Cyrenaica in 1926: in 1933 there were less than 100,000; the camel population had dropped from 75,000 to 2,600, horses had been reduced from 4,000 to 1,000. After their experience of Graziani's concentration camps, the nomads were sullen, frightened, and destitute. Balbo, for all his personal concern for their welfare, was never able to repair the psychological damage caused by the war, particularly in its later stages. The Cyrenaicans were completely pacified and gave no trouble, but they remained spiritually defiant until the end of the Italian occupation of their country.

The nomads were helped to rebuild their flocks (livestock in all Libya doubled from 980,000 head in 1936 to 1,900,000 in 1938), wells were dug, new mosques were opened, and health standards were improved when plague, cholera, and smallpox were eradicated and the eye infection, trachoma, controlled. Despite these services, Italian rule was no better liked, and the colonisation projects were as much feared and resented now that they were becoming reality as they had been when the nomads were fighting for their independence. Italian settlement, just as the nomads had always feared, was closing the traditional summer pastures on the Gebel Akhdar; they foresaw the appropriation of all the best land of northern Cyrenaica for Italian settlement, leaving only pre-desert pasturage for the flocks. The demarcation of a vast tract of the Cyrenaican steppe as a perpetual pastoral reserve closed to colonists did nothing to mollify the nomads, who had been grazing their flocks for centuries on that land which was, moreover, obviously useless for settlement. One of the colonial government's long-term plans was the settlement of all the nomads who, as unsupervised wanderers, were always considered a potential source of trouble. Early in 1938 Balbo announced the building of eight settlement villages, similar in organisation and finance to the Italian ones, for landless Cyrenaicans. The farms were not as good as Italian ones, 'because Arab requirements are less', it was explained. The scheme was not a success and did not outlive the Italian occupation.

Less was done for the Fezzanese living in the *Territorio Militare del Sud*. Balbo compared the southern tribesmen unfavourably with the people on the coast, and although military motor tracks were cleared between the main centres, a few wells dug, and a dozen elementary schools opened, the country remained a neglected and destitute backwater.

'Mussolini redeems the land', proclaimed the banners as a reminder of the desert reclamation programme. In the early 1920s sand dunes were piled up at Porta Benito, just beyond the southern suburbs of Tripoli. By the late 1930s, dune stabilisation with *Dis* grass, followed by planting with Australian eucalyptus (a successful import), acacia, pine, and cypress at the rate of over one million trees a year had pushed back the desert more than 20 miles in some places, but a plan for planting a line of forests across the Tripolitanian *Gebel*, which was expected to improve the climate of the Gefara Plain, was never carried through. By 1940 northern Libya was beginning to realise some of its agricultural potential and Balbo's 'policy of water', besides renovating many disused Roman wells, had shown that there were underground supplies sufficient for irrigated farming on a large scale. During their occupation the Italians planted a total of 3 million olive-trees, 3 million almonds, 1½ million fruit-trees, and 27 million vines.

Balbo was intensely proud of Libya and encouraged tourism by building hotels in Tripoli and other centres of interest. By 1938 visitors were arriving in the colony at the rate of 2,000 a month. Motor-racing at the Tripoli Grand Prix circuit at Mellaha attracted international crowds and racing aces; the Tripoli Fair was started as a showplace of Fascist colonial achievement; archaeological sites, Leptis, Sabratha, Cyrene, and others, were cleared of their accumulated sand and rubbish and were impressively, if at times excessively, restored to emphasise the past glories and present enterprise of Rome in Africa. (The fact that a Marshal Balbo was governing a province that a Roman General Balbus had subdued 2,000 years before seems to have escaped the notice of the slogan-writers of the new Roman empire.)

In March 1937, for the first time in eleven years, the Duce visited Libya. The occasion was the opening of the greatest of Balbo's civil engineering works, the *Litoranea*, or *Via Balbo*, which ran 1,132 miles from Tunisia in the west to Amseat on the Egyptian frontier in the east. In 1934 the easiest means of travel between Tripolitania and Cyrenaica was, as it had been since late Roman times, by sea. There were less than 1,000 miles of hard-top roads in the country, and there was not even a regularly used motor-track across the Sirtica. But for the Abyssinian war, the *Litoranea* might never have been built. As it was, the military planners foresaw the need to move large forces at short notice to the eastern or western frontiers in the event of British or French action from Egypt or Tunisia, or to any point on the coast threatened by naval attack. In March

1935 Rome authorised the building of the road at a cost of just over £1 million. (Ironically, the final instalment of this sum was included in the 1943–4 Italian budget, when the road had already carried the invading British Eighth Army from one end of Libya to the other.)

About 600 miles of highway, including 420 miles through the waterless Sirtica, needed to be built, for there were already roads from Zuara to Misurata and from Derna to Agedabia. Thirteen contracting firms employing 13,000 Italian and Libyan workmen, and some Libyan women, started work simultaneously on the road's sixteen sections in the winter of 1935–6. Shortage of water, particularly in the Sirtica, was the greatest problem and supplies often had to be taken many miles to the work-sites by truck. Sixty-five *Case Cantoniere* were built at regular intervals along the road and were first used as barracks for the roadbuilders and later as rest-houses and service centres for travellers. Apart from the desert heat and the problems of supply over great distances, there were no serious difficulties. Yet the project was publicised as a mighty Fascist enterprise, and on the most desolate stretch of the road, 120 miles west of Agedabia and near the traditional site of the burial place of the Philaeni brothers, Balbo ordered the building of a colossal triumphal arch to commemorate the work and to stand as a symbol of Italian power in that remote place. The Arch of the Philaeni, rising 100 feet above the desert and incorporating 350 tons of travertine, was a monstrous design by the architect Florestan de Fausto, who was responsible for many of the handsome 'Fascist colonial' buildings of the late 1930s in Tripoli, Benghazi, and the settlement villages. The monument, its architect explained, 'combines the lines of an Egyptian pyramid with those of Roman triumphal arches, and only in this way could the inviolate grandeur of Imperial Italy be symbolised'. It was capped by an appropriate quotation from Horace on the greatness of Rome.[5]

[5] The Horatian inscription was: ALME SOL POSSIS NIHIL VRBE ROMA VISERE MAIVS.

In 1957 the Libyan government replaced this with an Arabic text:

'The tyrants erected a monument to commemorate the glory of Rome, but God decreed their defeat.

'What had Rome to do with people of Arab origin who have lived by, and benefited from, the teaching of the Prophet?

'This country shall be defended by Islam when the cry of *Allah Akbar* echoes round its horizons.'

The *Litoranea* pierced the natural barrier of the Sirtica and united Tripolitania and Cyrenaica as one country. It was the colony's high street, passing through, or relatively close to, the main centres of population. It enabled motorised troops to move from one end of Libya to the other in less than thirty-six hours. Roadside air-fields laid out at regular intervals increased its strategic role both in defence and desert policing. Viewed in other lights, the *Litoranea* was Mussolini's highway to Egypt and the Suez Canal, and to Tunis and Bizerta.

The short stretches of railway built in Tripolitania and Cyrenaica in the 1920s and earlier were of little value because they went no-where of importance. But from the mid-1930s onwards the *Ala Littoria* developed civil air services under Balbo's encouragement and both Tripoli and Benghazi were linked by flying boat with Rome, Syracuse, and Italian East Africa.

After opening the *Litoranea* at Amseat in March 1937, the Duce went on a carpet-strewn tour of a colony that, according to the illustrated review *Libia*, he found 'morally and profoundly Italian'. The Muslims of Tripoli reportedly greeted him as 'the greatest man of the century and the sincere friend of Islam', a eulogy that hardly tallied with his image in the Islamic world. The Cyrenaican war and, to a lesser extent, Fascist policy in Libya afterwards, had done untold harm to Italy's standing among Muslims everywhere. It was during his 1937 visit to Tripoli, when Libyan notables went through the farce of presenting him with 'The Sword of Islam', that Musso-lini started seriously to play the curious role of 'Protector of Islam', the great leader who would defend the rights of Muslims both in Libya and beyond its frontiers.

Fascist Libya was not an African colony, but a colony of Euro-peans in Africa, where immigrants were encouraged and helped by the state to acquire and farm land, and where rule by the mother country was first and foremost in the interests of these settlers. The very definite Fascist programme for the colony was in contrast to the vague plans most European colonial powers had for their Afri-can territories in the inter-war years. This was partly the result of Libya's annexation a generation after the main European 'scramble' for Africa. While the typical African territory experienced full European colonialism over, broadly speaking, the eighty years from 1880 to 1960, in Libya the entire colonial cycle, from the first European sea-borne intervention to complete independence, was compressed into just half that time, the forty years from 1911 to 1951. The colonial achievement in Libya was largely the deliberate Fascist achievement of 1922–42; the effective conquest of the country, its pacification, and its intensive development as a colony were the uninterrupted work of those twenty years.

From the mid-1920s onwards, and increasingly so in the 1930s, colonialism in Libya was practised according to the theories of Fascism. The empire (founded in 1937) was, in the words of Mussolini, 'not only a territorial, military and mercantile expression, but a spiritual and moral one'. The tendency to empire, to the expansion of nations, was 'a manifestation of vitality'. Libya was subject to 'Fascistisation' (*Fascistizzazione*), so much so that, as a party propagandist enthused: 'No branch of social, political, economic or cultural life, no activity of the people, whether metropolitan or native, can be separated from the daily, continuous and precise influence of the Party which here, as in Italy, is the spirit of everyone.'[6]

Libyans provided a corps of manual and menial labourers; they were enrolled in the army and fought in Abyssinia; they gave the Fascist salute, wore black shirts, and cheered Mussolini, the king-emperor, and Goering through the streets of Tripoli and Benghazi; Libyan youth had its own Fascist organisation, the *Gioventù Araba del Littorio*, modelled on the *Balilla*. But the role the Libyans were expected to play in the Fascist scheme of things was never clearly defined. Balbo vaguely urged 'collaboration' between Fascist authorities, Italians, and Libyans for the progress of the country and the benefit of all; work was everyone's 'social duty' and there was the usual talk of 'corporatism'. In a matter of generations rather than years Libyans would presumably have been assimilated as citizens of the Greater Italy that Libya and all parts of the empire were to become. Balbo tentatively forecast something of this order when he declared: 'There will not be rulers and ruled in Libya; instead we shall have Catholic Italians and Muslim Italians, united in the common fold as constructive elements in a great and mighty organisation, the Fascist Empire. So does Rome still show herself to be the great and fruitful *Mater Gentium*.'

The Fourth Shore and the mother country were united in January 1939, when the four coastal provinces of Tripoli, Misurata, Benghazi, and Derna became an integral part of metropolitan Italy. One

[6] Lischi, op. cit.

of the reasons given for the creation of this nineteenth region of the kingdom was 'the continual manifestation of loyalty on the part of the Muslim population'. At the same time, Libyans were given their first opportunity to apply for *Cittadinanza Italiana Speciale* (Special Italian Citizenship). Applicants had to be literate (which was more than many Italian settlers could claim to be) and the petty privileges conferred by Special Citizenship were not valid outside Libya. It was also decreed that no Libyan could hold a post or practise a profession that would result in an Italian serving under him; it was this type of policy that caused there to be only sixteen Libyan university graduates in 1949. Assimilation, which was only an implied and not a declared policy, would be an unhurried process; there was no end in sight of Fascist Libya or, indeed, of any European colony in Africa in the late 1930s. The small Libyan intellectual class was either in exile or voiceless and all opposition had been too recently and ruthlessly stamped out for embryo independence movements to cause trouble. The traditional structure of tribal authority was deliberately weakened by the appointment of one 'leader' to as few as twelve tribesmen. In Fezzan the Italians abolished the *Jemaa*, or councils of family heads, which were genuine popular assemblies, and instead exercised authority through suitable *Mudirs*. Fascism taught Libyans, as well as Italians, to do as they were told. It was no duty of Fascism to give the reason why; Mussolini's 'You must because you *must*' was sufficient explanation.

In theory the Libyans were guaranteed justice, the right to work and education, and religious toleration. Of these, they probably had the least of justice. Islamic Law was administered by the *Sharia* courts that were concerned only with matters of personal status, family law, inheritance, and religious ritual; similar courts administered Jewish Law. All other cases were heard by Italian courts. In country districts and in Fezzan there were courts of Summary Jurisdiction, and even Italian sources acknowledge that impromptu justice was the rule in many parts of the country.

Balbo claimed that there was no unemployment in the colony, and public works and agricultural projects had indeed created an unprecedented demand for labour. Although, according to the fixed-wage scales laid down by Balbo's administration, Libyans were paid less than Italians doing the same work, many of them did earn good wages, by the standards of the country and the times.

In exercising political power, Italy was obliged to wield the religious power associated with it. Apart from the official ban on the Sanussi Order, however, there was religious freedom and the Italians, unlike the French, never tried to convert their Muslim subjects; indeed, the Church was strictly forbidden to proselytise in Libya. The colonial government, besides restoring many old mosques, built a number of new ones.

The United Nations Commissioner for Libya in 1950 quoted Libyans as saying: 'The whole policy of Fascist colonisation was to deny our people educational opportunities'. Yet the educational opportunities open to Libyans in 1940, although limited, were greater than those provided by the Turkish government thirty years earlier. The Italians concentrated on state primary education and also encouraged the opening of more private *katatib*, or Koranic schools. By the 1939–40 academic year there were over 20,000 Libyan pupils in 121 state elementary schools (fourteen of them for girls) and 629 *katatib*. In all, the Italians built 183 schools in the colony – 97 for Libyans, 81 for their own children, and five for Jewish children. But secondary and higher education for Libyans was definitely neglected. In 1939 there were only two Arab secondary schools in the whole of Tripolitania, the Higher Islamic School, with a strictly religious curriculum, and the Arts and Crafts School, a Turkish foundation, both in Tripoli; in Cyrenaica there was only the Benghazi Arts and Crafts School. By contrast, there were seven secondary schools for Italian children. A few Libyans were awarded scholarships for study in Egypt or Italy, but the main purpose of education policy in Libya seems to have been to produce relatively large numbers of Italian-speaking pupils, instilled with 'respect and devotion' for Italy, but knowing little more than the three Rs.

After 1934 the colony was ruled by a governor-general (renamed 'First Consul' in 1937) through a General Consultative Council and a Council of Government. A secretary-general supervised civil and political affairs, and various technical committees were responsible for public works, roads, and similar activities. The provinces of Tripoli, Misurata, Benghazi, and Derna were each administered by a prefect and were financially autonomous. The *Territorio Militare del Sud*, with its capital at Hon, was divided into five administrative zones.

In 1938 the colony had a population of just over 880,000, of which 10 per cent (89,000) were Italians and about 86 per cent (763,000) Libyan Muslims. There were also 30,000 Italian and

Libyan Jews and 6,000 non-Italian Europeans, mainly Maltese and Greeks.

Revenue was derived from customs and ports dues, state monopolies, and various taxes, but in 1938 these accounted for only 25 per cent of the colony's budget, which was balanced by subsidies from the mother country. Exports, mainly of wheat, hides, skins, esparto grass, and vegetable oils, were worth L. It. 109 million in 1938, but imports amounted to L. It. 882 million, of which L. It. 786 million worth came from the mother country. Exports of wheat for 1938, valued at L. It. 11·6 million, were offset by L. It. 54 million worth of wheat flour and pasta imports. Even building stone, as in Roman times, was brought in from Italian quarries. In 1940 the Information Department of the Royal Institute of International Affairs noted: 'In no sense can the colony be deemed self-supporting from its own resources; sufficient foodstuffs are lacking and practically all materials and equipment for the maintenance and development of the colony must be supplied by the Mother Country.'[7]

Investment in the colony, both in relation to the amount other European countries were then spending on their African territories, and to the poverty of pre-war Italy, was on a philanthropic scale, for all Balbo's complaints of Rome's parsimony. In the nine years up to 1938, Britain's African dependencies between them received only £4 million for development; Balbo spent more than that on the 1938 colonisation programme alone, but the difference was that Italy's money was being spent primarily for the benefit of her own people.

Libya was poor in natural resources, but the colony might in time have been made to 'pay' through its agriculture. As it was, the colonisation experiment was spoiled by war, which broke out just as the colonists of 1939 were bringing in their first harvest.

[7] The Italian Colonial Empire. Information Papers No. 27. RIIA, London, 1940, p. 32.

Chapter 16

War and Liberation

THE LOSS of the empire was one of the prices Italy paid for participation in the Second World War. By 1941 Italian East Africa had fallen to invading British forces, but Fascist rule in Libya was not finally ended until the spring of 1943. From Graziani's march of 70 miles into Egypt in September 1940, through the British 'Benghazi handicap' advances into Cyrenaica in the autumns of 1940, 1941, and 1942, to the retreat of the Axis armies into Tunisia early in 1943, western Egypt and Cyrenaica were the theatre of the longest campaign of the war.

In his *African Trilogy* the war correspondent Alan Moorehead wrote that: 'As a fighting arena, the desert is superb. You get there as close to a straight-out trial of strength as any battle-front on earth . . . neither side came into the desert for conquest or loot, but simply for battle.'

Yet Libya, and particularly northern Cyrenaica, suffered all the miseries of being repeatedly fought over. Compared with densely populated Europe, there was relatively little to be broken, but what was breakable – the towns and ports, the villages, airfields, roads, and installations built up by the Italians – was wrecked, and with it the hope of successful Italian colonisation in Africa.

During the first British advance into Cyrenaica in 1940–1, Moorehead found the towns and villages mostly intact, but the complete withdrawal of the Italian forces had given the Libyans some hours in which to pay off old scores against the unprotected colonists before the British arrived, although revenge-taking of any kind had been condemned by Sayyid Idris.

Rommel's first offensive in the spring of 1941 forced the British back to Egypt. By the winter of 1941–2, when the Axis was again driven out of Cyrenaica, the country was falling into ruin. Moorehead found the pleasant little town of Derna had been burned and sacked, colonial farms and farmland had been smashed and laid waste: 'The fight to maintain civilisation here was too unequal, too disappointing, too hard.' Benghazi as Moorehead saw it on Christmas Day 1941 was: 'no longer a city any more. The plague of high explosive had burst on the place and left it empty, apathetic and cold. The shops were shuttered, the markets closed and ruin succeeded ruin as we drove along.... For nearly a year the RAF had gone on and on, night after night, and here we were looking at the scoresheet – a ravaged, ruined city.'

Again the British were forced to evacuate Cyrenaica and not until the autumn of 1942 was the territory reoccupied for the third and last time. The colonists who had sailed in with such high hopes only three and four years before had been taken back to Italy for their own safety. Nearly all other Italian civilians had gone home or had fled to Tripoli by road, sea, or air.

By January 1943 two Allied armies were converging on Tripoli. From the east came General Montgomery's victorious Eighth Army while northwards across the Sahara dashed a fantastic force: 'They came', wrote the war correspondent Alexander Clifford, 'in filthy, rackety trucks tied together with wire, unkempt men incredibly sunburned with great, bushy, shapeless beards. Their own mothers could never have recognised them. But their trucks flew the tricolour of France and the cross of Lorraine.'[1] This was General Leclerc's Free French Brigade. Starting out from Chad, the French had entered Fezzan from the south and had systematically captured the oases from the surprised Italian garrisons before joining in the race for Tripoli. Very early on 23 January British tanks, with Highlanders riding on the hulls, rolled into the city. The people, who had been abandoned by the Germans and their own troops, and had been awaiting the arrival of the conquerors for three fearful days, were awakened by the rumble of armour and the skirl of pipes. Moorehead visualised how:

> 'At last, after thirty months of warfare, the ragged and dishevelled desert soldier stood with wonderment and emotion beside the playing fountains. If one excepts the entrance of the Germans into Paris, of the Japanese into Singapore, and the return of the Russians to Stalingrad, there can have been no moment in the war equal to this one.
>
> 'In the swaying battle of the desert, Tripoli had for two and a half years appeared as a mirage that grew strong and now faded

[1] *Three Against Rommel*, London, 1943, p. 355.

away again, and was for ever just beyond the Eighth Army's reach.'

The governor of Tripoli, Alberto Denti di Pirajno, tells how, before the formal surrender of the city, a diffident British captain came to his office to ask where the Military Police could be quartered: 'This was our first meeting with the British forces. We had imagined that it would be a solemn, probably a dramatic moment; we had expected the arrogance of the victor and had prepared ourselves to be firm and dignified. Instead, here was a meek man, certainly suffering from his liver, courteously asking us where he could lodge his men. I must admit we were rather disappointed.'[2]

Nevertheless, it was relief most Italians felt when they realised that Tripoli was not likely to be sacked by these conquerors.

The governor became one of many disillusioned Fascists that morning: 'Everyone had gone – the leaders who had sworn to defend the city to the last stone, the *di qui non si passa* authorities – all had left. The last hospital ship making for Zuara had been crammed, not with the wounded, but with gold braid and chests covered with ribbons and medals.'[3] He added bitterly that it was the civilians, who had no medals, who had stayed behind.

Later in the morning of 23 January, at the Porta Benito (now Bab Ben Gashir) crossroads on the eastern outskirts of the city, General Montgomery accepted the formal surrender of Tripoli. The governor, his deputy, and the mayor were present. (The governor, while watching Montgomery speaking, decided that 'the face of the enemy is never beautiful'.) Montgomery said there was to be no violence by troops; private property was to be respected; the Italian police was to remain in control; the civilian population was to be completely loyal; and there was to be no obstruction or treachery on the part of the Italians. The remarkable *Tripoli Times/Corriere di Tripoli*, which first appeared on 25 January as a single-page broadsheet, printed on one side in English and on the other in Italian, reported that the Italian officials listened to Montgomery impassively (the Italian translation added 'and with dignity') and had no questions.

The *Tripoli Times* continued: 'Back in the piazza, near the harbour, two highlanders climbed to the flag post and hoisted the

[2] Denti di Pirajno, *A Cure for Serpents*, London, 1955, pp. 248–9.
[3] Ibid., p. 250.

Union Jack. For a moment it caught in some wire, fluttered free, spread and waved triumphantly. To the crowd below who looked up and saw it flying over the statue of Romulus and Remus being suckled by the wolf, it meant the end of an epoch.' Such occasions are an excuse for mawkishness.

By February the Allies had occupied Zuara and Nalut. The *Tripoli Times* published a short article reassuring the Italians, who may have had doubts about collaboration, that the Fascists would not be returning. While Mussolini urged his people to bear the loss of Tripoli 'with manly and Roman courage', Richard Casey, the British Minister of State for the Middle East, announced that leading Fascists in Libya would be arrested, Fascist social organisations and clubs would be closed, and Fascist schooling would cease. (Most schools had been closed since 1940 anyway.) When he visited Tripoli in February, Winston Churchill called Rommel 'the fugitive of Egypt, of Cyrenaica and of Tripolitania', for the fighting had by then passed on into Tunisia. A newspaper correspondent who was a visitor about the same time reported: 'If ever there was an empire that demanded sacrifices of toil, sweat and tears, it was the Italian North African Empire. But as a reward for what must have been a colossal amount of grim and bitter toil, the colonists of Tripolitania and Cyrenaica have received only shame and ruin.'[4] The British have always had a talent for destroying other people's empires.

In the autumn of 1939 Libyan exiles saw Italy's expected involvement in the war as an opportunity to free their country from Italian rule. Fifty-one Tripolitanian and Cyrenaican leaders representing 14,000 exiles met in Alexandria in October 1939 to mend their differences and to discuss a common course of action, under the leadership of Sayyid Idris. When Mussolini entered the war the following May, many Tripolitanian exiles were reluctant to oppose and antagonise the Italians, who had apparently joined the winning side. But the Cyrenaicans, and particularly Idris, believed that in supporting the British war effort there was everything to be gained – the liberation of Cyrenaica – and little to lose, for Libya could be expected to remain an Italian colony if the Axis was victorious. The British had for some time been considering the possibility of enlisting the support of Libyan exiles, and after Italy's declaration of

[4] *Tripoli Times/Corriere di Tripoli.*

war, Sayyid Idris was invited by General Maitland Wilson, commander of British troops in Egypt, to raise a Sanussi force from among his followers.

At a second meeting of exiles, in Cairo on 9 August 1940, resolutions were passed calling for participation in the war alongside the British army and under the banner of the Sanussi Amirate. (The foundation of the Sanussi army is now celebrated as a national holiday on 9 August in Libya.) At the same meeting, a Sanussi Amirate in Cyrenaica and Tripolitania was proclaimed. It was also resolved that representatives of both provinces were to form the Amir's advisory council, and that a provisional Sanussi government was to be set up; Britain was expected to finance the Sanussi war effort and administration, and the Amir was empowered to make political, military, and financial agreements with the British government to further the cause of Libyan independence. A British-organised recruiting office was opened in Egypt and five infantry battalions of volunteers were mustered as the Libyan Arab Force; 10,000 men eventually joined it. Officered by British and Libyans, it fought under its own flag and took an active part in the campaigns of 1940–3. Libyan civilians helped and sheltered Allied troops cut off behind Axis lines and, when they had the chance, Libyan troops deserted from the Italian army to the British.

Some Tripolitanian leaders, who resented Sanussi claims to leadership over their province, were critical of the Sayyid's decision to collaborate with the British before he had obtained sound guarantees of independence for Libya. In fact, during 1940 and 1941, Sayyid Idris kept pressing the question of independence with the British authorities in Egypt. Although they shared his views on the desirability for a self-governing Libyan Amirate, governed with the help of British advisers, they were not prepared to make definite promises until the war was over. But, if Sayyid Idris was apparently satisfied with private verbal assurances from the British, his followers, and particularly the Tripolitanians, were not, and their pressure on him was such that he even threatened to withdraw from active collaboration with Britain. It was to give the Sayyid and his followers some sort of official public assurance that the British Foreign Secretary, Anthony Eden, made a statement in the House of Commons on 8 January 1942. After briefly outlining the development and scope of Sanussi collaboration and paying tribute to this contribution to the British war effort, he concluded: 'His Majesty's

Government is determined that at the end of the war the Sanussis in Cyrenaica will in no circumstances again fall under Italian domination.'

The Eden statement, which did not even hold out the promise of independence for Cyrenaica and failed to mention Tripolitania, was, Sayyid Idris complained at the time, negative; indeed, it might have been taken as a forewarning of intended domination by Britain or another power. Nevertheless, after the British rejection of his outright demand for Libyan independence, made in February 1942, Sayyid Idris professed himself satisfied with the oral promises he had been given. The fact was, as Dr Majid Khadduri has quoted him as saying almost twenty years later, that the British did not want to give written pledges that they might not have been able to honour after the war, as was the case with the Middle East settlement after the First World War.

Following the third and final British occupation of Cyrenaica, General Montgomery on 11 November 1942 announced in a message to the people that the province would be administered by a British military government until the end of the world war and not, he was careful to stress, merely until the end of the fighting in North Africa. He added: 'The military government will not enter into questions relating to political affairs of the future, but will endeavour to rule with firmness, justice and consideration for the interests of the people of the country.'[5]

Only a month later, from his headquarters at Agedabia, he issued a proclamation declaring as yet unconquered Tripolitania to be under British occupation. By January 1943 Libya had indeed been 'liberated' and was under the military administration of two occupying powers, the British in Cyrenaica and Tripolitania and the French, according to the terms of an agreement reached between General Alexander and General Leclerc, in Fezzan.

[5] Quoted in Rodd, *British Military Administration of Occupied Territories during the Years 1941–47*, London, 1948, p. 249.

Chapter 17

The Years of Debate

OF ALL THE COUNTRIES that have become independent since the Second World War, Libya's way to independence was unique. By 1943 Italian forces and authority had been withdrawn and replaced by those of Britain and France. At the end of the war, the United States and the Soviet Union joined Britain and France as powers deemed to have an 'interest' in, and competence to decide on, Libya's future. As a result, the movement for independence was directed not, as in other colonial territories, against the ruling colonialist power, but against the proposals thrown up by the international debate on the country's future. The one point of agreement in this debate was the Libyans' unreadiness for self-rule and independence. During four post-war years it seemed highly likely that Libya would be split up and placed under the administration of two, or even three, trustee powers. So, up to 1949, when the Libyan case was given a relatively disinterested hearing by the United Nations, it was the prospect, rather than the fact, of division and rule by foreigners that the Libyans and their sympathisers had to resist as best they could.

In 1945 the case against Libyan independence was overwhelming, as even the Soviet Union agreed. The one guarantee the Libyans had been given about their future was the Eden statement, and that only precluded the return of the Italians to Cyrenaica. The people, numbering just over one million, were politically inexperienced, under-educated, untrained, and extremely poor: *per capita* income was between £15 and £16 a year. Economic collapse and serious inflation had followed the stopping of Italian development funds and the withdrawal of the bulk of the free-spending wartime armies. The banks had been closed since the middle of the war; there was no trade with Italy and but little with Egypt and Tunisia. The strongest sector of the Tripolitanian economy was the Italian colonial farms, but they were only beginning to reach self-sufficiency; in Cyrenaica the Italian farms had been abandoned or taken over by

Libyans. There was no proper industry and unemployment was widespread. Towns, villages, communications, and installations, particularly in Cyrenaica, had been destroyed in the fighting (Bardia and Tobruk had been laid flat and three-quarters of the buildings in Benghazi had been damaged or destroyed) and the land was sown with mines and littered with battle scrap. Yet, until the future of the country was decided, no recovery or development could start. Occupied by troops of three nations and ruled by three stop-gap governments of soldiers, Libya was in 1945 a war victim more in need of all the foreign political supervision and economic aid available than a fit candidate for independence.

The British military administration in Tripolitania and Cyrenaica, and the French administration in Fezzan, governed under the terms of the 1907 Hague Convention on the conduct of war. Libya was Occupied Enemy Territory and its government, in accordance with international law, was on a 'care and maintenance' basis. Laws and institutions in force at the time of occupation remained in effect, although stripped of their Fascist and racialist aspects. The administrations were not, and were never intended to be, anything but temporary, and it was Libya's misfortune that they lasted for so many years, for colonels do not necessarily make the best rulers. The British military administration's legislative, administrative, and political powers, roughly those of a colonial governorate, were derived from the Commander-in-Chief, Middle East Land Forces. In 1944, when operational control was no longer necessary, the C-in-C's deputy Chief Civil Affairs Officer, Brigadier T. R. Blackley, was appointed Chief Administrator of Tripolitania; Brigadier Duncan Cumming had already taken up a similar post in Cyrenaica. Cumming's view of military government in general was that: 'There is no question about its right to rule; it can legislate with maximum ease and it can avoid becoming involved in politics even though it must be keenly alive to the political atmosphere.'[1]

The former provinces of Tripoli and Misurata were divided into three new provinces – Tripoli, eastern, and central – with capitals at Tripoli, Misurata, and Garian respectively. The provinces, divided into a total of fifteen districts, came under the command of senior Civil Affairs Officers with the rank of Lieutenant-Colonel. A small, mainly British, staff was assisted by Italian and Libyan local advisory councils. The twenty-one *Municipii* in the towns and settlement vil-

[1] Quoted in Rodd, op. cit., p. 249.

lages continued to work on the Italian model. In Cyrenaica, there were seven districts, later reduced to three, in place of the Italian provinces of Benghazi and Derna.

The B.M.A. thought well of itself and, in its own opinion, its greatest handicap was the uncertainty over its future. Even so, it did go beyond its brief of 'care and maintenance' by fostering some developments of the social services and particularly Libyan education. Italian and Libyan children had been untaught since the closing of the schools in 1940; by the end of 1943, over one hundred schools with 10,000 pupils had been reopened and for the first time significant numbers of Libyans began to receive a secondary education. But in 1947, although there were 21,000 children at school in Tripolitania, there was still no formal education for the majority of young Libyans. In Cyrenaica, the B.M.A. started to form a native civil service in 1943 and within two years there were about 450 Libyan government officials. In Tripolitania many Italian civil servants kept their jobs, and only the leading Fascists were purged. In outlying areas, Italian officials were usually replaced by British ones because of Libyan resentment of continued Italian authority. Yet by 1951, as a result of British training, 80 per cent of the civil servants in Cyrenaica and 71 per cent in Tripolitania were Libyan. Despite the shortage of skilled labour, the British tended to award manual and lower clerical jobs to Libyans rather than to Italians, and the Italians complained that their wages had dropped to 'Arab level', instead of Arab wages rising to 'Italian level'. One of the most successful achievements of the B.M.A. was the creation of the Libyan police. As the strength of the Italian police was gradually reduced, the British built up a body of well-trained young Libyans, organised on the same lines as many British colonial police forces.

The French administration, headed by a resident at Sebha, ruled Fezzan through the old enemies of the Italians, the paramount Saif al-Nasir family. Three local administrations were responsible to two Ministries in Paris. As in the French Saharan territories, local civil government and political affairs were the duties of the district garrison commanders. Most of the 40,000 people the French found living in Fezzan in 1943 were neglected, ignorant, and half-starved. Nine out of ten were suffering from trachoma, one in four from malaria. The French cured the malaria cases and reduced the incidence of trachoma by half; they also raised wages, shortened working hours, and opened schools.

According to Soviet and other commentators, the French isolated Fezzan from the rest of Libya. This charge seems to have been based on the evidence that the oases of Ghat and Ghadames were administered as part of southern Algeria and southern Tunisia respectively, that Tunisian officials were sent to work in Fezzan, that Fezzanese finances were included in the Algerian budget, and that the Algerian franc replaced the Italian lira. Yet it was a fact that Fezzan, securely garrisoned by French troops, was a convenient 'buffer territory' protecting an exposed flank of the French African empire.

To Britain, as to Italy, Tripolitania and Cyrenaica were strategically valuable. Tobruk, visited intermittently by the Royal Navy at the beginning of this century, could rather belatedly have become a link in the chain of British bases on the sea route from Gibraltar to Singapore, while the nearby airfield at El Adem was a staging post on the route to East Africa, the Indian Ocean, and the Far East. It was thought that Cyrenaica could become an alternative, if less effective, Middle East base when the Suez Canal zone was evacuated on expiry of the Anglo-Egyptian treaty.

Before the end of the Second World War, two occupying powers had in effect been increased to three with the establishment of an American 'presence' at the old Italian airfield of Mellaha, east of Tripoli. According to the *New York Times*, the United States had by February 1945 spent $100 million on developing Wheelus Field, as Mellaha was renamed in honour of a young U.S.A.F. officer killed in Iran. The oldest American air base in Africa, Wheelus by the 1950s was playing its part in Cold War strategy, as one of a series of U.S. bases in western Europe, North Africa, and South and East Asia encircling the communist bloc.

When, two days after the British occupation of Tripoli in January 1943, Sayyid Idris asked the British government for nothing less than immediate independence for Cyrenaica, he was told that the future of the country would be decided at a conference to be held after the war. The British would have preferred the postponement of all political activity until the fighting was over. But by 1943 Britain's war was no longer Libya's and the people, excited by their 'liberation', could not share Whitehall's desire for a delayed settlement of their future. Embryonic political parties, founded in the days of Italo-Libyan negotiation at the end of the First World War, re-emerged, and new ones were formed by groups of returning exiles. Nationalism, fertilised by the war, was already a healthy growth in other parts of the Arab world, but was still little understood in Libya in 1943; it was, for the most part, transplanted from Egypt, Syria and Lebanon, and elsewhere by homecoming exiles. Yet, such was its rapid growth, only six years later the Libyans, and particularly the Tripolitanians, were demonstrating something very like a true national consciousness.

Cyrenaica, as if in compensation for its resistance against the Italians and recent use as an international battlefield, emerged from the war with a convincing and accepted leader. Sayyid Idris had the advantages, for a national leader seeking independence for his country, of the genuine support of the majority of the people and the respect and recognition of the British authorities. Tripolitania, by contrast, had enjoyed longer and greater prosperity under the Italians and had been less harmed by the war, but was in danger of becoming, as in 1919–22, the leaderless victim of its own factious politics.

After twenty-two years of exile, Sayyid Idris returned to Cyrenaica in July 1944. He was widely acclaimed during a short tour of towns and tribal areas but, despite British and local appeals to do so, he refused to live in the country until he became its acknowledged and actual ruler. In the meantime, he urged the people to co-operate with the British and continued to direct his followers from Cairo. Renewed calls, endorsed by him, for an independent but British-guided and assisted Cyrenaica under his leadership were officially ignored in London. But he was privately assured that Cyrenaica's case would be favourably considered once the question of the future of the Italian colonies had been settled by peace treaty.

In August 1946 Sayyid Idris approved the formation of a National Front representing both the townsmen and tribes of Cyrenaica. In November the Front repeated the demand for British recognition of the Sanussi Amirate under Sayyid Idris and sought permission to form an interim government. While the older generation of dignitaries and tribal leaders was thinking mainly in terms of early independence for Cyrenaica alone, the younger men, with their wider, pan-Libyan nationalist outlook, included union with Tripolitania in their programme. They already had a forum in the Omar Mukhtar Sports Club (the name was merely a cover for a political organisation) founded in 1942 under the patronage of Sayyid Idris.

As early as 1944 the club had become outspokenly critical of the British administration, mildly republican in outlook, and a supporter of the Tripolitanian call for national unity. By the autumn of 1946 the British had recognised the need to grant Cyrenaica a measure of self-government under Sayyid Idris and, after touring the country, a five-member War Office Commission in January 1947 recommended a three-stage programme for independence under British guidance.

While Cyrenaica made some progress towards self-rule, Tripolitania's future was still an open question. There was no guarantee that the territory, with its large and vocal Italian community having rights and aspirations of its own, would not again come under Italian rule. In face of the very real possibility of renewed Italian government, the Tripolitanians were politically weak, leaderless, and divided. Political groupings, where they existed at all, were based on old tribal and family loyalties and nationalism was an insignificant, albeit growing, force. There were some, looking back to the early 1920s, who believed that only by accepting Sanussi leadership in Tripolitania as well as Cyrenaica could Italy be held off and Libya united. The United National Front, founded in Tripolitania in 1946 to oppose an Italian return, was the main advocate of Sanussi rule over a united Libya. The Front's plans were presented to Idris in the summer of 1946, but early in 1947 negotiations over unity broke down because the Cyrenaicans were not prepared to jeopardise their chances of independence should the Tripolitanians fail to have their own case for independence accepted, as indeed seemed likely.

If there was discord in Libya, there was more of it in the world outside. And, paradoxically, Libya was put on the road to independence because international disagreement was greater than her own national disunity. At the end of the war, Italy still held legal sovereignty over Libya, Italian Somalia, and Eritrea. The question of their future had been raised at the Potsdam Conference and came up for detailed consideration at the meeting of the Council of Foreign Ministers of Britain, France, the Soviet Union, and the United States in London in September 1945. Because of disagreement, a settlement was postponed until the council's next session in Paris in the summer of 1946, when it was agreed that a decision would be taken within one year of the Italian peace treaty coming into effect on 15 September 1947.

Seventeen words of the treaty that Italy actually signed on 10 February 1947 stripped her of her African empire. Section IV, Article 23, stated: '1. Italy renounces all rights and claims to its African possessions; that is, Libya, Eritrea and Italian Somalia.' The treaty then stipulated: '2. The said possessions will remain in their present state until their future is decided.'

It was the second clause that provoked angry reactions in Libya. Both the Libyans and the Italian colonists, who up to then had been the least consulted of all the interested parties, took up their own cases with an outburst of political activity; indeed Tripolitania and Cyrenaica have never known such free and diverse political expression as was allowed under the British military administration. The majority of the parties and factions in both territories were agreed on the need for a unitary state, and not the federation that Libya eventually became. Outside that common ground there were wide divergences of regional and party opinion. While Cyrenaica was strongly monarchic, a considerable section of Tripolitanian opinion was republican. The proposed Libyan Amirate was seen by many Tripolitanians as the potential tool of foreign interests, while a republic was judged to be the more patriotic and pan-Arab alternative.

Following the recommendations of the 1947 War Office Commission, Sayyid Idris brought further political stability to Cyrenaica by settling there permanently with authority to wield certain powers. But the Omar Mukhtar Club had become increasingly critical of the British and the traditionalist leaders co-operating with the British administration. At the beginning of December 1947 Idris banned all political parties and, in January 1948, a National Congress was formed under the leadership of his brother, Mohammad Rida al-Sanussi, to present Cyrenaica's case with one voice. The congress, although supposed to represent all Cyrenaican opinion, was mainly composed of the older generation of tribal and other conservative leaders.

While Cyrenaica could show a certain enforced unity, Tripolitanian politics had become a babel of opposing opinions. There were at least a dozen political parties, groups, and clubs offering a wide variety of programmes. The Labour Party, founded in September 1947, and the United National Front wanted Sanussi leadership for a united Libya. The Nationalist Party, which was formed by a small group of nationalists in 1944 but was not officially recognised by the B.M.A. until 1946, was divided over the Sanussi leadership issue. The former Nationalist Party leader, Ahmad al-Fiki Hassan, in 1946 organised the Free National Bloc, which was opposed to Sanussi leadership and mildly republican in outlook. The Egyptian-Tripolitanian Union, which emerged at the end of 1946 as a breakaway from the Free National Bloc, advocated a union of Tripolitania and Cyrenaica under the Egyptian Crown, and was said to be financed by Egyptian royalists.

The main disagreement between these and other parties was the Sanussi leadership issue, for they all advocated independence, union of Tripolitania, Cyrenaica, and Fezzan, and membership of the Arab League. The Libyan Liberation Committee, founded in March 1947, lost many potential supporters in both Cyrenaica and Tripolitania through its temporary failure to take a clear stand on the Sanussi issue. The party was organised in Cairo with Arab League support and later moved to Tripoli to present a co-ordinated, popular programme under the leadership of Bashir Bey al-Sadawi, an experienced freedom fighter and a leading figure of the old Misurata republic. The Istiklal Party, an offshoot of Sadawi's party, was created in 1948 and excluded close co-operation with the Arab League from its programme. Membership of parties was counted in hundreds, if not in dozens, and the majority of Tripolitanians never became involved in party politics.

The 48,000-strong Italian community (which had been increased since the war by illegal re-immigration from Italy) was itself divided into right- and left-wing factions. In 1947 a Tripolitanian landowner, count Ulderico Sottocasa, set up the neo-Fascist Italian Representative Committee which was well-supported by Italian settlers, landowners, and *nostalgici*, and advocated Italian trusteeship for Tripolitania. It was opposed by the Italian Association for the Progress of Libya, led by an ex-Fascist official, Dr Enrico Cibelli, who after the war reportedly took to calling himself a 'Social-Marxist'. In 1948 and 1949 the association co-operated with Libyan groups in opposing proposals for Italian trusteeship. Complete Libyan independence was advocated by the Popular Democratic Front, led by Alvaro Felice and supported mainly by Italian artisans and labourers.

When the Italian peace treaty was signed, the Four-Power Council of Foreign Ministers agreed to send missions to 'ascertain the views of the local populations' in the Italian colonies before a final decision on their future was taken. A Four-Power Commission accordingly arrived in Libya in the spring of 1948 and spent eleven weeks touring the three provinces. Considering the prevailing political disharmony in Tripolitania, the commission found an amazingly unanimous desire, both among political leaders and the politically uncommitted, for national unity, independence, and membership of the Arab League. Most of those interviewed by the commission in Tripolitania were strongly opposed to the prospect of foreign, and particularly Italian, rule, but party leaders said they were prepared to recognise equal rights for the Italian community after independence. The commission also heard the views of the Italian Representative Committee and the Italian Association for the Progress of Libya.

Cyrenaica, through its National Congress, was able to impress on the commission an apparently unanimous desire for independence and Sanussi government. The Cyrenaican view of union with Tripolitania, as expressed to the commission, was that it would be acceptable only under Sanussi rule, and that the Italians should not be allowed to return to Cyrenaica under any circumstances or in any guise. In Fezzan, the commission heard a few pleas for national unity and independence from a largely inarticulate population.

The commission's report, which was studied at the Four-Power Conference of deputy Foreign Ministers in London in the summer of 1948, put on record the almost unanimous Libyan desire for complete independence, but concluded that Libya was neither economically self-supporting nor ready for independence. It expressed particular doubt about Fezzan's prospects. Probably most significant and damaging to Libyan hopes were the harsh economic and social truths brought to light in the report. The commission estimated that 94 per cent of the population was illiterate, and it was no estimate, but fact, that there were barely a dozen Libyan graduates and not one doctor of medicine among them; that *per capita* income was in the region of £15 a year; that the infant mortality rate was a horrifying 40 per cent and that, disturbing as the current economic situation was, the future held out little hope for real improvement.

Under the terms of the Italian peace treaty, the Council of Foreign Ministers was obliged to consult all 'interested governments' before deciding the future of the Italian colonies. The governments consulted were the eighteen that had signed the treaty, plus Egypt.

There had already been various proposals, some surprising, others expected, for trusteeships over the three Libyan provinces.

From the outset, Britain's attitude had been governed by the pledge in the Eden statement that Cyrenaica would never again come under Italian rule. A British-sponsored Cyrenaican Amirate, British trusteeship over Tripolitania, and French trusteeship for Fezzan was therefore Britain's logical, and in effect existing, solution to the problem of who should govern whom.

The United States took an apparently disinterested stand by suggesting that the whole country be placed under United Nations trusteeship for ten years. The United States, presumably, would have kept the Wheelus air base and other military 'facilities'. Britain was prepared to accept the American proposal, but France was not.

France was perhaps the least disinterested of all the 'interested' powers; even more so, perhaps, than Italy. France was reluctant to evacuate her garrisons from Fezzan and had misgivings about the example an independent Libya might set the neighbouring and more 'advanced' French territories of North Africa, where there had lately been outbreaks of strong nationalist activity. A French-occupied Fezzan shielded southern Algeria, Tunisia, and French Sudan from Egyptian and Asiatic nationalist influence and French trusteeship over Fezzan was therefore, to the French, a highly desirable goal. Paris had no objection to British trusteeship over Cyrenaica, and was willing to support the Italian case for the return of Tripolitania, probably on the understanding that Italy would adopt a policy of 'good neighbourliness' towards the adjacent French territories of Tunisia and Fezzan. Italy was, in effect, to serve French interests by making Tripolitania another buffer territory isolating the French African empire from the outside world.

The Soviet Union at first favoured the American plan for United Nations trusteeship, but later proposed a ten-year Soviet trusteeship for Tripolitania, stressing that, if this came about, the 'Soviet system' would not be introduced there. Neither Britain nor France received the offer sympathetically.

When Italy had changed sides in the war in 1943, she had suggested that all her African possessions, except Ethiopia, be returned to her. But after the war it became clear that trusteeship over Tripolitania would be the most she could hope for in Libya.

Although Egypt offered union with Libya, she did not make a claim to trusteeship; but the Arab League did, on Egypt's behalf, and at the same time proposed collective League administration as an alternative.

Not one of these proposals was unanimously approved; nor was the suggestion by the British Foreign Minister, Ernest Bevin, made at the Council of Foreign Ministers meeting in Paris in 1946, that Libya be granted immediate independence. Several modified proposals were heard, including one for joint Soviet-Italian administration of Tripolitania, but the outcome by the autumn of 1948 was a complete deadlock.

The possibility, indeed the likelihood, of stalemate had at least been foreseen. At the signing of the Italian peace treaty in February 1947, the Four-Power Council of Foreign Ministers had stated in a joint declaration that if no agreement was reached within one year of the treaty coming into effect (i.e., by September 1948): 'the matter shall be referred to the General Assembly of the United Nations for a recommendation, and the Four Powers agree to accept the recommendation and to take appropriate measures for giving effect to it.' So it was that Libya's case, after three years of fruitless wrangling, was taken to the United Nations.

There was a delay of six months before the fully occupied General Assembly was able to start reviewing the question in the second part of the third session at Lake Success in April 1949. The head of the Soviet delegation, Andrei Gromyko, opened the debate by making a blistering attack on the records of the British and French administrations, and then renewed the Soviet call for U.N. trusteeship and independence after ten years. There was no response from the western powers and the case was referred to the Political and Security Committee and to sub-committee.

It was at this stage that the western powers made a final attempt to reach a solution of their own. On 7 May 1949 came the announcement that the British Foreign Secretary, Ernest Bevin, and the Italian Foreign Minister, count Carlo Sforza, had agreed on a plan for the future of the Italian colonies. The so-called Bevin-Sforza Plan was a compromise intended to satisfy British, Italian, French, and, to a lesser extent, United States interests. Trusteeships were to be granted to Britain in Cyrenaica, to Italy in Tripolitania, and to France in Fezzan. Libya was to become independent after ten years, subject to the approval of the United Nations General Assembly.

When it was submitted to the United Nations, the plan was supported by Britain, the United States, and the formidable voting power of the Latin American delegations, which at that time represented roughly one-third of U.N. membership of fifty-seven countries; Italy, of course, was not then a member state. Eighteen Latin American delegations were prepared to accept the plan as a whole because they favoured Italian trusteeship for Tripolitania. The plan was opposed by the Soviet, Arab, and Asian blocs on the grounds that it ignored the interests of the Libyans and would further divide a country whose people wanted unity. Nevertheless, a resolution based on the plan was approved by the First Committee (Political) by 34 votes to 16, with 7 abstentions.

Meanwhile, news of the plan had reached Libya, where mass demonstrations left no doubt as to popular feeling against it. Large but orderly, and for the most part silent, crowds marched through the streets of Tripoli protesting in particular against the proposed Italian trusteeship over Tripolitania. An estimated 60,000 people, including demonstrators from other Tripolitanian towns, took part in the biggest of the marches, which appeared to have been entirely locally organised. The demonstrations were given wide publicity and aroused international, and particularly Arab, sympathy for the Libyan case.

It was during these demonstrations that the Nationalist Party, the United National Front, and other groups merged as the Tripolitanian National Congress Party under the leadership of Bashir Sadawi. The National Congress Party continued to organise demonstrations and protests until the final rejection of the Bevin-Sforza Plan by the United Nations and, as a result, emerged as the leading political force in Tripolitania.

The signs were that the resolution based on the plan would secure the two-thirds majority vote in the General Assembly necessary for its adoption. Yet when the vote was taken on 18 May 1949, the delegate of Haiti, Emile Saint Lot, who had abstained from voting at the committee stage, opposed the clause proposing Italian trusteeship for Tripolitania. The result was failure, by one vote, to secure a majority (33 in favour, 17 against and 8 abstentions). The six Arab delegations, sympathetic to the popular feelings expressed in the Tripoli demonstrations, had without difficulty persuaded the Soviet and Asian delegations to oppose the clause; Emile Saint Lot had been personally lobbied by the Libyan representatives at the United Nations.

With the failure of the vote on Italian trusteeship, the Latin

American bloc had no reason to support the remainder of the resolution and actually voted against it, causing its defeat by 37 votes against 14 in favour, with 7 abstentions.

The Bevin-Sforza Plan had tried to sail against the rising post-war anti-colonialist tide. It had been put forward at a time when such newly independent countries as India, Pakistan, Syria, and Lebanon were beginning to support the cause of independence of such countries as Libya, and when the attitude of the colonial powers to empire was changing. The rejection of the plan by the United Nations was probably in the best long-term interests of all concerned. Italy was at first dismayed at the failure to regain even Tripolitania, but count Sforza adopted a wise and generous policy of support for Libyan unity and independence. The main Italian backing for the plan seems to have come from officials of the Ministry of Italian Africa, people with commercial ties and investments in Libya, former Fascists, and other small, self-interested groups.

Italy's failure to return to Tripolitania after the war was surely no misfortune. The enthusiasm with which Libyans greeted the news of the Bevin-Sforza Plan's rejection showed how difficult the restoration and maintenance of Italian rule over an unco-operative, if not hostile, population might have been. The Libyans who still quietly express regret at the passing of Italian rule must surely outnumber those who would have applauded its restoration. Italy, emerging from her own post-war economic difficulties, would have found herself committed to relieving Britain of the expense of administering Tripolitania and subsidising the economy. No matter how good or bad her trusteeship record in Tripolitania, Italy would have laid herself open to charges of 'colonialism', to the detriment of her relations with the Afro-Asian 'Third World'; as it is, Italy is now remembered as having emerged from the Second World War purged of colonial 'guilt'.

It has been suggested that in the United States a large body of public opinion considered that the Jews had been given an unfair share of international support in Palestine and that the granting of Libyan independence would serve as a gesture of redress towards the Arabs. Perhaps it was a similar attitude that prevented British troops from restoring order during the anti-Jewish riots in Libya in 1945.

The Soviet attitude had undergone some curious changes over the years. From advocating Soviet trusteeship for Tripolitania (a fact not noted by Soviet writers) and, at one time, the return of Libya to Italy, the Soviet Union by 1949 was calling for Libyan independence within three months and evacuation of all foreign troops.

Although Britain had supported the Bevin-Sforza Plan, there may well have been second thoughts in London about the Tripolitanian and Fezzanese trusteeship proposals, which promised to open the way to a Franco-Italian alliance in western Libya. It has been suggested that the Tripoli demonstrations against the plan were actually British-organised; certainly the British administration did not prevent their taking place; but if Perfidious Albion was in fact at work, it was because Perfidious Gaul was in the background. Britain had been sympathetic to early Italian claims in Libya, seeing them as a balance to French expansion in the Mediterranean, and the prospect of a French-administered Fezzan and an Italian-administered Tripolitania together holding the eastern flank of the French North African empire was not, perhaps, a desirable one. Independence for the whole of Libya was preferable, especially if British bases could be maintained in Tripolitania and Cyrenaica, and if an independent Cyrenaica remained under some sort of semi-official British 'patronage'. It can have been no happy accident of timing that within two weeks of the General Assembly's rejection of the Bevin-Sforza Plan, Sayyid Idris, with Britain's full approval, announced the independence of Cyrenaica and his assumption of authority as Amir. Under a Transitional Powers Proclamation issued by the chief administrator (who was from then onwards to be known as the British Resident) on 16 September, the Cyrenaican government became responsible for internal affairs, although certain legal and financial matters were still decided by British advisers. Foreign affairs, defence, and the question of the disposal of Italian property remained under British control. The British government had already promised that 'in taking these steps... nothing will be done to prejudice the eventual future of Libya as a whole'. In fact, a great deal had already been done.

The Cyrenaican constitution was promulgated on 11 October 1949. According to its provisions, the Amir was Head of State and Commander-in-Chief of the Armed Forces. He appointed the Council of Ministers and could veto legislation initiated in the one-chamber parliament, ten of whose sixty deputies were appointed by him, and the remainder elected by adult male suffrage. Civil and religious courts and a court of appeal were independent of the executive. The constitution was not a model of modern democratic principles, but in giving wide powers to the Amir it was judged to be better suited to the traditional tribal form of government familiar to the majority of Cyrenaicans.

With the rejection of the Bevin-Sforza Plan, independence for Libya seemed the only acceptable solution. Britain, the United States, Italy, and France came round to this view and, indeed, Italy went so far as to support the Soviet Union and the Arab-Asian bloc in calling for immediate independence. Both Britain and the United States thought a pre-independence transition period of anything up to five years would be needed; France, perhaps hoping that Fezzan might at least remain within the French sphere of influence, was for independence, but without unity of the three provinces.

Within a few weeks the United Nations was to reach the general agreement on Libya's future that had eluded the Four Powers. The Libyan question was again passed to the U.N. Political Committee in the summer of 1949. Italy, not then a member state, was allowed to take part in the discussions and the committee also interviewed representatives of the Cyrenaican National Congress and the Tripolitanian National Congress Party and Istiklal Party, together with representatives of the Tripolitanian Jewish community. In October a sub-committee started drawing up a resolution embodying all the main points in proposals made by the delegates of India, Iraq, Pakistan, and the United States. The resolution was overwhelmingly approved by the Political Committee on 12 November and a week later it was presented to the General Assembly. The Pakistani Foreign Minister, Sir Zafrullah Khan, described the draft as 'a fair compromise between what each delegation might regard as ideal and what was practicable from every point of view.'

It was on 21 November 1949 that the General Assembly, with a vote of 48 to 1 (Ethiopia) and nine abstentions (including France and five Soviet bloc countries) adopted the resolution:

1. That Libya, comprising Cyrenaica, Tripolitania and Fezzan, shall be constituted an independent and sovereign state;

2. That this independence shall become effective as soon as possible and in any case not later than January 1, 1952;

3. That a constitution for Libya, including the form of the government, shall be determined by representatives of the inhabitants of Cyrenaica, Tripolitania and Fezzan meeting and consulting together in a National Assembly;

4. That, for the purpose of assisting the people of Libya in the formulation of the constitution and the establishment of an independent government, there shall be a United Nations Commissioner in Libya appointed by the General Assembly and a Council to aid and advise him;

5. That the United Nations Commissioner, in consultation with the Council, shall submit to the Secretary-General an annual report and such other special reports as he may consider necessary. To these reports shall be added any memorandum or documents that the United Nations Commissioner or a member of the Council may wish to bring to the attention of the United Nations;

6. That the Council shall consist of ten members, namely (a) One representative nominated by the government of each of the following countries: Egypt, France, Italy, Pakistan, the United Kingdom and the United States; (b) one representative of the people of each of the three regions of Libya and one representative of the minorities in Libya;

7. That the United Nations Commissioner shall appoint the representatives mentioned in paragraph 6 (b), after consultation with the administrative powers, the representatives of the governments mentioned in paragraph 6 (a), leading personalities and representatives of political parties and organisations in the territories concerned;

8. That, in discharge of his functions, the United Nations Commissioner shall consult and be guided by the advice of the members of his Council; it being understood that he may call upon different members to advise him in respect to different regions or different subjects;

9. That the United Nations Commissioner may offer suggestions to the General Assembly, to the Economic and Social Council, and to the Secretary-General as to the measures that the United Nations might adopt during the transitional period regarding the economic and social problems of Libya;

10. That the administering powers in co-operation with the United Nations Commissioner: (a) Initiate immediately all necessary steps for the transfer of power to a duly constituted independent government; (b) Administer the territories for the purpose of assisting in the establishment of Libyan unity and independence, co-operate in the formation of governmental institutions and co-ordinate their activities to this end; (c) Make an annual report to

the General Assembly on the steps taken to implement these recommendations;

11. That upon its establishment as an independent state, Libya shall be admitted to the United Nations in accordance with Article 4 of the Charter.

Two weeks later the General Assembly appointed the United Nations Assistant Secretary-General, Adrian Pelt, of the Netherlands, as U.N. Commissioner in Libya.

Chapter 18

Towards Independence

INDEPENDENCE was due in just over 700 days when the United Nations Commissioner started his assignment. On his arrival in Libya for a three-week exploratory visit on 18 January 1950, Pelt outlined his terms of reference as: 'To assist the people of Libya in the formulation of their constitution and in the establishment of an independent government.' It was not, he stressed, 'my function to govern your territory; that remains within the competence of the Administering Powers until you assume it yourselves.'

His first duty was to complete the membership of the council, provided for in the General Assembly resolution, that was to advise him. The representatives of Egypt, France, Italy, Pakistan, the United Kingdom, and the United States had already been appointed by their respective governments. Pelt asked for one agreed candidate for each of the three Libyan provincial seats and the one seat of the combined Italian, Jewish, Maltese, and Greek minorities of Tripolitania.

Only Fezzan submitted the name of one candidate. At the end of March, Amir Idris put forward eight names of possible Cyrenaican representatives and asked Pelt to choose one of them. The political parties of Tripolitania proposed seven different names, and the minorities four. After consultations with the administering powers and the six foreign representatives on the council, Pelt named Ali Assad al-Jirbi, the Cyrenaican Minister of Public Works and Communications, as the representative for Cyrenaica; Mustafa Mizran, vice-president of the Tripolitanian National Congress Party, for Tripolitania; Ahmad al-Haj al-Sanussi, the *Qaid* of Murzuk, for Fezzan; and Giacomo Marchino, the Italian vice-president of the Savings Bank of Libya, for the minorities. The Council for Libya (the 'Council of Ten' was its popular name) was established on 5 April 1950. It had, besides its three Libyan members, two representatives of independent Muslim states (Egypt and Pakistan), *two* Italians (one representing the Italian government and the other the minorities), and three representatives of the western powers, Britain, France, and the United States. Its membership, therefore, had a distinctly 'western' bias, in the ratio of seven to three, for the only Libyan representative who could be considered free of British or French 'influence' was Mustafa Mizran of Tripolitania.

The council met for the first time in Tripoli on 10 April 1950. The representative of Pakistan – he and his Egyptian colleague were to raise dissenting voices at many sessions – almost immediately asked whether Britain and France were prepared to transfer their administrative powers to the Libyan people. Pelt replied that the administering authorities were 'solely responsible to the General Assembly for their actions', and pointed out that the General Assembly resolution did not provide for any transfer of powers during the transitional period 'but only to a duly-constituted independent government'.

At this stage serious controversy arose over the commissioner's and the council's respective powers and responsibilities. Mainly for the benefit of the Egyptian and Pakistani representatives, Pelt made it quite clear that the members of the council were his advisers, whom he was obliged to consult. But he was not their executive officer 'bound', as the Egyptian representative had claimed, 'to accept and to follow the advice of the Council in all cases'. Yet not until September did the council at least hide its differences behind a unanimously adopted resolution that: 'In the interest of Libya, the only, practical solution is for the Council and the Commissioner to co-operate on the basis of mutual confidence respecting each other's views as to their respective duties and responsibilities and to reach agreement from case to case as circumstances might require.'[1]

Meanwhile, Pelt had started putting into operation the third paragraph of the General Assembly resolution: 'That a constitution for Libya, including the form of the government, should be determined by representatives of the inhabitants of Cyrenaica, Tripolitania and Fezzan meeting and consulting together in a National Assembly.' He drew up an eighteen-month plan of action which he submitted to the advisory council. Local assembly elections were to be held in Cyrenaica and Tripolitania in June 1950; a Preparatory Committee of the National Assembly was to meet by July 1950, 'for the purpose of recommending the method of election, including the composition, of the Libyan National Assembly, and of drafting a

[1] Pelt, First Annual Report.

constitution'. The National Assembly, elected and convened by the autumn of 1950, would establish a provisional government early in 1951. This would be followed by the adoption of a constitution laying down the form of government. Independence was to be proclaimed and a definitive government formed before 1 January 1952.

Pelt's plans for elections in Tripolitania were criticised, and eventually abandoned, for two main reasons. There was considerable opposition to participation by the Italian and other minorities (although the Italians pointed out that they were among the 'inhabitants' of Libya referred to in the General Assembly resolution), and there was fear that the British administration would interfere in the voting.

In the middle of June a formula for the selection, and not election, of a twenty-one-member National Assembly Preparatory Committee was accepted by a majority of the advisory council. Amir Idris was to propose seven Cyrenaican representatives; after consultations with Tripolitanian political leaders, Pelt was to choose the names of 'seven outstanding personalities of Tripolitania', and was also to ask the *Chef du Territoire* of Fezzan to nominate seven Fezzanese representatives. But before the committee could be formed a decision had to be reached on the representation of the Tripolitanian minorities, to which both Cyrenaica and Fezzan were opposed. The Cyrenaican objection stemmed from anxiety over the possibility of renewed Italian political influence. The issue was settled when Amir Idris agreed to representation on condition that it would not 'prejudice the settlement of the legal status of the Italians after the country has promulgated its constitution and attained its independence'. Ahmad Saif al-Nasir of Fezzan was also persuaded to accept these terms.

Meanwhile, five Tripolitanian political parties had offered identical lists of Arab candidates, and four of the parties had also proposed an Italian as representative of the minorities. Pelt's own consolidated short-list, which 'took into account the personal competence of the candidates' was submitted to the advisory council on 11 July. There was an objection to the inclusion of the Mufti of Tripoli, Mohammad Abu al-Isaad al-Alim, because he had not been proposed by his own party, the Tripolitanian National Congress, of which he was vice-president. Pelt's list, with one change, but still including the Mufti, was nevertheless approved by the advisory council by six votes to four abstentions.

The Preparatory Committee (or 'Committee of Twenty-One') met for the first time on 27 July under the chairmanship of the Mufti and with the minorities duly represented by an Italian. By 7 August the committee had reached agreement on the composition of the National Assembly, which was to have sixty members, twenty from each of the three territories. This principle of equal, and not proportional, representation was emerging as a fundamental issue between the provinces and indirectly predetermined the form of the future state. The committee's fourteen Tripolitanian and Cyrenaican representatives were in favour of a nominated National Assembly; they had argued that elections would need too much preparation and might be 'influenced' by the British administrations. But not until October were the Fezzanese persuaded to agree to nomination. On the 23rd of that month the committee decided that: 'Representation in the National Assembly will be by means of selection, consideration being given to the equitable representation of the national Arab parties in the various areas as also of independent individuals and leading personalities, particularly where the territory of Tripolitania is concerned.'[2]

Amir Idris was to select the Cyrenaican representatives and Ahmad Saif al-Nasir those of Fezzan. The Mufti of Tripoli, 'after the necessary consultations and conversations', would nominate the members for Tripolitania. The committee also decided that: 'Non-national minorities will not be allowed to participate or be represented in the National Assembly. There is, however, a genuine intention and a general feeling that all civil, religious, and social rights of all minorities and foreigners should be fully safeguarded in the future constitution of Libya.'[3]

The Mufti presented his list of National Assembly candidates on 30 October and it was approved by sixteen votes of the committee. One Tripolitanian member voted against it, one abstained, another Tripolitanian member and the representative of the minorities were absent, as also was one Cyrenaican member. In other words, the Mufti's nominees had been approved by only three of the seven Tripolitanian members. Cyrenaican and Fezzanese representatives were accepted without comment.

At the end of November the committee completed its work and the majority of its members congratulated themselves on their deci-

[2] Pelt, Second Annual Report.
[3] Ibid.

sions which, in their view, had shown 'compromise in the interests of Libyan unity' and had made concessions 'on all sides'. But in March 1951 the way the Tripolitanian delegates to the National Assembly had been chosen became the subject of a bitter debate among members of the advisory council. The Tripolitanian representative, Mustafa Mizran, criticised the entire principle of nomination of National Assembly members by the Preparatory Committee, since the committee's brief had actually been only 'to prepare a plan whereby the representatives of the inhabitants of Cyrenaica, Tripolitania and Fezzan should meet in a National Assembly'.

The Egyptian representative, Kamil Salim, claimed that the committee had 'deviated' from, and had 'flagrantly violated', its terms of reference. Because decisions had been accepted by a two-thirds majority of the committee, the fourteen representatives of 350,000 Cyrenaicans and Fezzanese had been able to override the seven representatives of 800,000 Tripolitanians. The fifteen-member quorum rule had enabled the Fezzanese representatives of 5 per cent of the population to hold up the committee's work for weeks. Salim then attacked the Mufti's membership of the committee, charging that he was the only member who had been neither proposed nor supported by any Tripolitanian political party, but had in fact been nominated by the British administration and seconded by Pelt. Yet the Mufti, 'assisted by the British Administration', had drawn up a list of twenty Tripolitanian National Assembly delegates and had submitted it to the committee, where it had been supported by only three of the seven Tripolitanian representatives. Salim continued: 'Thus, thirteen Cyrenaican and Fezzanese members of the Committee had ensured that the Mufti's appointments were accepted despite objections from some of the Tripolitanian members; while Cyrenaica and Fezzan were free to appoint their own twenty members of the National Assembly, the Tripolitanian members, representing two-thirds of the population, had been selected by the other third.'[4] The 'Committee of Twenty-One', Salim said, had produced not a plan, but a National Assembly. Pelt and the 'Council of Ten', who had been out of the country at the time, had returned to find a *fait accompli*.

Nevertheless, Salim found himself opposed by the representatives of the United States, the United Kingdom, France, Cyrenaica, and Fezzan, and even Pelt was prepared to endorse the methods used

[4] Ibid.

and the results achieved by the committee. The Cyrenaican representative, Ali Assad al-Jirbi, seemed to touch on the truth when he said no discussion had been heard until the names of the Tripolitanian delegates of the National Assembly had been announced 'and it was therefore permissible to wonder whether the present objections were not based on personalities rather than politics.'

The composition of the Tripolitanian bloc in the National Assembly was also attacked by Bashir Sadawi, the Tripolitanian National Congress Party leader, who claimed that most of the Congress Party delegates in the assembly were bogus. Although he ordered all Congress Party members to withdraw from the assembly, only two actually did so, and from then onwards the party, supported by the Egyptian and Pakistani members of the 'Council of Ten', were bitterly critical of the assembly and its work.

Even the United Nations Political Committee, when it considered Pelt's first Annual Report in October 1950, criticised the way the National Assembly had been formed. The following month Arab delegates in the U.N. General Assembly attacked the National Assembly as 'undemocratic and unconstitutional', and criticised the increasing tendency towards Libyan federation. At the same time, the Soviet delegation introduced a resolution calling for Libyan unity and the withdrawal of foreign forces.

Invited to address the General Assembly, Pelt declared that he felt bound to say that since the Libyan National Assembly was appointed and not an elected body, 'there are grave doubts in my mind as to whether it will have the necessary moral and political authority to elaborate a final and definite constitution for Libya'. But when the Egyptian delegate urged that the National Assembly be made an elected body, Pelt replied that there was no time for elections if Libya was to become independent by the end of 1951.

On 17 November 1950 the General Assembly adopted a resolution submitted by the *ad hoc* Political Committee, reaffirming the original 1949 resolution on Libyan independence and calling on the National Assembly to set up a provisional government before 1 April 1951. The administering authorities were to transfer powers progressively to the provisional government before 1 January 1952. The resolution, in effect, expressed the General Assembly's approval of the constitutional developments achieved to date by Pelt, the 'Council of Ten', and the 'Committee of Twenty-One' recognised the National Assembly as a lawful body, and, for the time being, closed the debate on the legality of the 'Committee of Twenty-One' and its actions.

Empowered to decide the structural and constitutional form of the future state, and to select from its own members a committee to draw up a constitution, the National Assembly held its first meeting in Tripoli on 25 November 1950. After sending Amir Idris its respectful greetings, it elected the Mufti of Tripoli as its president. Within a week it had agreed that Libya was to be established as a democratic, *federal*, and sovereign state, and that the form of government was to be a constitutional monarchy. The principle of federation was strongly supported by Cyrenaican and Fezzanese delegates, but the Tripolitanians, although outvoted and powerless to reject it, accepted it without enthusiasm. At the same time, the Libyan throne was offered to Amir Idris. Although he accepted it in principle, he asked for the postponement of his proclamation until the constitution had been promulgated and transfer of powers by the administering authorities completed. In the meantime, he preferred to be known as king-designate.

The longest and most passionate debate of all the Libyan independence negotiations was over the form of the future state. In the 1930s the Italians had united Libya, but for most of their history Tripolitania, Cyrenaica, and Fezzan had been ruled separately and by foreigners. Even under what could have been the unifying rule of the Romans, the Sirtica had been a frontier and not a bridge between the western and the eastern empires. After the Second World War the three territories, with varying degrees of poverty and 'advancement', with different political outlooks and population densities, had agreed to become one state. But, owing to their very diversity, they long failed to agree on the form of the proposed union.

Idris wanted federation and equal representation; indeed this was the only form of Libyan state he was prepared to rule. Both he and his British advisers feared that a unitary state would be dominated by Tripolitania, the most populous, the least destitute, the most republican, and politically the least stable of the three territories. Federation, by contrast, would safeguard the Sanussi character of Cyrenaica and, so long as the Cyrenaicans approved of them, of the British bases there. The Cyrenaican National Congress gave its reasons for supporting federation as 'in order to ensure that Cyrenaican internal affairs as such remain inviolate.'

In transferring power to Idris in Cyrenaica shortly after the rejection of the Bevin-Sforza Plan in the summer of 1949, Britain had virtually decreed that if there was to be an independent Libyan state (and in November that year the United Nations decided that there was) it would be under the Sanussi Crown. So much for the British assurance, given at the time, that nothing was being done 'to prejudice the eventual future of Libya as a whole'. Because Idris wanted it, federation was the only possible form of Libyan state, and in Cyrenaica even the Omar Mukhtar group, which had originally favoured unity, had by 1949 come round to the view that federation was 'essential'.

The majority of vocal Tripolitanians were apparently in favour of unity. Moderates attacked federation for its added administrative complications and expenses; extremists denounced it as a ruse by the British and the French to continue their influence in Cyrenaica and Fezzan. The most ardent advocate of unity was Bashir Sadawi; he also favoured closer links with Egypt and the Arab League. Trade unionists were among his responsible supporters and xenophobic troublemakers among the irresponsible ones. The Fezzanese, of whom all but a handful were politically passive, showed no signs of sharing Tripolitania's concern for the drawbacks or dangers of federation, and supported the Cyrenaican stand.

In his second Annual Report, Pelt describes how he found that:

> 'As the debates in and outside the National Assembly on this point continued, it became more and more clear that those who were in favour of the unitarian form of state were mainly inspired by the fear that federation would mean excessive autonomy for each of the three territories. They feared that it might be stretched to such a degree that foreign or local influence would possibly be given an opportunity to offset or even undermine the authority of the central Government. Those in favour of federation, while anxious to reinforce the powers of the Federal Government to a sufficient extent to offset the dangers of decentralisation, argued that federation was the form of State best calculated to bring about and maintain Libyan unity.'

News of the National Assembly vote for federation was greeted with violent demonstrations in Tripoli on 5 December, which was to have been a day of national rejoicing for Amir Idris's acceptance of the throne. A fortnight later, Tripolitanian National Congress

Party supporters demonstrated in front of the Islamic Arts and Crafts School building in the centre of Tripoli where the National Assembly was meeting. The demonstrators shouted their loyalty to the king-designate, but denounced federation as a 'divide and rule' plot by the 'colonialist' powers. British military police broke up the crowd and the Tripoli newspaper *Al-Mirsad*, which had criticised federation, was suppressed. The dispute became more widespread when Bashir Sadawi, in appeals to the United Nations and the Arab League, questioned the competence of the National Assembly. With the National Congress Party behind him, he continued throughout the first half of 1951 to charge the assembly with incompetence. In doing so he attracted the sympathetic support of an old political campaigner in Tripolitania, Abd-al-Rahman Azzam, who from baiting the Italians during and after the First World War, had graduated to the Secretary-Generalship of the Arab League.

In an interview with *Il Tempo* of Rome, Azzam attacked the National Assembly and its decisions as 'illegal' and contrary not only to the wishes of the Libyan people, but also to the United Nations General Assembly resolution on Libyan independence. The Political Committee of the Arab League, when it debated the question, decided that there was no need for federation in a country united by race, language, customs, and religion, and, moreover, that an assembly not elected by the people had no power to decide on matters affecting the future of the country. Such was the apparent hostility of the League towards not only the National Assembly but also Pelt and the 'Council of Ten', that the assembly sent a mission, headed by the Mufti, to Cairo to placate the League. Although the Council of the League in March passed a resolution recommending Arab states not to recognise any régime created by the National Assembly, the League's hostility slowly died down.

Further attacks on the National Assembly and federation were made by members of the 'Council of Ten'. The Egyptian representative said federation was 'the fundamental policy of Britain, France and the United States', but was condemned 'by the majority of Libyans'. Federation – the very word had no equivalent in Arabic – had never been intended for people such as the Libyans and 'merely paved the way to foreign exploitation'. The representative of Tripolitania denounced the National Assembly and every stage of Libya's constitutional development to date as illegal. But the Italian representative pointed out that the National Assembly's decision to invite Amir Idris to accept the Libyan Crown appeared to have met with general approval, even among the Tripolitanians. This was an important guide, he argued, for the Amir had accepted the assembly in its present form.

On 4 December 1950 the National Assembly approved the Libyan flag of red, black, and green horizontal stripes with a white crescent and star in the centre. More important, on the same day it elected a 'Committee on the Constitution', with six members from each territory, entrusted with the preparation and submission of a draft constitution. The committee in turn formed a six-member working group to write the draft and submit it chapter by chapter to the committee. Pelt and other United Nations experts were available to offer advice when the working group first met on 11 December. The constitutions of eleven federations, including the Indian, Swiss, and Venezuelan, were studied and compared before the group decided that foreign affairs, defence, finance, communications, justice, public education, and health were to be the responsibilities of the federal government. The constitutions of Egypt, Iraq, Jordan, Lebanon, and Syria, as well as the Universal Declaration of Human Rights, were taken as models for the chapter on fundamental freedoms. The working group then went on to discuss Libyan nationality, language, powers of the king, ministerial responsibility, parliament, composition of the Senate, and electoral law. Few changes were made when the completed chapters were passed up to the committee on the constitution and the entire draft was presented to the National Assembly in September 1951.

For three weeks the assembly debated the draft, but made little progress. At the end of the month the deputies moved to quieter surroundings in Benghazi, but Pelt was beginning to fear that independence might be delayed if the constitution was not soon approved. There were several points of disagreement between the deputies. The Cyrenaicans were insisting, 'with some vehemence', Pelt noted, that Benghazi be the future capital. The Tripolitanians, supported for once by the Fezzanese, were equally vehement in their insistence on Tripoli. The obvious choice was Tripoli. It was at the centre of the most populous and highly developed region and was nearer than Benghazi to western Europe, with which independent Libya could be expected to have close links. Tripoli had been the capital of Italian Libya and was still the country's main commercial, social, and cultural centre, and the chief port. It had the added advantage of looking more like a capital than smaller, war-damaged Benghazi. But, as the chief city of Cyrenaica, Benghazi's claim was an emotional one, through association with the Libyan resistance and early independence movements.

The Cyrenaicans were also pressing for greater powers for the king and less for parliament. They argued that as Libya was politically inexperienced, a completely democratic parliamentary form of government was not in the best interests of the country. The Tripolitanians felt otherwise, and their view prevailed after they had pointed out that only a democratic parliamentary régime would conform to the spirit and purpose of the United Nations resolution. By 3 October the National Assembly had approved all the articles of the constitution, except those concerning distribution of customs revenue, naming of the capital, and succession to the throne. The choice of capital was still an open question and Pelt felt obliged to warn bluntly that it 'might bring about a rift between the three territories and thus delay their independence'. Alarmed into action, the National Assembly on 6 October announced a compromise solution that was to be a source of much expense and inconvenience in the future: Tripoli and Benghazi were to be joint capitals. The following day, the assembly reached agreement on all outstanding points and duly approved the whole constitution of 213 articles. As Pelt commented in his second Annual Report: 'Ten months to write a constitution by people none of whom had any previous comparable experience in this field is indeed a remarkable accomplishment.'

At the beginning of November the assembly discussed the draft Electoral Law and unanimously approved it on the 6th. The assembly remained in session until Independence Day, but no further business was done.

Pelt, in his second Annual Report, recorded: 'One of the most notable developments during the deliberations of the National Assembly was the gradual strengthening of a sense of Libyan national consciousness.' He found that the deputies were: 'All one in their decision to establish a united Libya and as their labours progressed their mutual understanding of each other's views grew and helped them to overcome differences which at the outset appeared almost insurmountable.' He added: 'As the work of the National Assembly on the definition of the words "federal powers" progressed and took shape, the Commissioner [Pelt] felt more and more that the issue of "federalism" versus "unitarianism" was gradually being solved by way of compromise.'

The constitution approved by the National Assembly declared that: 'Libya is a State having a hereditary monarchy, its form is federal and its system of government is representative. Its name is "The United Kingdom of Libya".'

Cyrenaica, Tripolitania, and Fezzan were 'Provinces' of the kingdom, the word 'Province' being chosen in preference to 'State' to emphasise national unity. Legislative power was vested in the king and in a parliament consisting of a Senate and a House of Representatives. The Senate was to have twenty-four members, eight from each province, half of them appointed by the king and half elected by the provincial Legislative Assemblies. Members of the House of Representatives were to be elected by adult male suffrage in the ratio of one deputy for every 20,000 inhabitants, which gave Tripolitania thirty-five and Cyrenaica fifteen deputies; the 40,000 Fezzanese were allowed five. A federal government of Ministers was to be selected from the federal parliament; the Prime Minister was to be appointed by the king. Each of the three provinces was to have a governor (*Wali*), also appointed by the king. Three-quarters of the members of the Tripolitanian and Cyrenaican Legislative Assemblies were to be elected by the people, and the remainder appointed by the *Wali*; all members of the Fezzanese assembly were to be elected. Each province was to have an Executive Council of eight *Nazirs* holding Internal, Finance, Justice, Agriculture, Public Works, Communications, Education, and Health portfolios. A new administrative system, based on the Ottoman model, divided the provinces into districts (*Mutașarrifiyya*) governed by a *Mutasarrif*; these were subdivided into *Mudiriyas*, each under a *Mudir*. The cities were to have a municipality (*Baladiya*) headed by a mayor (*Rais*). A Supreme Court was established to hear disputes between the federal government and the provinces, or between provinces, and to act as the highest appeal court; its judges were appointed by the king.

The planning of transfer of powers from the British and French administrations to the future Libyan federal and provincial governments started early in 1951. On 8 February a Co-ordination Committee met in Tripoli under Pelt's supervision to consider the transfer of administrative and financial powers, but not constitutional ones. Powers were divided into four main groups for transfer in four stages between September and the end of the year.

While Cyrenaica had had a native administration since the summer of 1949, Tripolitania had nothing more than native municipal councils with limited powers. In January 1950 the French administration in Fezzan had invited village leaders and the *Jemaa* (traditional assemblies of heads of families) to appoint three representatives for each of the seventeen Fezzanese *Mudiriyas* and three for the oasis of Ghadames. This 54-member assembly had duly met in Sebha in February and had elected Ahmad Saif al-Nasir *Chef du Territoire*. Fezzanese counsellors were also appointed, but the French still wielded effective authority.

In February 1951 the National Assembly passed a resolution setting up local governments that were to receive powers transferred by the administering authorities. The king-designate was asked to select members of the Tripolitanian and Fezzanese provisional governments and to request the administering authorities 'to enable those persons to receive and exercise their powers as a preliminary measure towards the establishment of a federal Libyan State.' With the approval of the king-designate, the British Chief Administrator on 5 March issued a Transitional Powers Proclamation setting up a local government in Tripolitania. A five-member Council of Regency (in effect a Council of Ministers) was appointed on 8 March. At the same time, the British Chief Administrator became British Resident, with powers shared with Tripolitanian Ministers. Departments were headed by Libyan officials with British advisers, and the future transfer of all responsibilities to Libyans was provided for. This temporary administration was inaugurated on 15 May 1951 and remained in office until Independence Day. Pelt, who seems to have felt that too much had been done without his knowledge or advice, stated in his second Annual Report that he 'did not regard these measures with unmixed favour'. The Tripolitanian National Congress Party felt even more strongly about them, and said so, both in a petition to Pelt and during the course of street demonstrations.

When the king-designate made his first official visit to Tripoli with his new title on 19 May 1951, there were angry demonstrations by crowds protesting against the new Tripolitanian administration and calling for a united Libya. Two bombs were thrown at Idris's

Rolls-Royce, injuring several policemen. Over 800 people were arrested, in addition to more than one hundred potential trouble-makers who had already been detained.

Ten days later the king-designate authorised publication of an official statement which mildly pointed out that the throwing of bombs injured the state as well as people because it provided material for anti-Libyan propaganda. The statement invited the people to collaborate in forming the new state, gave assurances to the minorities of the good intentions of the new rulers, and concluded by expressing thanks 'for the homage shown us'.

Meanwhile, a National Assembly resolution had established a provisional federal government to receive powers progressively transferred by the British and French administrations. The same resolution named Mahmud Muntasser of Tripolitania as Prime Minister, Minister of Justice, and Minister of Education. The Ministries of Foreign Affairs and Health went to the former Public Works and Transport Minister in the Cyrenaican administration, Ali Assad al-Jirbi; National Defence to Omar Shannaib (Cyrenaica); Finance to Mansur bin Gadara (Tripolitania). Mohammad bin Othman, a Fezzanese and future Prime Minister, was named Minister of State. 'For the first time in Libyan history,' Pelt recorded, 'there had come into existence a government composed of Libyans from the three territories.'

The actual transfer of powers to the provisional federal and provincial governments started in the autumn. The first and second groups of powers, defined by the Co-ordinating Committee as those having no financial implications, were transferred on 12 October. Transfer of the third group, mostly financial powers, was delayed by discussions on foreign aid after independence. But by 15 December, Pelt reported, 'virtually all powers were vested with the Provisional Libyan Government or the provincial administrations, with the exception of those relating to foreign affairs or defence.' Final powers giving Libya 'the attributes of sovereignty' were not to be transferred until Independence Day.

Throughout his mission, Pelt was very conscious of Libya's economic and social problems, in addition to the political ones. He believed that the United Nations had a special responsibility to help the Libyans 'not only in formulating their constitution', as he wrote, 'but also in establishing sound administrative services fitted to the needs and resources of the country, and in promoting a viable economy that the State might endure.'

Libya had, Pelt noted in his first Annual Report, 'a marginal agricultural economy basically handicapped by inadequate rainfall and poor soil'. The crop surplus for export was 'small and irregular', of low quality and high price. After diagnosing other economic ills, he reported: 'The Arab population of Libya stands in need of as much financial and technical assistance as the United Nations can supply... it is obvious that the country requires very substantial outside assistance in order to maintain even its present standards, and yet more for development in the economic and social fields.' Further on in his report he warned that: 'Unless means are found to improve the agricultural techniques of the country and to bring in new capital investment, there is a grave danger that the Libyan economy will sink back towards a pastoral economy of nomadism, with inevitable social and political consequences which may jeopardise the very existence of the new State.'

The Secretary-General of the United Nations, the U.N. Food and Agriculture Organisation, the International Bank for Reconstruction and Development, the International Monetary Fund, and the U.N. Educational, Scientific, and Cultural Organisation all promised to help. But it was plain that until the machinery of international bureaucracy had been suitably primed with detailed technical studies of Libya's problems, little practical aid would be forthcoming.

As Pelt saw them, the country's most pressing needs in 1950 were training of civil servants; establishment of budgetary and fiscal services; development of agriculture, animal husbandry, and soil, water, and forestry resources; expansion of education; and improvement of public health services. He judged health conditions to be 'relatively good if compared with other African territories, but low in comparison with many other parts of the world'. There were in 1950 three French doctors in all Fezzan, eighteen doctors, most of them British, in Cyrenaica, and eighty Italian doctors in Tripolitania.

Pelt recommended an overall planning survey to reveal the greatest needs of the country and the people, bearing in mind that the first object of the United Nations Technical Assistance Programme was 'to help people help themselves'. The United Nations granted funds for the recruiting of a few agricultural and financial experts and to pay for a small pilot survey. Limited help also came from UNESCO, FAO, and the World Health Organisation. But Pelt found that: 'The Libyan public is not yet entirely aware of the extremely limited capacity of the United Nations and its specialised agencies to render financial assistance to under-developed countries, of which Libya is one among many.'[5]

When serious discussion of the finances of independent Libya started in 1951, there were some harsh truths to be faced. It became clear, for instance, that a standing army even of the suggested strength of one thousand men would cost more than the country could afford. The three separate currencies that had been introduced by the British and French forces in 1943 were still in circulation: the Egyptian pound in Cyrenaica, the Mal (Military Administration Lira) at 480 to the pound sterling in Tripolitania, and the Algerian franc in Fezzan. Britain put forward a good case for Libya's admission to the Sterling Area. There were French and other objections, but the British suggestion was accepted, mainly because Britain was, at the time, the only country to have made any fairly definite proposals for post-independence financial aid. Libya was to join the Sterling Area with a federal unit of currency, the Libyan pound, on a par with sterling and divided into one hundred piastres, each of 10 mils.

Pelt had already called on the governments of Britain, Egypt, France, Italy, and the United States to send experts to discuss future economic aid with him, and a firm offer to cover the ordinary budget and balance of payments deficits came from Britain. Pelt, who sensed more than altruistic motives behind the offer, expressed his misgivings diplomatically: 'The foreign aid required to cover the deficit of the Libyan budget may give rise to difficulties of a somewhat different nature, namely, that this aid when rendered by one single Power will grant that Power a predominant influence in the country's internal affairs.'[6]

It was also decided to channel some foreign aid through a Public Development and Stabilisation Agency. The PDSA was to finance the type of development project that under other circumstances would have been included in the capital or extraordinary budget of the government; no repayments of capital or interest were envisaged. The main purpose of the PDSA was to develop national resources, carry farmers through droughts, and stabilise the balance of

[5] First Annual Report.
[6] Second Annual Report.

payments. A Finance Corporation, with a capital of £1 million subscribed by foreign governments, was set up at the same time as an investment bank offering low rates of interest.

Under its expanded Programme of Technical Assistance, the United Nations was meanwhile assessing how, as Pelt put it, 'independent Libya would have the economic, social and administrative means for independent survival'. Studies and surveys by the U.N. and its specialised agencies had shown up the extreme poverty of the country, which was expressed by Pelt as:

> 'A lower *per capita* income than any other country in the Middle East, a very high birth rate... marginal or sub-marginal land, low and "capricious" rainfall and frequent droughts, absence of minerals or fuel and, above all, of skill and education – these are the hallmarks of a country in the greatest need of help.
>
> 'The deficit in the public finances of nearly £2 million cannot be met by increasing the taxes on an estimated $35 *per capita*, and subvention is therefore necessary to preserve the present standard of living. The adverse balance of trade, amounting to a shortfall of nearly £3 million yearly, cannot be righted by a reduction of imports without yet further reducing the level of the economy; and this, too, must therefore be made good by external aid until it can be corrected by expanded internal production. The balance of payments position... shows receipts for exports equal only 45 per cent of payments for imports. Of the credits, only 40 per cent come from military expenditures, while budgetary grants-in-aid account for another 20 per cent.'[7]

Yet U.N. reports did speak of prospects for development, and for extending dry-farming and irrigated cultivation without large capital investment. Pelt believed Libya might yet 'attain a position of economic viability, gaining at the same time in social and political security and health.'

He was nevertheless aware that the Libyans were disappointed that the United Nations were unable to give needed administrative and development funds, which had to come instead from Britain and France. A temporary aid agreement was signed by Britain and the provisional government in December 1951. Britain undertook to provide the Public Development and Stabilisation Agency with not more than £500,000, guaranteed the financial backing of the

[7] Second Annual Report.

initial issue of Libyan currency, and promised economic aid up to 31 March 1952 to the Tripolitanian and Cyrenaican administrations, which were in turn expected to finance the federal government. Britain also undertook to make good the federal, Tripolitanian, and Cyrenaican budget deficits for the 1952–3 financial year, if requested, and France made similar provisions for Fezzan. Libya could therefore embark on independence with financial aid guaranteed for the following fifteen months.

Education, Pelt judged, was the most important of the country's social needs, and he considered that 'the principal untapped resource of Libya is its human skill.' He advised a speedy reduction of the 90 per cent illiteracy rate and training of teachers, farmers, artisans, and workshop and handicraft apprentices. Agricultural development he considered to be in part a matter of training, improved techniques, and increased irrigation. Other priorities, in his view, were the repair of war-damaged installations, particularly ports, water supply systems, and power plants; work-training for the blind (an estimated 10 per cent of the population); and slum clearance. 'The approach must be to increase the productivity of the Libyan people so that their poverty is alleviated', he said. But he also foresaw the need for foreign aid for many years to come.

Libyan independence was declared on 24 December 1951, one week before the deadline set by the United Nations. In the early hours of the morning the last powers held by the British and French Residents were transferred to the provisional government. At the same time, the foreign administrations were brought to an end and the National Assembly was dissolved. The provisional government was fully in control, the constitution was ready to go into effect, and the way was open for the formal Declaration of Independence. This was done by the king-designate at a ceremony at the Manar Palace, Graziani's former residence in Benghazi:

> 'We joyfully proclaim to the noble Libyan people that ... our beloved country has, with the help of God, attained independence ... We formally proclaim that Libya has, from today, become an independent sovereign state and ... we take henceforth the title of "His Majesty the King of the United Kingdom of Libya".
>
> 'We welcome also the coming into force at this moment of the Constitution of the country.... It is our wish, as you well know,

that the life of the country should conform to constitutional principles, and we intend henceforth to exercise our powers in accordance with the provisions of this Constitution ... it is our duty one and all to preserve what we have gained at so dear a price, and to hand it down carefully and faithfully to posterity.

'At this blessed hour we call to mind our heroes of the past. We invoke God's mercy and reward upon the soul of our righteous martyrs, and we salute the sacred banner, the legacy of our fathers and the hard-earned symbol of our unity....'

The king then sent for the Prime Minister of the provisional government, Mahmud Muntasser, whose resignation was tendered and accepted. He was thereupon asked by the king to form the first national government. Muntasser, in addition to the premiership, took over the Foreign Affairs portfolio. He named Fathi Kikhia his deputy premier and Minister of Justice and Education; Omar Shannaib, who had held the Defence portfolio in the provisional government, was dropped from the new cabinet and was later appointed head of the Royal *Diwan*. Ali Assad al-Jirbi took over the Defence Ministry, Mansur bin Gadara and Ibrahim bin Shaaban remained at the Ministries of Finance and Communications respectively, and Mohammad bin Othman took over the Health Ministry. The king also appointed the *Walis*, or governors, of the three provinces and Libya applied for membership of the United Nations, FAO, UNESCO, and WHO, and a U.N. Technical Assistance Agreement was signed by the Prime Minister.

Muntasser returned to Tripoli on the evening of 24 December and asked Pelt to notify the president of the U.N. General Assembly of the Declaration of Independence. In a letter to the president, Muntasser himself wrote: 'Our thanks to the General Assembly must be directed above all to its agent, the United Nations Commissioner in Libya, Mr Adrian Pelt. We have come to regard him not only as our beloved friend and wise counsellor, but as one who toiled without regard for personal convenience or health for our interest.'

No streets in any Libyan town or city are named after Wavell or Montgomery or Leclerc, but in both Tripoli and Benghazi the *Lungomare*, the main sea-front avenue, is named after Adrian Pelt. During his two years in the country, Pelt had only the moral authority of the United Nations behind him. He had no executive powers; he was an adviser, a conciliator, a co-ordinator, supplying, as he put it, 'the necessary motive power and guidance to ensure that Libya followed the right path to independence and in the set time limit.'

In his Supplementary Report, Pelt expressed satisfaction with what had been achieved within the extraordinarily short time of two years, and with the constitutional and other provisions made under his guidance. He pointed out that: 'Libya has made its entry into the family of nations without any ties which its Government will not be free to sever, modify or continue in the light of the country's interests or affinities.' To criticism that the political system that had been worked out was too advanced and democratic for the country's needs, he replied with a formidable metaphor: 'When a politically adolescent people acquires its first constitutional garment, it seems wiser to allow a size permitting a degree of political growth, rather than to select one of such tight-fitting proportions as to risk congestion of the body politic.' And he warned that the country's survival would depend, above all, on the development and consolidation of unity.

Libya's attainment of independence under United Nations supervision made excellent publicity for the organisation. As Pelt noted in his Supplementary Report, the original General Assembly resolution on Libyan independence was welcomed as: '. . . a test of the ability of the United Nations to arrive at solutions of difficult international problems which had previously escaped settlement and as the inauguration of a new method for the peaceful and orderly transfer of a colony into an independent state.'

The United Nations passed this test and Libya became, with Egypt, Ethiopia, Liberia, and South Africa, one among the five independent states of Africa.

Chapter 19

Independence—The First Ten Years

WITHIN TWO MONTHS of independence, the new state was thrown into a potentially disastrous internal crisis. In reverse of normal procedure, the constitution had been drafted and independence proclaimed before general elections had been held. The Electoral Law laid down that elections were to take place by 20 February 1952 and the national government accordingly set 19 February as polling day. At the beginning of that month the Tripolitanian National Congress Party announced its platform and the names of its candidates, and started an intensive election campaign. The party, which was contesting all of the 35 Tripolitanian seats in the 55-seat House of Representatives, seemed set to win an overall majority. Although the Tripolitanian results, announced on 20 February, did give the party convincing majorities in seven constituencies in Tripoli and neighbouring districts, they also recorded heavy losses to independent 'government' candidates in the countryside, where the ballot was not secret. The national results gave the government 44 out of the 55 seats in the House.

Alleging 'manipulation' of voting in the rural and tribal constituencies of Tripolitania by government officials, the party organised demonstrations in Tripoli on 20 and 21 February. Groups of armed men entered the city, public property was damaged, and there were signs that more was intended than a mere display of protest. Police action was prompt and decisive, but order was not restored before at least a dozen people had been killed and one hundred injured. Party leaders were arrested and Sadawi was deported to Egypt on the excuse of his having lost his Libyan citizenship because of his earlier political service in Saudi Arabia. He returned to the court of king Saud as an adviser and died, still in exile, in 1957. Dr Enrico Cibelli, the Italian – Tripolitanian 'Social-Marxist' labour leader who had supported the National Congress Party, had been deported at the end of 1951.

Although the elected National Congress members were allowed to take their seats in the House, the party was dissolved. The crisis had been contained, mainly by the police, but the outcome was the disappearance of an effective parliamentary opposition and of all political parties both inside and outside parliament. In its future relations with the provinces, the federal government was to be deprived of support for central authority that the National Congress Party, with its policy of national unity, might have provided. The party's fatal mistake had been its organisation of the post-election riots; but the fact remained that it had failed in the elections through its inability to arouse the politically unresponsive country voters and ally them with its more articulate and bourgeois supporters in the city.

Both Houses of the first all-Libyan parliament in history were ceremonially opened in Benghazi by the king on 25 March. The speech from the throne, read by the Prime Minister, Mahmud Muntasser, promised a legal code and education reform on the Egyptian model, and development of communications and the economy; stressed the ideal of independence and sovereignty; paid tribute to the United Nations and the countries that had helped Libya to gain independence; and expressed the government's desire to protect the rights of foreigners living in the country.

Libya was now provided with the trappings of independence, an independence that was the result of compromise between opposing foreign interests and rival national aspirations. Outside the country, more than inside, there were serious doubts as to whether this fragile independence could be maintained. In addition to its grave economic and social problems, the new state had to steer a passage between the Scylla of internal disunity and the Charybdis of foreign domination.

Internal disunity was characterised by clashes of authority that broke out between federal and provincial politicians and the palace entourage soon after independence. These led in the autumn of 1953 to the resignation of the Prime Minister in protest against the friction between the provincial governors appointed by the king, and the federal government. Muntasser, whose resignation the king was reluctant to accept, finally gave up his office in February 1954, on the additional plea of ill-health. He was succeeded by Mohammad al-Sakisli, the former governor of Cyrenaica and Head of the Royal *Diwan*. Sakisli's appointment was not apparently intended to be a long one, and his ministry actually fell within two months. In

January the king had dissolved the Tripolitanian Legislative Council, constituted nine months previously, for alleged failure to co-operate with the federal government. But when, in April, the newly-established Supreme Court ruled that the order of dissolution was unconstitutional, the ruling was made to appear as a deliberate attempt to oppose the king's authority. Sakisli resigned and was succeeded by his Minister of Communications, Mustafa bin Halim, a thirty-three-year-old engineer and businessman who had spent most of his life in Egypt and was little known in Libya. He had served in the Cyrenaican administration from July 1950, until he was invited to join the Sakisli government. Bin Halim, a British visitor to Libya noted, had the virtue of seeming 'so totally undismayed by the vast problems lying ahead of his country.'

Ever since the Tripolitanian National Congress Party had been dissolved, national and local politics, for lack of parties, had revolved around personalities and family and business cliques within the federal and provincial parliaments and the Royal *Diwan*. Oligarchic politics, coupled with a family quarrel involving some of the thirty-eight royal princes, erupted into another major internal crisis in October 1954. Ibrahim al-Shalhi, for some forty years the king's loyal and very close personal adviser and Controller of the Royal Household, wielded a degree of influence at court and outside that was deeply resented by many members of the collateral branch of the royal family. As the king had no surviving children by his wife Fatima, the daughter of Sayyid Ahmad al-Sharif (the king's cousin who had been Head of the Sanussi Order during Idris's minority from 1902 to 1916), Sayyid Ahmad's descendants claimed the succession for their side of the family. But to Idris, the Libyan monarchy and the leader of the Sanussi Order were two distinct and separate institutions, the monarchy having in effect been established by himself. It was his view that, while any competent relative could become the next Head of the Order, the successor to the throne had to be a member of his side of the family: his brother, Mohammad al-Rida, in fact. To Sayyid Ahmad's descendants, Shalhi was the one responsible for originating and perpetuating this restrictive view, which excluded them from the royal succession and alienated them from the king.

Among the younger princes who resented Shalhi's unique relations and influence with the king was a grandson of Sayyid Ahmad, nineteen-year-old Al-Sharif bin al-Sayyid Muhi al-Din al-Sanussi;

there is no doubt that he was much influenced by other members of his family. In September 1954 there had been an unsuccessful attempt to alienate the king from his adviser by trying to implicate Shalhi in the visit of an Italian ex-landowner to his former estates in Cyrenaica, a visit that had already caused considerable embarrassment to the king. On 5 October Sharif shot and killed Shalhi in a street in Benghazi, and was arrested immediately. As soon as the king realised that other members of the family were implicated, a state of siege was proclaimed and all members of the Sanussi family were put under house arrest, perhaps partially for their own safety, for it has been suggested that the Barasa tribe of Cyrenaica, to which Shalhi was related, was preparing to avenge his murder. Two weeks later it was announced that seven younger members of the family were to be exiled to the oasis of Hon and that all the family, except those in direct line of succession, were to lose their titles and their right to hold government posts. On 20 October the line of succession was restricted by royal decree to the king's branch of the royal family. Shalhi's son, Busairi, succeeded his father and, up to his death in a motor accident in 1964, wielded almost as much influence. Sharif was tried for murder, was found guilty, and was executed in February 1955; the body is said to have been exposed in public for twenty minutes at the exact spot where Shalhi was shot.[1]

The king moved permanently from Benghazi to the British garrison town of Tobruk, where he is reported to have found the climate more agreeable. The events of the autumn, and the king's swift and decisive deployment of his authority, had undoubtedly strengthened the monarchy and had ended family rivalries, if not permanently, then at least for many years to come. But the question of the succession remained an open one. A solution, offered by Bin Halim and quite seriously considered by the king, proposed replacing the federal state with a united republic; Idris was to be its president for life. The main opposition to the plan came from Cyrenaican tribal leaders, and it was eventually shelved, although the imminent replacement of the Libyan monarchy by a republic has since been frequently reported by the Beirut press in particular. In June 1955 the king married Alia Abd-al-Kadr Lamlum, the daughter of an Egyptian merchant, but the marriage was childless and was dissolved in 1958. The heir apparent, Mohammad al-Rida, the brother of Idris, died suddenly in 1955 and the king the following year chose

[1] Carrington, *East from Tunis*, London, 1957, p. 129.

Mohammad's second son, Amir Hasan al-Rida, as his heir. In 1959 Amir Hasan strengthened the royal family's links with Tripolitania by marrying a Tripolitanian and by making his home in the province.

The object of Libyan foreign policy in the 1950s was to take an independent and unassuming stand between the western powers, on whose support the economy depended, and the fellow Arab states. Not until February 1953 was the first formal approach to either bloc made, when Libya applied for Arab League membership. Despite the unexplained delay of fourteen months in making the application, the newcomer was warmly welcomed as the League's eighth member in March that year. Having made this necessary gesture to Arab solidarity, Libya then turned to the west and in July signed a twenty-year Treaty of Alliance with Britain which was promptly, but not unexpectedly, denounced by the press of some Arab countries as a blow to Libyan independence and sovereignty. The treaty, which was signed after some eighteen months of negotiations, and in the face of a certain amount of opposition in Libya itself, provided for 'peace and friendship' between the two countries and mutual aid in the event of war or armed conflict. In two separate agreements Britain was granted 'facilities within the territory of Libya for military purposes' (providing Libyan sovereignty was not compromised) and in turn promised annual grants of financial aid for the duration of the agreement. In the first five years there was to be a £1 million annual grant for economic development and £2,750,000 a year in budgetary aid; British arms supplies were also pledged. The treaty was approved by parliament and ratified by the king in December. It gave Britain alternative Middle East bases to those in the Suez Canal zone, evacuation of which started in 1954, and provided staging posts at Idris Airport near Tripoli and at El Adem near Tobruk on the strategic air corridors to East Africa, the Indian Ocean, and the Far East. When the treaty went into effect Britain started to build up a complete division, the Tenth Armoured, in Libya.

Britain had granted the Americans the use of Wheelus air base near Tripoli towards the end of the war. The U.S. Air Force had retained possession and the base, the largest outside the United States, later came to 'play a part in the defense arrangements of the Free World'. Negotiation of an agreement with the Libyan government for continued use of the base started soon after independence, but not until September 1954, following a visit to Washington by Bin Halim, were the two sides ready to sign. According to its preamble, the agreement reflected the desire of the United States and Libyan governments 'to strengthen the firm friendship and understanding now existing between them'. In return for a lease on the base and other areas to the end of 1970, plus concessions covering the movement of personnel, aircraft, and surface transport, the United States undertook to pay $42 million in cash over the period 1954–71 and to supply $3 million worth of grain for immediate drought relief. The base was 'not primarily designed for retaliation ... in the event of war', but acted as a U.S. Military Air Transport Service staging post and, in conjunction with the Al-Watiyah range in western Tripolitania, as an aerial gunnery practice centre for American fighter crews based in western Europe. In 1956 the headquarters of the U.S. Seventeenth Air Force was transferred from Morocco to Wheelus. The agreement was not approved by parliament until considerable opposition had been overcome; the king was forced to dismiss the president of the Senate, Omar Mansur, who had publicly criticised its terms. The agreement was passed by parliament on 30 October after Bin Halim had put forward a persuasive case for the economic advantages to be gained, and it went into effect the same day. It was described by the first U.S. ambassador to Libya, Henry Serrano Villard, as 'the keystone of the bridge between the two countries and the best example of Libyan orientation [*sic*] toward the West'. As a foreign commentator put it, Libya was through its base-lending arrangements with Britain and the United States 'living on its geography'.

Even as the American agreement was being finalised in June, Bin Halim went to Cairo for talks with Colonel Gamal Abdel Nasser, who had recently replaced General Neguib as head of the Egyptian revolutionary government. Nasser was apparently satisfied with Bin Halim's explanation of Libyan policy towards the west, and particularly towards the United States. In November Bin Halim was again in Cairo, and agreed to the secret passage across Libya of arms supplies for the Algerian revolution, which was just starting. Inevitably, Egyptian influence was strong in Libya, where the administrative, judicial, and educational systems were partly based on the Egyptian model; judges, teachers, and officials were recruited in Egypt; Egyptian newspapers were in general circulation and Cairo Radio was heard all over Libya. Relations between the two countries were probably at their best in 1955, the year the king married Alia Lamlum.

At the end of 1954, against a background of growing Libyan and Arab hostility towards France as a result of events in Tunisia, Morocco, and above all Algeria, parliament put pressure on the government to have French troops evacuated from Fezzan. Under a special three-monthly arrangement reached shortly after independence, France maintained garrisons, totalling about 400 men, at Sebha, Ghat, and Ghadames, and in return made good the Fezzanese budget deficit. These troops, stationed at strategic oases at the junctions of desert tracks, could intercept the flow of arms from Egypt to Algeria far more effectively than a greater force of men patrolling the 600 miles of unmarked Libyan-Algerian frontier.

The French would have liked nothing better than an agreement similar to those already reached by Libya with Britain and the United States. But the Libyan government was prepared to negotiate only on the assumption of the total evacuation of Fezzan. Although the special arrangement with France was ended on 31 December 1954, not until August the following year was a treaty of 'friendship and good-neighbourliness' signed. The garrisons were to be withdrawn by 30 November 1956 and France was guaranteed certain limited air and surface transit rights in return for contributions to Libyan development spending in 1955 and 1956 amounting to nearly 500 million francs. Although the agreement was ratified by the Libyan parliament in April 1956, the French National Assembly did not do so until the following November. All French troops left Fezzan before the end of the year and in due course the worst French fears were fulfilled when Fezzan became a supply line for the revolutionary forces in Algeria. Libya's diplomatic success in ending the French occupation set a precedent that Tunisia and Morocco were to follow with similar demands for evacuation of foreign troops. Franco-Libyan relations were not improved by the occasional hospitality Tripoli gave to Algerian exiles and the provisional Algerian government, and they became very much worse after French and Algerian forces fought an engagement on the Libyan frontier, if not in Libya itself, in October 1957. As a result of further incidents in 1958, a Franco-Libyan commission was set up to investigate frontier violations.

The decline of Italian influence in international politics after the Second World War was reflected in the agreement on outstanding issues reached with Libya in 1956. The agreement was a purely economic settlement between two countries that up to a few years before had been ruled as one. The negotiations, which had been opened on Italian initiative in 1953, were held up by disagreement over compensation for Libyan war damage, but a settlement was reached after Italy had offered £2,750,000 in economic aid in the name of 'friendship and collaboration'. A draft treaty signed in Rome on 2 October erased all outstanding differences between the two countries. The promised Italian aid (or compensation) was to be paid as a contribution of £1 million in cash within three months of the treaty going into effect, and as a credit of £1,750,000 in three annual instalments for the purchase of Italian industrial goods. The transfer of most Italian public property to Libya was confirmed, but Italy retained some buildings for diplomatic and consular use, as well as several schools. Certain Italian commercial rights were recognised and the agreement allowed for the completion of development work on colonisation schemes by 1960 at Italian expense. As had been the Italian government's intention in 1938, colonists were to become owners of their land, regardless of how it had been acquired. But those who had returned to Italy, or who planned to do so by 1960, could sell their property to Libyans and, in most cases, freely transfer their capital to Italy.

The treaty, which was ratified in March 1957, affirmed that 'all questions relative to... the transfer of sovereignty' had been settled. For the first time since the beginning of the Second World War, the future of the estimated 15,000 colonists still occupying farms in Libya (apart from the 30,000 Italians in the towns) had been clarified. Many of them took advantage of the generous terms of the treaty to sell out to Libyans and return home. But many others decided to stay on and become the owners of the land they had developed through so many unsettled and uncertain years; their decision to do so was an act of faith in Libya's future.

Early in 1955 came the announcement that Libya and the Soviet Union had agreed to open diplomatic relations. The western powers were taken by surprise (officially, at least) because the negotiations had been held in secret. Soviet diplomatic missions were set up in Tripoli and Benghazi, but offers of Soviet economic aid, cheap machinery, and facilities for the transport of pilgrims to Mecca were all turned down, and the United States quickly reacted by increasing economic aid and spending. Bin Halim denied that there was any connection between the rejection of aid from the Soviet Union and acceptance of more from the United States. His reported comment at the time was 'We do not like to change our friends'. He had no intention, as he told the first Soviet ambassador, of opening the country to communist influence. His main objects in flirting with Moscow were to show that Libya was not wholly tied to the west and to win Soviet support for Libya's admission to the United Nations.

Although a child of the United Nations, Libya nearly four years after independence was still not a member. An application for membership had been made on Independence Day and had immediately been added to the list of thirteen other national applications sponsored by the Soviet Union, but not all acceptable to the Security Council. The deadlock continued until December 1955, when Libya and fifteen other states were admitted under a compromise 'package deal' between the Soviet Union and the west, for Bin Halim had not, after all, been able to persuade the Russians to give preferential treatment to the rather special Libyan application.

By the autumn of 1956 Libyan foreign policy had begun to be modified by new contacts in the eastern Mediterranean. Although a trade and payments agreement was reached with Egypt in May, relations with Cairo became distinctly cooler after king Idris in August visited first Turkey and then Lebanon, neither of which were at that time on close terms with Egypt. Nevertheless, Libya fully supported the Egyptian nationalisation of the Suez Canal in July; Bin Halim hailed it as a 'wise and courageous step'. The government also sought a British guarantee that bases and troops in Tripolitania and Cyrenaica would not be used against Egypt, and assurances to this effect came from London on 30 October. There was wholehearted Libyan sympathy for the Egyptians when Britain and France joined Israel in attacking Egypt the following day. Anti-western feeling in Libya ran high and had to be allowed some expression for fear that repression might possibly antagonise Egypt and even bring the government under attack by extremists. Bin Halim's position was almost untenable, and not the least of his fears was that fighting would break out between British and Egyptian forces on the Cyrenaican frontier. A state of siege was proclaimed and Libyan troops were quietly moved into eastern Cyrenaica. There were some attacks by demonstrators on British and American military installations, ten Libyans were wounded in an explosion at the Tripoli branch of Barclays Bank, and British families were evacuated. A home-made bomb was planted in the editorial office of the English-language *Sunday Ghibli* newspaper in Tripoli, but the editor tossed it outside, where it exploded; he was later given a small fine for letting off explosives in the street.

The sudden end of the fighting in Egypt saved Libya from further crisis. After the cease-fire, the Egyptian military attaché in Tripoli, Colonel Ismail Sadik, was declared *persona non grata* for 'activities damaging to Libya and of no honour to Egypt'. He had for some months been supervising the trans-shipment of arms to Algeria; according to reports published later, he had been distributing some of these arms, and explosives, in Tripoli; he had allegedly incited demonstrations and had threatened security men with a gun. There were the usual rumours of a plot against the king, and Sadik's name was linked with an underground organisation, the Arab Liberation Committee. Sadik was escorted out of the country on 12 November and President Nasser sent a formal apology to king Idris. At about the same time, the First Secretary at the British embassy in Tripoli, Cecil Greatorix, was also expelled from Libya, probably as a gesture to Arab opinion, as no reason was given.

Bin Halim had apparently brought Libya through the crisis with both its Arab and western ties virtually intact. The British bases had been effectively neutralised, yet it had not been thought necessary to break off diplomatic relations with either Britain or France. Nor had the Anglo-Libyan treaty even been denounced, although Libya did for a while press for its revision. But immediate Egyptian reaction to Bin Halim's role in the crisis was not reassuring, and on 1 June 1957 he was denounced by the Cairo newspaper *Al-Ahram*, the semi-official government mouthpiece. He was accused of having allowed British aircraft to use the El Adem airfield for raids on Alexandria and, although the Libyan government denied the charge, Bin Halim's resignation a week earlier on a matter of domestic policy proved in the light of the *Al-Ahram* attack to have been unfortunately timed.

Meanwhile, Tunisia had become independent, giving Libya for the first time a chance to match its links in the Arab Middle East with others in the Arab Maghrib. The Tunisians, perhaps the best-educated and most prosperous of the Maghrib peoples, had a traditional attitude of condescension towards the Libyans, but Libyan initiative in establishing closer relations was appreciated by President Habib Bourguiba. In January 1957 Bin Halim and Bourguiba signed a twenty-year treaty of friendship and co-operation that Bin Halim called 'the cornerstone of North African unity', and which provided for co-operation and co-ordination of policies. It marked the practical start of the drive for greater Maghrib unity, a policy regarded by Tunisia, in particular, as a potential counterweight to Egyptian influence in Arab North Africa.

Seeking further contacts outside the Egyptian sphere of influence, Bin Halim at the end of January 1957 welcomed the Turkish Prime Minister, Adnan Menderes, on a four-day official visit to Libya, a visit that was attacked by Cairo Radio. Reports that Turkey had been asked for arms were confirmed the following November when Ankara supplied military equipment worth $5,500,000; Egypt had made an arms delivery the month before. In March the United States Vice-President, Richard Nixon, visited Libya to explain the purpose of the recently announced 'Eisenhower Doctrine', the economic and military aid programme designed to counter communist influence in the Middle East. Bin Halim welcomed the doctrine in principle, and two days later President Eisenhower's special envoy, James P. Richards, arrived in Tripoli for further talks. The outcome was Libyan acceptance of the 'Eisenhower Doctrine', with a resultant increase of $7 million in American economic aid and the promise of American military equipment. Bin Halim countered criticism by pointing out that Libya was receiving more aid without in any way increasing its commitment to the west.

Bin Halim's foreign policy was neither particularly pleasing, nor manifestly hostile, to any other government. Reflecting as it did almost total economic dependence on the west, obligations to the Arab world, and concessions to various shades of opinion at home, it was well suited to Libya's needs at the time. In refusing to commit himself too decidedly to any one camp (not even to the Arab Maghrib in favour of the Arab east), Bin Halim was inevitably criticised at home and abroad. But the fact that Libya fell out with no one, never broke off diplomatic relations, maintained political independence, and received many more marks of favour from foreign powers than were offered in return, said something for the success of a modest policy of all-round passive co-operation.

Bin Halim was Prime Minister for thirty-seven months, but almost continual oligarchic in-fighting and manoeuvring caused no less than five cabinet reshuffles during that time. The swopping of portfolios on average once every seven and a half months was decided more by personalities than by policies, as also were the general elections of January 1956. Voting went off quietly, mainly because no less than 30 of the 55 deputies were nominated unopposed, especially in the case of Tripolitania. One of the most able leaders of independent Libya, Bin Halim resigned in May 1957 over the old question of legislation by royal decree that had already caused the downfall of two Prime Ministers.

Abd-al-Majid Kubar, a Tripolitanian and the Speaker of the House of Representatives almost continuously since independence, was invited by the king to form a new government. Kubar persuaded both the United States and Britain to increase their economic aid, while he at the same time rejected a Soviet offer of $2,800,000 in cash, plus health and educational aid. At the end of April 1958, he went to London to discuss financial aid up to 1963 under the terms of the Anglo-Libyan treaty. On his return, he was able to announce the promise of £3,250,000 a year in British subsidies for the next five years, as well as supplies of British military equipment and free military training. No conditions were attached. He also announced that Britain's annual contribution of £1 million to the Public Development and Stabilisation Agency, made since 1953, would end, but that the United States would pay $5,500,000 to the agency over the next five years instead. Kubar's reputation for attracting foreign aid was further enhanced in July 1960, when a technical and economic co-operation agreement was signed with Federal Germany; it was followed up by a long-term German loan of £5 million for agricultural and industrial development.

Like Bin Halim, Kubar also had to allay Arab suspicions of Anglo-Libyan motives. On 18 July 1958, four days after the revolution and overthrow of the monarchy in Iraq, British troops were landed in Cyrenaica. The purpose, it was announced, was to reinforce British units under the terms of the Anglo-Libyan treaty and in view of the Middle East situation. Meanwhile, the king and, somewhat reluctantly, the government, had declined to recognise the new Iraqi régime of Brigadier Abd-al-Karim Kassim, and the country was officially in mourning for the death of king Faisal II. The presence of additional British troops and the official attitude towards the new Iraqi government was strongly criticised at home and abroad and, as a result, Libyan recognition of the Kassim régime was declared on 4 August. Ten days later the government sent an appeasing note to Cairo, affirming for the first time that 'Libya is an integral part of the Arab nation',[2] and that 'Libya will continue to oppose foreign armed intervention in the Middle East'. Once again, the right gesture had been made, and in Cairo the note received official approval by being described by *Al-Ahram* as Libya's most positive action since independence. Understandably, Kubar refused to take part in the dispute between Tunisia and Egypt in the Arab League in 1958. In a press interview, he merely said that Libya 'deplored' such quarrelling, and expressed hopes for a speedy settlement.

The Kubar administration was brought down in October 1960 after forty months in office by a long-threatened financial scandal. A forewarning had come in July when the king had sent a letter to members of the federal and provincial governments in which, quoting from the Koran and mincing no words, he had denounced bribery and nepotism in official circles. Two years earlier the contract to build a much-needed road from Bu Grain on the main coast highway to Sebha, a distance of 410 miles, had been awarded by Kubar, acting without parliament's approval, to a leading Libyan company. The work was to be completed in three years, apparently at a cost of £1,900,000. News of the award was not well received and, as rumour had foretold, in 1960 the firm asked for, and received, a further £4 million (a quarter of it in advance) from the government for completion of the project, only one-third of which had so far been finished at a cost of £1,900,000. First the press and then parliament took up the matter, determined to use the scandal as a platform for a general attack on the government's administrative record. At an extraordinary session of parliament on 10 October the government was collectively attacked by an amazingly united House. A motion cancelling both the contract and the government's undertaking to pay the additional £4 million, and calling for full technical and financial investigations, was passed by 53 votes to one. A motion withdrawing confidence in the government was also put down for debate after the statutory interval of eight days. During this breathing space, Kubar unsuccessfully tried to persuade the king to dissolve parliament; then, rather than attempt to defend himself before the House, he resigned. Parliament had lived up to its responsibilities; for the first time, deputies from the three provinces had united for a political purpose and had brought not merely an individual but a whole government to account.

[2] A statement to this effect was not written into the constitution until 1963.

Kubar's successor was Mohammad bin Othman. He was the first Prime Minister from Fezzan and had served in all but two previous cabinets. The main policies of his administration were the restoration of public confidence in government, greater understanding of government policy by the people, and better relations between the provinces.

National unity had not been achieved during the long struggle against the Italians – it was actually they who had united Tripolitania and Cyrenaica as a single colony – nor in the years of debate culminating in an independence voted for by member states of the United Nations. Only after 1951 did unity begin to emerge from the difficulties and daily routine of self-government. By the time the tenth anniversary of independence was celebrated, the supposedly brittle Libyan federation had been shown to have considerable resilience, largely due to wise interpretation put on his own powers by king Idris. The king, the bespectacled, rather frail scholar, aged sixty-one when he came to the throne, found himself theoretically divided between loyalty to Cyrenaica and to Libya as a whole. Yet in practice it was he, and not the federal government, who provided the real link, and a flexible one, between the unevenly matched team of the three provinces. Three Prime Ministers, Muntasser, Sakisli, and Bin Halim, resigned because the king, putting national stability before any individual, had overruled them by royal decree. Secluded after 1954 in his palace near Tobruk, the king became the remote and wise guardian of his country, a figure of great prestige, wielding the ultimate power.

Unity and the centrifugal rivalry of the provinces, the powers of the king and his Ministers, were still matters of contention at the tenth anniversary of independence, but were steadily becoming less disruptive, and the fact that the Libyan federation had survived to celebrate that anniversary gave hope for the future. Yet the rulers, both at court and in the federal and provincial governments, had failed to communicate with the ordinary citizen, although Bin Othman had at least tried to explain his government's motives. The country was ruled by an oligarchy of prominent families who, whenever they swopped appointments or portfolios, generated a mild sense of crisis, and renewed misgivings about administrative competence. Government was a remote affair over which the urban voter had little control and the country folk, represented in the national and provincial assemblies by their traditional leaders, neither expected to control, nor hardly felt the need to do so. (This sense of remoteness from the affairs of state was emphasised when the administrative capital was transferred to Baida, four hours' drive from Benghazi; Ministers and officials became more inaccessible as much of their time was taken up with travelling between Tripoli, Benghazi, and the Gebel Akhdar, and their whereabouts was often uncertain.) With political parties banned and elections offering only a choice of candidate and not of programme, votes were cast according to tribal, family, and personal loyalties. There was little opportunity for voices to be raised, let alone heeded, except during street demonstrations, and even parliamentary deputies, with their provincial outlook, tended to put local interests above national ones. It was, nevertheless, a form of government that gave Libya, the first of the ex-colonial territories of Africa to become independent, a record of rather tremulous stability.

In the first three years of independence, imports averaged well over £11 million, while only in 1953 did exports rise above £4 million. The adverse trade balance crept up from about £7 million in 1952 to nearly £10 million in 1955, and by 1960 had reached £56,400,000, although a large part of the total was by then accounted for by deliveries of oil industry equipment. An important export commodity, and a source of considerable wealth to those enterprising enough to organise its collection and shipment to Europe, was the battle scrap still lying in the desert. Exports of salvaged metal earned between £400,000 and £500,000 in foreign exchange a year for several years until the more accessible battlefields were picked clean.

Aid by foreign countries and spending by British, French, and American troops not only covered the trade gap, but also outgoing payments for invisible transactions, and every year there was a surplus on current account. Spending by foreign military establishments was alone worth £6,200,000 in 1955. Official foreign economic aid increased from £1,458,000 to £10 million between 1951 and 1956. The annual budget deficit was met by foreign assistance. Of the £11,500,000 of estimated federal revenues for 1956–7, only £3 million represented internal revenue. The balance was provided by a British grant-in-aid of £3 million and by other foreign aid, contributed mainly by Britain and the United States, totalling £5,200,000. American Point Four aid was worth about $1,500,000 a year, and contributions were also made by Egypt, France, Italy, and Turkey. From the mid-1950s onwards spending by foreign oil companies brought further large sums into the country. By 1953 the United Nations Technical Assistance Programme in Libya was, in proportion to the population, larger than in any of more than ninety countries and territories where the U.N. was active.

Libya's need for money, advice, and administrative guidance was only equalled by the need for the education that had for so long been neglected. In 1950, when there were about 26,000 pupils in primary schools, Adrian Pelt estimated in his first Annual Report that 'the number of students for whom education would have to be provided would considerably exceed 100,000'. By 1953 40 per cent of Tripolitanian children were at school, but of the 800 teachers in the province, only 200 had been trained as teachers, and about the same number had themselves had only one or two years' schooling. A Libyan University was founded in Benghazi in 1956 with faculties of Arts and Education and thirty-one students. Foreign teachers, the majority of them Egyptian, were imported, teacher-training colleges were opened, and a start was made in providing technical and higher education. The budget for education was more than two and a half times higher in 1956–7 than in 1952–3, for the government shared the view of the United Nations economic expert, Benjamin Higgins, that 'education is the core of both economic and social development in Libya.' In 1960–1 the school population rose to a figure roughly corresponding to the target proposed by Pelt ten years before: 131,000.

In the 1950s Libya did have an advantage in its tiny population (although the manpower shortage was to create new problems in the following decade). £10 million in foreign aid, which may have little overall effect in such countries as India or Indonesia, go a long way among one million people. If the incidence of trachoma and illiteracy was high in Libya, only hundreds of thousands, and not millions, were asking for treatment and education. The economic and social problems were great, but not overwhelming, and once work started on them, results could be hearteningly swift. John Gunther found in 1955 that 'Libya does not cost very much' to the foreign-aid donor. Then, in October 1961, king Idris inaugurated the first Libyan oil terminal at Marsa Brega, and at the tenth anniversary of independence two months later, he was able to announce: 'The coming years will be years of abundance, owing to the wealth God has given us from our soil.'

Chapter 20

Oil

IRONICALLY, it is the desert, inhospitable, unproductive, and sterile, abused as 'a crate of sand' and as 'the abomination of desolation', that has yielded the greatest source of wealth Libya has ever known. Yet, until the 1950s, the presence of oil in North Africa was barely suspected; the oil and gas fields of the Sahara do not betray their presence by such obvious clues as the 'Eternal Fires' of Azerbaijan or the asphalt ponds of Iraq.

Libya's first recorded hydrocarbon strike was in 1914, when a trace of methane gas was found at a depth of 480 feet during the drilling of a water well at Sidi Mesri, near Tripoli. The intensive Italian search for underground water supplies in the 1920s and 1930s led to several more, but valueless, finds. The pioneer of the Libyan oil search was Professor Ardito Desio, who had made a comprehensive geological map of Italian North Africa before Balbo inaugurated the 'Policy of Water' in the mid-1930s. Desio decided in 1935 to watch for oil and gas traces in water wells being drilled under his supervision. Two years later, while sinking a well near Tripoli, he found both methane and 'blackish drops of crude oil', and in 1938 he collected enough oil to fill a bottle with the first sample of Libyan crude. After finding further traces in water wells on the Gefara Plain and in the Misurata area, he submitted a confidential report to the Italian government. The *Azienda Generale Italiana Petroli* (AGIP) sent out a prospecting team, and a Tripolitanian exploration programme was drawn up. Early in 1940, Desio divided the country into twelve geological zones and, with shrewd judgement, pointed to the Sirtica as one of the most likely oil-bearing areas; that major oilfields were found there twenty years later surprised him less than anybody. But when the Italians moved rigs into the Sirtica in 1940, neither the equipment nor the techniques then in use were sufficient to stand up to the appallingly tough desert conditions, nor to reach the relatively deep deposits. Some traces of oil were found, but in the summer of 1940 war ended further exploration.

After the war, Standard Oil studied the results of Italian exploration and two company geologists made a brief survey of the country. But the oil industry is particularly sensitive to political atmosphere, and the post-war uncertainty over Libya's future delayed further prospecting until after independence. It was only on publication of a Minerals Law in 1953 that prospecting permits were granted to nine major international companies and small teams of geologists were sent out into the desert to make preliminary surveys.

Two events of 1955 started the Libyan oil rush: oil was struck at Edjeleh in the Algerian Sahara, providing the first real evidence that North Africa was an oil-bearing region, and in June the government passed the first Petroleum Law, much praised for its fairness and foresight. It declared all subsurface mineral resources the property of the state; it divided the country into four exploration zones; it laid down rules for the granting of concessions and set out concession terms, rents, and relinquishment arrangements; it decreed that government revenue was to be 50 per cent of the income from company operations after deduction of operating costs, and that revenue was to take the form of fees, rents, and royalties, plus surtaxes due under other laws.

The first concessions were granted in November 1955 and over the next three years 55 per cent of the land area of the country was allocated to fourteen international oil companies. Unlike some Middle Eastern states, Libya did not surrender itself as a single concession to one company or one consortium of companies. The rush for territory in Libya in the 1950s, at a time of world oil surplus and falling prices, was very largely the result of the industry's policy of continual diversification of sources. No company, nor any government of a consumer country, likes to depend on a single, or only a few, sources of crude oil; ideally, no source should be indispensable. The need to diversify supplies was stressed by the Abadan crisis of the early 1950s and the blocking of the Suez Canal in 1956–7, events that stressed the vulnerability of Middle East oil supplies to political crises. Oil found in Libya, a country with which Britain and the United States had treaties, and in which they maintained military bases, would not have to pass through the Suez Canal, nor indeed any narrow waterway, on its relatively short journey to the large and rapidly growing oil markets of western

Europe. By the late 1950s, with oil already flowing from the Algerian Sahara, Libya was the 'big play' that the Middle East in the 1930s, and Canada in the 1940s, had been, and that Nigeria, Alaska, and the North Sea were later to become.

Writing about the Libyan oil search Christopher Tugendhat says: 'As soon as a discovery is announced in some previously unconsidered territory, the scramble for concessions begins as each company tries to ensure that none of its rivals secures a decisive advantage. The rushes are usually successful at finding large new reserves within a very short time, since they would not have begun unless the prospects looked extremely bright in the first place.'[1]

In fact, the early geological reports were not particularly optimistic, but the companies were prepared to invest in exploration because of Libya's nearness to European oil markets, relatively stable politics, and favourable concession terms; seismic exploration was under way by June 1956.

Probably the greatest hazard to exploration, apart from the harshness of the climate and terrain, was the unexploded mines sown across the desert. During the Second World War the British, German, and Italian armies had laid about 4 million mines between El Alamein in Egypt and Mareth in Tunisia; in 1957 an estimated 3 million were still untouched and ready to be stepped on or driven over. In the minefields, some of which extended inland for 100 miles, clearing parties went ahead of the geological crews to sweep and mark 'safe lanes'.

Because oil had already been found in Algeria (one field was almost on the Libyan frontier) western Fezzan was the first main centre of interest. Esso Libya spent a year on geological and geophysical exploration in Concession One, between the Ubari Sand Sea and the Algerian frontier, and in June 1957 decided to drill. The company, not given to underrating its achievements, has described some of the difficulties of placing the unwieldy 100-feet-high drilling rigs on site:

> 'Moving in the drilling rigs meant bringing them across country rough enough to test even camels. To keep the rigs from bogging down completely, Esso Libya's transportation division devised a special truck-trailer, using giant, oversized tires that could maneuver over both sand and hard rock... Even with the big wheels,

[1] Tugendhat, *Oil – The Biggest Business*, London, 1968.

however, the drilling caravan had to detour 980 miles to reach the well site, which was only 480 miles from Tripoli on a straight line.'[2]

The first two holes in Concession One were dry, but in January 1958 came proof that there was oil in Fezzan, when Atshan Number Two well started flowing at the rate of 500 b.p.d. (barrels of oil per day). This well was so remote that its low output was not worth exploiting. Another eleven wells drilled in Concession One failed to make any significant strikes.

In April 1956 Esso had moved geological parties into its 10,000 square-mile Concession Six, which stretched southwards from the Gulf of Sirte to Gebel Zelten. Drilling started in the concession early in 1958, the blackest year for Libyan oil. Despite extensive exploration and drilling costing £24 million in 1958, not one commercial find had been made by the end of the year, and Esso alone had drilled a dozen unproductive wells. At the beginning of 1959 the industry had spent a cumulative total of £42 million, drilling had been going on for over eighteen months, and the only rewards for this time, effort, and expense were the one Atshan strike, nearly 500 miles from the coast, and a few other 500 b.p.d. wells. There seemed to be no commercial oilfields in the Sahara east of Algeria. Discouragement set in; more than one company was preparing to abandon the search; and a current industry joke was that Libya was enjoying the biggest dry-hole boom the world had ever known.

If 1958 was the year of frustration and disappointment, 1959 was the year of achievement. Down in Esso's Concession Six, near a lonely landmark known as Bir Zelten, a preliminary test made on the C1-6 exploration well on 18 April gave promising results. C1-6, known also as Zelten Number One, was completed in June, and when tested by geologist Joe Brown on 11 June, flowed at 17,500 b.p.d., a rate that compared favourably with Saudi Arabian and Kuwaiti oil wells. One of the world's largest oilfields had been found, but at the time Esso could only guardedly announce that a 'promising' discovery had been made in the Sirtica where, nineteen years before, Ardito Desio had said oil was likely to be found. In August came confirmation of a major discovery when Zelten Number Two was brought in at 15,000 b.p.d. At Zelten, a thick oil-bearing stratum (or 'pay zone' in the expressive jargon of the

[2] *Esso in Libya*, Tripoli, 1965, p. 6.

industry) lay at less than 6,000 feet, and it was there that the industry found the first convincing pointer to a possible abundance of oil in the Sirtica.

Then, still in that wonder year of 1959, reports of strikes began to come in from all over the Sirtica. Even before Zelten Number Two had been completed, the Oasis Group (the Libyan operator for Continental Oil, Amerada, Shell, and Marathon) was drilling the first producer in Concession 59, which covered some of the Sirtica's most prolific structures. This first well in what was later to be known as the Waha Field came in at a reluctant 226 b.p.d., but later holes in the same structure flowed at up to 7,000 b.p.d. In 1959 Oasis also made the first unpromising strikes in what was to become the Dahra Field in Concession 32. In August, the Esso Sirte/Libam/Grace group found the Mabruk Field in Concession 17; at the end of September Amoseas (the operating company for Texaco Overseas and California Asiatic) completed the first producer in the Beida Field in Concession 47; and on 1 November the German-American consortium, Mobil-Gelsenberg, brought in the first producer in the Amal Field, in Concession 12.

The year 1959 will go down in the history of the industry as that in which six major Sirtican oilfields (Amal, Beida, Dahra, Mabruk, Waha, and Zelten) were found. In 1960, a year of consolidation, there were fewer new discoveries. Oasis found the small Defa Field in Concession 59, and at the end of the year Shell made the first strike in the low-yielding Antelat Field in Concession 51. But drilling activity was higher than ever as fields found the previous year were evaluated. It was noted that parts of Libya were geologically similar to the mid-continent region of the United States, and Esso's magazine *The Lamp* quoted a geologist as saying: 'It's as if we were moving into Oklahoma in 1900 before a single well had been drilled.'

Zelten was the first big find and the first, by almost a year, to be exploited. The story of the development of Libyan oil discoveries is largely a repetition of Esso's pioneering work at Zelten and on the Gulf of Sirte. Having found oil, Esso then had to move the output of its scattered wells from the field to the coast for shipment to market. The company has recorded: 'If this problem had its thorns, they were at least more bearable than those that went with the empty days of search and the succession of dry holes.' When it had been cleared of mines, Marsa Brega, a former Italian outpost 30 miles east of El Agheila and on the most southerly curve of the Gulf of Sirte, was chosen as the site for an oil shipment terminal. It was 'about as good a site as could be found' on that exposed and dangerous coast. In June 1960 the contract for the 105-mile, 30-inch pipeline from Zelten to Brega was awarded, and in July the first shiploads of 40-foot lengths of pipe began arriving off the terminal site. As there were no harbour facilities, the pipes, which had been plugged at both ends, were floated into the sea, towed to land by boats, and manhandled ashore. (Early experiments with wooden plugs proved disastrous because the wood tended to shrink during the voyage from Europe.) By August 1961 nearly 16,000 sections of pipe had been welded, wrapped, and buried to form the complete pipeline. Its initial capacity was about 200,000 b.p.d., but by 1964 had been nearly trebled. In the late summer of 1961 Zelten was ready to go 'on stream'. At Brega, meanwhile, a harbour for small supply ships had been dredged, and a wharf and breakwater built with 2,200-ton submersible caissons floated from Italy. Sea-loading berths had been laid out into the Gulf and connected to the shore by underwater pipelines. On land, where a few months before there had only been a huddle of surveyors' tents, there had appeared a sprawling terminal complex: a hideous industrial landscape set between the sea and the desert, but a striking example of American organisation and initiative.

Zelten production started on 8 August. Half a million barrels of oil were pumped before the pipeline filled completely, and not until 17 August did oil begin to reach Marsa Brega. On 12 September 1961, twenty-seven months after the first test at Zelten and fifteen since the start of work on the Zelten–Brega 'transportation system', the first oil to be shipped from Libya was loaded aboard the *Esso Canterbury* bound for England. Libya had become an oil-exporting state, although the flow was, initially, a mere trickle by Middle Eastern standards; total exports in 1961 amounted to a mere 6,670,000 barrels.

Esso's achievement was duly acknowledged on 25 October when the Marsa Brega terminal was officially inaugurated by king Idris.

After the opening of the first terminal the 'legend' of Libyan oil, in the words of the former Minister of Petroleum Affairs, Fuad Kabazi, was to 'outpace imagination'.[3] Between October 1961 and the spring of 1968, five major Libyan oil terminals were opened,

[3] With his administrative ability Kabazi rather unusually combines such talents as translating Arabic poetry into Italian and designing postage stamps.

giving an average rate of one opening every fifteen months. Esso exports had been flowing for less than a year when, in May 1962, oil started moving along an 85-mile, 30-inch pipeline from the Oasis Group's Bahi and Dahra Fields in Concession 32 to a terminal at Es Sidra, 100 miles west of Marsa Brega by road. Then, in December 1964, a third terminal was opened at Ras Lanuf, near Marble Arch, and only 20 miles east of Es Sidra. The 24/30-inch, 170-mile Ras Lanuf line was built to take production from the Amoseas Beida and the Mobil Hofra and Ora Fields. Meanwhile, the Esso Sirte/Libam/Grace consortium had started running crude from its Raguba Field, near Marada, through a 20-inch spur-line to the main Zelten–Marsa Brega pipeline; Esso had started production at the Jebel Field south of Zelten and Oasis had extended the Dahra–Es Sidra line by another 260 miles out to the Samah, Waha, Zaggut, and Gialo Fields in Concession 59.

The years 1965 and 1966 were a period of consolidation in the Sirtica, and for twenty-six months no new terminals were opened. But there was much activity away to the east, in the wilderness of shifting sand-dunes not far from the Egyptian frontier. In 1957 an American oilman, Nelson Bunker Hunt, had been awarded Concession 65, a 33,000 square-kilometre territory sprawling across the plain and sand sea of Calanscio. The concession lay fallow for the next three years while the Oasis Group was making its series of strikes in the prolific and neighbouring Concession 59. Then, in September 1960, British Petroleum bought a half share in Concession 65 from Hunt, reportedly for £10 million. The company, which desperately needed west-of-Suez supplies, and had had little luck in eight concessions of its own, also took on the job of operator for the partnership with Hunt. It proved to be a worthwhile gamble. On 27 November 1961 the C1 well was completed at 3,910 b.p.d., C2 came in at 2,840 b.p.d. in March 1962, and ten weeks later C3 was tested at 8,500 b.p.d. By mid-1963 eleven wells with a total production of over 25,000 b.p.d. had been drilled in what came to be called the Sarir Field. Further evaluation showed it to be the largest-known field in Africa and twice the size of the greatest in the United States, the East Texas.

Sarir was further from the coast than any other productive field. Possible terminal sites on the Gulf of Sirte were surveyed, but it was at Tobruk, on the Gulf of Bomba, that the most promising one was found. It has been suggested that the presence of a British garrison at Tobruk influenced its selection by B.P. as a terminal port; physics and meteorology were actually the deciding factors. Marsa Hariga, opposite Tobruk, stands on a deep-water bay forming probably the best natural harbour in Libya. Loading could continue there during spells of rough weather that frequently hold up operations at the Gulf of Sirte terminals. The water was deep enough to allow tankers to moor close inshore and load from surface pipelines. This was a key feature of a terminal that was to handle the waxy Sarir crude, which had to be heated before it would flow, and could have solidified in the type of submarine pipeline necessary at other terminal sites. The Marsa Hariga project was not approved until 1965 and only in the middle of that year was B.P. able to start work on the site. The laying of the 320-mile, 34-inch pipeline, part of it through the Great Sand Sea of Calanscio (Sarir Kalanshu al-Ramli al-Kabir in Arabic) was finished at the end of 1966. By then, some seventy wells were ready to start feeding oil into the pipeline, which had an initial capacity of 100,000 b.p.d. The first shipment of Sarir crude left Marsa Hariga on 12 January 1967 and on 14 February king Idris went down from his nearby palace of Dar al-Salaam to inaugurate the terminal. Sir Maurice Bridgeman, Chairman of B.P., said at the opening ceremony that the Sarir Field had been found 'by a combination of luck, scientific judgement, inexhaustible patience and financial resources'; the company had reportedly spent £85 million on exploration, development, and installations, of which the pipeline and terminals had accounted for £35 million.

There was a seven-year gap between B.P. buying a share in Concession 65 and the first exports of Sarir crude; yet when Marsa Hariga was opened in February 1967, another company was halfway to achieving similar results in just over two years. In May 1965 the government had invited offers for some promising new concessions. They were composed partly of acreage not previously assigned and partly of territory 'handed back' under a clause in the Petroleum Law requiring concession-holders to relinquish 25 per cent of their holding five years after its being granted. Allocations were announced in February 1966, and two coveted concessions, 102 and 103, went to Occidental of Libya Inc. Within fifteen days of the award, the company had started seismic operations in Concession 102, and in mid-July the first wildcat well was spudded in. The fourth well to be drilled, the D1, struck oil in November and flowed at 14,860 b.p.d. on test. The strike was made only 6 miles south of

Amoseas' Nafoora Field in Concession 51, to the north of the Oasis Gialo Field in Concession 59, and in territory handed back from Concession 59. In January 1967, the D2 step-out well came in at 7,732 b.p.d. and the discovery of another major field, the Augila, was claimed soon after; small wonder that nineteen companies had bid for Concession 102 in 1965. Almost as soon as Occidental had announced its first strikes, oilmen stopped discussing the possibility of a company giving away an undiscovered oilfield with hand-back territory, for it had obviously happened. By the end of April 1967 seven Augila wells were between them producing 61,000 b.p.d.

Augila was only the start of Occidental's brilliantly successful Libyan operation. In May 1967 a strike was made in former Mobil territory in Concession 103. The A1 wildcat, drilled about 40 miles west of Augila, came in at a magnificent 40,080 b.p.d. in a 'pay zone' of oil-bearing sands almost one thousand feet thick (the average thickness of 'pay' in other Libyan fields is about 100 feet). Occidental had been planning to pass Augila production into existing pipelines, but with the new discovery the company began to plan the building of its own 'transportation system' and terminal. The new Idris Field very soon proved to be a 'humdinger', as the Tripoli *Sunday Ghibli* called it: the A2 well came in at the fabulous figure of 53,349 b.p.d., and the A3 at only 2,000 barrels less.

In the space of about ten months, and despite delays caused by bad weather, Occidental built a 135-mile, 40-inch line (Libya's biggest) from the Idris Field to Zuetina, on the Gulf of Sirte near Agedabia. A 24-inch spur-line brought in Augila crude, and production started in February 1968 at 150,000 b.p.d., although the full capacity of the pipeline was one million b.p.d. The Zuetina terminal was inaugurated by king Idris in April 1968.

Late in 1967 Occidental brought in the D1 well, 15 miles south of the Idris Field, at the enormous flow-rate of 74,867 b.p.d., and a 40-inch spur-line was built to link this find with the main Zuetina pipeline.

Few oil companies have been as successful as Occidental. The Umm Farud Field, found by Philips Petroleum in 1962, by 1967 had production problems, and output in that year was down by 46 per cent compared with 1966. A similar percentage drop in output was registered by Pan American's declining Khuff Field. And there are companies that have drilled for years in Libya without making a single significant strike. Oil is the biggest business, but it is one of the chanciest.

The Libyan government and the companies have always had a good working relationship. Changes in operating terms and revenue payments have come about through negotiation, rather than by more drastic methods. In 1961 government revenues from oil were just over 60 U.S. cents a barrel; by 1965 they were over 80 cents a barrel, and by 1967 had risen to one dollar. That the government has over the years won itself better terms without provoking a breach with the companies is a tribute to the goodwill and moderation of both sides.

The government's first move to increase revenues was made in July 1961, only two weeks before exports from Zelten started. By a royal decree amending the Petroleum Law, the taxable income of the companies was redefined and increased by allowing fewer deductions. According to figures quoted by Abdul Amir Kubbah, the government's share of Esso's 1962 profits would have been £9,500,000 under the 1955 law, but were actually an estimated £13 million as a result of the amendments. The royal decree, besides changing concession terms, also ruled that concessions were in future to be granted by competitive bidding. Although the established companies were not bound to accept the amendments, failure to do so would have disqualified them from bidding for new concessions, and all the companies in fact agreed to the new terms.

In December 1965 eighteen companies accepted a further amendment to the Petroleum Law under which taxes were to be paid on the full posted price (the price at which a given quality of crude is offered for sale at a given place) and not on the very much lower realised price; big discounts offered by the 'independent' companies in particular had cut the average price of Libyan crude from $2·19 a barrel in 1961 to $1·80 or thereabouts in the first half of 1965, compared with a posted price of $2·21 for Zelten crude at Marsa Brega. The government had threatened to stop exports by companies that did not accept the new terms, which were based on a formula drawn up by O.P.E.C., the Organisation of Petroleum Exporting Countries, which Libya had joined in 1962. The main objects of the 1965 amendment were to increase government revenues, stop price-cutting on the European markets, and bring Libyan oil-pricing laws into closer harmony with those of other O.P.E.C.

member-countries. The enormous increase in Libyan production since 1961, coupled with progressive price-cutting, had threatened selling prices elsewhere; there were also scare stories of Libyan fields being 'skimmed' by excessive and physically damaging production rates by 'independent' companies seeking a quick return on their investments.

The six-day Middle East war of June 1967 and its aftermath emphasised the geographical advantages of Libya as an oil-producer. In September, when the oil-supply situation in western Europe was beginning to recover from the selective Arab embargo on exports and the closure of the Suez Canal, *The Times* commented: 'It is difficult to over-emphasise the importance of the near-at-hand Libyan oil to the fuel economies of all the West European nations.' For the importing countries were by then taking full advantage of these west-of-Suez supplies. Even with the Canal open, Libya's favourable situation was obvious: the round journey from one of the Gulf of Sirte ports to the south European pipeline terminal near Marseilles is under 2,000 nautical miles; the comparable trip from the eastern Mediterranean terminals is 3,200 miles, and from Kuwait via the Canal, 9,200 miles. Accordingly, the companies in the autumn of 1967 agreed to waive allowances off posted prices so long as the Canal remained closed. This somewhat delayed financial recognition of Libya's geographical advantages gave the government an estimated increase in revenue of 8·5 cents a barrel, or almost $80 million extra in the full year.

With negotiating skill, a nice sense of timing, and a little pressure, and aided by rivalry between companies, the government has been able to improve its share of oil income substantially. Moreover, as the *Financial Times* pointed out in March 1968: 'Because foreign oil companies are so anxious to secure concessions, the Government is able to insist that they should undertake various forms of capital investments as part of their price of entry.'

Occidental, in winning Concessions 102 and 103 in competition with nearly twenty other companies in 1965, committed itself to spending 5 per cent of pre-tax profits on an agricultural scheme in Kufra Oasis, and to the setting up of a $30 million ammonia fertiliser and urea plant in co-operation with the government.

The Libyans, as has been said of other Arab producers, cannot drink their oil: they must sell it if they are to maintain the pace of economic development and their rising standard of living. The state of the Iranian industry after the Abadan closure of the early 1950s was a standing warning of what can happen when governments and companies fall out. Although Libyans were taking over technical and administrative jobs in the industry from foreigners, the country was in 1968 still very dependent on the foreign expertise and equipment which found and exploited the oil in the first place to keep it flowing.

It has been stated that: 'The most dedicated mercantilist of the eighteenth century could not have tied a colonial economy more closely to that of its mother country than the oil-producing nations are tied to the companies that exploit and export their resources.'[4] Yet the majority of Libyans seemed to be satisfied with letting gross revenue increase, while leaving effective policy and management control to the companies. After the war of 1967 there was talk of attacks on oil installations, but none took place; as it was, the Libyan oil export embargo cost the country an estimated £500,000 a day.

Following two rapid changes of government, there were signs in 1968 of a new and more independent Libyan oil policy. The formation in April of the Libyan General Petroleum Corporation (LIPCO) gave the government a chance to take the initiative in national oil development. With the former Under-Secretary of the Petroleum Ministry, Mohammad Geroushi, as its full-time chairman and general manager, LIPCO was authorised 'to engage in all aspects of the oil industry, both within and outside Libya either on its own or in participation with others'. It was to collaborate 'with the authorities concerned' in planning and executing national oil policy and in setting and maintaining price levels. It also took over the government's rights to participate in existing and future concessions.

No sooner had LIPCO been formed than the Prime Minister, Abd-al-Hamid Bakkush, announced at the end of an official visit to France on 5 April that LIPCO was to associate with the French E.R.A.P. and S.N.P.A. companies in exploration and exploitation in Libya. The *Financial Times* welcomed the agreement as 'Libya's first departure from the old type of concession'. It was suggested that French staff in the Petroleum Ministry had, as the *Financial Times* put it, 'pressed the virtues of joint ventures in general and French partnership in particular.' The French did not break in cheaply: not only were they to bear all of the $22,500,000 cost of exploration over ten years, but they were to spend at least $1 million

[4] Tugendhat, op. cit.

on offshore drilling in the Zuara area. The Libyan share of any production was to be 25 per cent, later rising to 50 per cent. Indeed, the terms accepted by the French were rumoured to have upset the established 'Anglo-Saxon' companies already concerned about royalty payments.

The June war of 1967 and its aftermath forced the industry to recognise some basic truths. The two-month selective embargo on exports was a practical demonstration of how Libyan oil could be prevented from flowing by political pressure, both domestic and foreign. In effect, by bringing the economy nearly to a standstill, Libya had showed solidarity with the Arab cause. Although Libyan exports had since 1961 given European oil sources greater *geographical* diversity, the embargo made it clear that there had not been the *political* diversification, the disengagement from Middle Eastern politics, that the industry had looked for when it moved into Libya in the mid-1950s. At the same time, the Libyans realised that when they and other Arab producers cut off their exports, the importing countries of western Europe had been able to turn to the United States, Venezuela, and Iran for alternative supplies, but that the producer-countries had had no immediate alternative markets and sources of revenue. The events of 1967 provided some salutary lessons, and before the end of the year production was again rising rapidly as the government and the companies took advantage of the demand placed on Libyan crude by the closure of the Suez Canal. In the first four months of 1968, production was up by 40 per cent compared with the same period of 1967, and still the government was calling for greater output.

A common, but embarrassing, by-product of many oil wells is natural gas, which has been found at Zelten and elsewhere in the Sirtica. Unless a market is found for it, natural gas is useless and has to be 'flared' (burned) at the oilfield as a constant reminder that this is 'the most wasted raw material in the world'. So sensitive were Esso about the flares at Zelten that the company would not allow photographs of them to be published. As there were in 1962 an estimated American trillion (million million) cubic feet under the ground at Zelten, and a further five trillion cubic feet at other productive fields, it seemed that much gas was to be used to warm the desert air. But in 1964, the year that Algeria started selling liquefied, frozen natural gas to Europe, Esso announced plans to export

Zelten gas, subject to government approval. In November the following year the company signed contracts for the supply of 235 million cubic feet of gas a day to Italy and 110 million cubic feet a day to Spain. Work started at Brega that year on building one of the largest 'gas-processing facilities' in the world, at a cost of $300 million. The plant, which was opened in January 1969, liquefies the natural gas piped from Zelten by cooling it to minus 260° Fahrenheit. It is then shipped aboard four specially built refrigerator ships for delivery to Italian and Spanish receiving terminals. Esso claimed that 'these sales of Libyan gas represent the largest liquefied natural gas transaction in the world and one of the largest gas sales ever made by the international petroleum industry.'

In the early summer of 1967, Esso opened a 10,000 b.p.d. refinery at Marsa Brega. This prestige installation had been completed in 1963 after being floated *en bloc* from Europe and dug into its site on the sea shore, but negotiations over the price to be charged on the home market for refined products lasted for four years. When it did start production, the refinery was able to supply half the country's demand for petrol, paraffin, and diesel, and enough fuel oil to provide a surplus for export.

In July 1968 Libyan oil output amounted to 85·2 million barrels of oil and, for the first time, overtook Kuwait, which had that month produced 80 million barrels.

TOTAL OIL PRODUCTION
(millions of barrels)

1961	6·7
1962	67·2
1963	169·4
1964	315·5
1965	419·7
1966	550·2
1967	636·4
1968	916.6

These figures show a boom greater, in terms of sheer annual expansion, than any in the industry's history. At the beginning of 1969, Libya was the world's sixth oil producer and fourth oil exporter, and was expected to be the third producer by 1970.

In early 1968, the Oasis Group was the largest producer, nearly half of its crude coming from the Gialo Field. Next were the Esso companies (which lifted their thousand-millionth barrel of Libyan oil in February 1968). Zelten, in its seventh year of production, was flowing at 525,000 b.p.d. In third place was Mobiloil-Gelsenberg, followed by B.P./Hunt, with increasing output from the Sarir Field, and Amoseas, whose Nafoora Field was yielding about two-thirds of the total company output. Occidental exports were only just starting, but the potential for rapid increase was enormous.

In 1968 most Libyan oil was sold to the nearest big market, western Europe. Since 1963, West Germany had been the biggest buyer, and in 1968 shipments there represented 28 per cent of the total. Italy, Britain, and France were also important customers.

In less than a decade a country that had been classified as 'the poorest in the world' had become a major supplier of fuel to those same countries that a generation before had fought each other over the oil-bearing desert of Libya for the possession of the oilfields of West Asia. No wonder that in 1966 a *Giornale di Sicilia* headline complained: 'We never knew it: Millions of Barrels of Oil in Libya.'

Chapter 21

The Kingdom of Libya

AT THE TENTH anniversary of independence, on 24 December 1961, king Idris acknowledged 'the wealth God has given us from our soil', but warned: 'the struggle ahead will not be less strenuous than during the past ten years. Prosperity has its own problems....' He could foresee that a terrific pace of change and progress was to be set in the 1960s. Libya was to cease being a 'poor-poor' nation and was to become a 'rich-poor' one, in the sense that, despite the opportunities for greatly increased development spending, the effects of poverty were not to be erased overnight. The unprecedented and unpredicted growth in oil revenues, which from £13,700,000 in 1962 had by 1965 multiplied six-fold to £81,500,000, and in 1968 reached £303,000,000, consolidated the new situation. The king's words echoed *The Economic Development of Libya*, the report of an International Bank for Reconstruction and Development mission to Libya, which noted in 1960 that: '... the discovery of oil does not provide an easy or a complete solution to the problems of economic development.' The old problems remained, and oil could provide only the financial means of solving them.

Yet oil revenues, which relieved the country of its most pressing financial problems, were the catalyst that brought about national unity, which became an officially acknowledged reality with the abolition of the federal system in 1964. The provincial administrations had been made subordinate to the federal government in December 1963. Then, in April 1964, a month after Bin Othman had been succeeded as Prime Minister by Muhiaddin al-Fikini, further constitutional amendments passed by parliament abolished the provincial administrations and the federal government altogether, and entrusted all authority to one central government. The provinces of Tripolitania, Cyrenaica, and Fezzan were replaced by ten administrative districts, namely Benghazi, Derna, Gebel Akhdar, Gebel Gharbi, Homs, Misurata, Sebha, Tripoli, Ubari, and Zavia, each under an appointed administrator. The abolition of the federal state was formally proclaimed by the king on 27 April, the new system went into effect on 2 September, and the name of the country was changed to the Kingdom of Libya.

For twelve years, 1½ million Libyans had been ruled by *four* governments sitting in the national and provincial capitals of Tripoli and Benghazi, and in the provincial capital of Sebha, an extravagant, cumbersome, and inefficient arrangement. In addition to the fifteen federal Ministries, the provinces had had an average of eight Ministries each, and Tripolitania and Cyrenaica had each employed more civil servants than the federal government. Liaison between the provincial and central administrations had been poor and the provinces, frequently acting independently, had followed their own policies. During the years the federal system had been in operation, prejudice against a unified state was broken down, and when parliament voted for unity, the vote was acclaimed with apparently popular enthusiasm.

In January 1963 an observer of Arab affairs, H. B. Sharabi, noted that: 'So far, the two sources of upheaval and revolution in the political life of the Middle East, the students and the army, have remained calm in Libya.' He maintained that the 'predominant ideology' among the more educated was the *Baath* (Arab Renaissance Party) version of socialism and Arab nationalism. Pro-Nasser feeling was strong among students and other young people.

When, in January 1964, President Nasser called a conference of Arab states in Cairo to plan action against Israel's proposed diversion of the River Jordan waters, king Idris broadcast in favour of the conference, at which Libya was represented by the Crown Prince and the Prime Minister. On 16 January high school and university students in Benghazi demonstrated their support for the meeting. The Cyrenaica Defence Force was called out to clear the streets and, according to the most reliable accounts, two students were killed and several were injured in the ensuing clashes. (Because no official announcement was made, the number of killed and wounded was rumoured to be far higher; the *Cyrenaica Weekly News* could only report that 'several' youths had been shot in Benghazi.) On 22 January there were demonstrations in Tripoli, where several hundred students took part in a mock funeral symbolising mourning for those killed in Benghazi. The crowd marched to the Prime Minister's office, where a tearful Fikini publicly expressed deep sorrow and regret for the Benghazi incidents. That night, after the demonstrators had been dispersed, Fikini's resignation was announced. He had reportedly been to see the king (who was in residence at Suani ben Adem, near Tripoli) on 21 January and had requested the resignation of Mahmud Bukuwaytin who, as commander of the Cyrenaica Defence Force, was technically responsible for the police action in Benghazi, although he had been out of the city at the time. Bukuwaytin was the brother-in-law of the king's adviser, Busairi Shelhi, and the king preferred to ask for Fikini's resignation rather than Bukuwaytin's. It seems that one of several alleged plots against the régime had recently been uncovered, the country was in a restless mood, and, at a time when loyalties were in question, a man of Bukuwaytin's calibre was less dispensable than a Prime Minister.

Fikini's successor was Mahmud Muntasser, the first Prime Minister and the only man to hold the office twice. Significantly, he was made responsible for internal security on his appointment. The announcement of his new cabinet, coupled with Fikini's resignation, started a second round of demonstrations and on 24 and 25 January crowds which a few days before had demanded Fikini's dismissal, shouted for his return. On 27 January the Prime Minister, in a broadcast to the nation, blamed the recent disturbances on a 'small, evil minority'.

Calm was restored. But on 22 February (United Arab Republic day) assurances that foreign bases in Libya would not be used against Arab states in the event of war with Israel were demanded by President Nasser in a speech broadcast throughout the Arab world by Cairo Radio. Taking its cue from Nasser, the Libyan press raised the cry for liquidation of the bases. In mid-March Muntasser, under pressure from both Houses of Parliament, informed Britain and the United States that the government was not prepared to renew or extend the base agreements. (France had given up her rights to operate a limited number of military flights at Ghat, Ghadames, and Sebha in 1963.) According to Soviet sources: 'It was well known that in 1962 atom and hydrogen bomb depots were being built, and rocket-launching pads set up, at Wheelus Field. Fourteen thousand American soldiers and officers were concentrated in the base area.'[1] According to the same sources, British forces in Libya in 1964 amounted to between 12,000 and 15,000 men. These 'well known' facts may have been based on popular rumour, or vice-versa.

[1] Bodyanski and Shagal, *Sovremennaya Liviya*, Moscow, 1965.

On 21 March, reportedly after a stormy meeting between the king and the cabinet at the new administrative capital of Baida, it became known that the king had decided to abdicate, and had shut himself up in his palace at Tobruk. The reason given for the decision was ill-health and rumours of differences with the government were denied. But it seems that the abdication was the ultimate gesture of disapproval of the proposal to break the twenty-year-old British connection that had sustained Sanussi interests up to, and beyond, independence.

The government's position was clarified (or modified) on 23 March by the Minister of State, Omar Baruni, who said that, despite the desire to have the bases closed, Libya wished to maintain economic and trade relations with Britain and the United States, and to continue the British training of the navy and the army and the American training of the air force. The government merely wanted, Baruni said, 'to modify agreements that had become outmoded'. Later, after a moving demonstration of loyalty outside the palace by Ministers, Senators, deputies, and Cyrenaican tribesmen, the king was persuaded to change his mind, for it was plain that the country had no acceptable alternative leader.

Britain and the United States opened talks on the future of their bases later in the year and in August the Prime Minister announced that evacuation had been agreed in principle. Britain had undertaken to withdraw garrisons within eighteen months; evacuation started in 1965 and was completed in Tripolitania in the spring of 1966. In October 1964 two Libyan-American commissions started discussing the evacuation of Wheelus Field, but there seemed to be no sense of urgency to the negotiations.

In 1963, certainly for the first time in this century, Libya had a favourable trade balance, due almost entirely to oil exports. This fact, symbolising growing national wealth, helps partially to explain the events of 1964: the demonstrations, Fikini's fall, the yielding to outside pressure over the foreign base issue, and the abortive abdication.

In response to the demand for labour created by the oil industry and, more particularly, by the expanding service industries, thousands of country and oasis folk were uprooting themselves and migrating to the cities in expectation of immediate participation in the national economic miracle; the rush was probably greatest in the late 1950s. Housed in shanties on the outskirts of Tripoli and Benghazi, the newcomers who found work also found the value of their wages constantly eroded by inflation. Although *per capita* annual income was officially stated to have risen four and a half times (from £13 to £57) between 1950 and 1962, and the wages of many skilled and semi-skilled workers were high for North Africa, the cost of food, housing, and other basic necessities was rising rapidly, and unemployment among the entirely unskilled remained high. Oil revenues were multiplying from year to year, the business classes and enterprising individuals were obviously prospering, and there was no further financial necessity to rent bases to foreigners. But there was a suspicion among the urban proletariat that the new wealth was not being fairly distributed. The mood of resentment was not allayed when the Prime Minister reported to the United Nations General Assembly in September 1962 that: 'The declared aims of the [1963–8] Five-Year Plan are to raise the standard of all Libyans and to lay the foundation of future economic growth'; nor was it allayed by the knowledge that under the Petroleum Royalties Law of 1958 70 per cent of oil revenues were to be devoted to economic expansion. It seemed to many Libyans that the pace of economic and social advancement was matching neither national income nor popular demand, and that the existing régime offered no immediate prospect of closing these gaps; indeed, it could not, for the distribution of national income was bound to take time. If many people were unable to make their impatience known, there were foreign voices ready to do it for them, and to others with half-digested grievances and no clear-cut remedies, the street demonstration was the only form of expression.

A year of unrest culminated in general elections in October. The country's fourth elected parliament was opened in November and was dissolved by the king the following February. Among the few official reasons given was that the House had been 'top heavy' and that there were too many constituencies. While new elections were being prepared in April, it was announced that the number of constituencies would be reduced from 103 to 91. Elections held in May 1965 returned sixteen candidates unopposed and 75 other pro-government members. (King Idris, unlike king Hassan of Morocco, who dissolved his parliament in June 1965, was not prepared to rule without an elected assembly.)

Mahmud Muntasser had resigned in March and was succeeded by his Foreign Minister, Hussain Mazigh. For more than two years after Mazigh took over, the country was placidly prosperous, and the benefits of oil revenues did begin to filter through to many sections of the population.

As of the late 1960s, no government had shown any desire to fashion a new political order. Libya was not even a one-party state. There was no ideology of 'Idrisism', and the king had never been known to make a major policy statement. Certain Baathists were given mild prison sentences in 1964, and the alliance of the monarchy and the governing oligarchy, which had brought the country safely through the first decade of independence, still seemed to offer the best guarantee of stability in the second. 'A working constitutional monarchy, which is best suited to the nation's genius', is how the system of government has been described and, in the first seventeen years of independence, at least, no practical alternative to the system was offered.

FOREIGN POLICY

In a memorable cable from Tripoli in 1961, a foreign news agency correspondent reported: LIBYAN REACTION TO SYRIAN COUP COLON NOT MUCH – a reflection, perhaps, on the degree of interest then shown to events not directly affecting the country's own affairs. Until the mid-1960s, foreign policy was largely one of good neighbourliness towards the various blocs, western, Arab, African, Maghrib, or Islamic, to which Libya was bound by economic, racial, geographical, religious, and other obligations.

Genuine Libyan enthusiasm and support for the concept of a Greater Maghrib, a vague and structurally undefined union of Morocco, Algeria, Tunisia, and Libya, was slow to develop. While the three other would-be partners specifically affirmed their 'Maghribism' in their constitutions, the 1963 Libyan constitution merely defined the kingdom as 'a part of the Arab Home-Land and a portion of the African Continent'. Libya was only represented by an observer at the 'Conference for the Unification of the Arab Maghrib' in Tangier in 1958, and thus had no say in the decision that a Maghrib federation was best suited 'to the realities of the participating countries'. Unity was to be a long-term objective of which, after 1958, 'joint action', 'solidarity', and 'co-operation', rather than 'federation', became the guide-lines. Although Libya continued to be the least involved of the four states, government Ministers did make an increasing number of public statements affirming their faith in Maghrib unity. Along with Morocco, Algeria, and Tunisia, Libya at the end of 1964 played a full part in the meeting in Tangier, under the auspices of the United Nations Economic Commission for Africa, that agreed on the establishment of three permanent institutions to plan and implement regional economic development and integration, and Libya from then onwards became a more active supporter of Maghrib unity.

As a 'portion of the African Continent', Libya also officially supported the cause of African unity, and in 1961 was represented at the Casablanca conference attended by Morocco, the United Arab Republic, Ghana, Guinea, Mali, and the Algerian provisional government. But the spirit of positive pan-Africanism of the 'Casablanca Group' was too strong for current Libyan thinking, and it was at the conference of moderate African states held at Monrovia, Liberia, the same year that aims closer to Libya's own were expressed, particularly the desire to put the solution of internal problems before continental unity. Both Libya and Tunisia withdrew from the second meeting of the 'Monrovia Group' at Lagos in 1962 because of differences with other states over Algeria. Growing awareness of the community of independent African states, however, was shown by sending a delegation to the 1964 Organisation of African Unity Conference in Cairo, representation at later O.A.U. meetings, and solidarity with other African states in condemning and boycotting South Africa, Portugal, and Rhodesia. Nevertheless, the first attempts to form foreign links on geographical grounds rather than on economic, religious, or ethnic ones were not very rewarding and diplomatic and other ties with Africa south of the Sahara were few. Although Ghana appointed a resident ambassador to Tripoli shortly after gaining independence in 1957, there seemed to be little justification for having done so.

Following the king's own ideas, Libya refused to become involved in Arab polemics. 'Do not enter into disputes lest you fail and lose all your power' was an adage of the Prophet that provided a cautionary policy guide. As a result, Libyan participation in Arab councils, up to the 1967 Khartum Summit Conference, was colourless, cautious, for the most part uninfluential, and occasionally a source of annoyance to others. But at least once national economic interest was put above Arab solidarity: in 1965, following the *rapprochement* between Federal Germany and Israel, Libya did not join some Arab states in breaking off diplomatic relations with Bonn: West Germany happened to be the best customer for Libyan oil. There was always sympathy for Arab causes, but national resources and energies were devoted to economic and social developments at home, and not to foreign ventures.

Relations with Italy remained cordial and, as the future Prime Minister, Muhiaddin al-Fikini, publicly stated in 1959, they were based 'on mutual respect and fructuous co-operation in the framework of dignity, equality, and the respective independence of the two countries [and] illustrate the best example of the manner in which relations between some of the Western Powers and the African peoples should be settled.' Italy retained considerable trade and economic interests in her former colony, particularly in Tripolitania, and was the foremost supplier of imports. Although Cyrenaica had but a few reminders of the Italian occupation, Tripoli and parts of northern Tripolitania retained much of their Italian character; certain quarters of Tripoli were almost entirely Italian-occupied, and the dome and *campanile* of the Roman Catholic Cathedral continued to dominate the city skyline. Personal relations between Tripolitanian Libyans and Italian townspeople and farmers (who kept their Italian citizenship) were good, and at no time after independence were there any significant demonstrations of anti-Italian feeling.

The greater economic independence gained through oil revenues, and a willingness to do business with all but a few blacklisted countries, enabled Libya in the 1960s to make new foreign contacts outside the narrow circle of necessary friends of the 1950s. If oil revenues hastened the process of economic and military decolonisation, those very revenues were paid by American and other western oil companies, and Libya was closely linked to the western economic system. In 1964 the Minister of State, Omar Baruni, was quoted by the *New York Times* as saying: 'We are not a Socialist country. Our wealth in oil we intend to exploit by permitting full activity of private enterprise.'

Yet, with loyalties to the neutralist and developing 'Third World' of Afro-Asia, the government and the press tended to take the conventional, 'anti-imperialist' stand on international issues, particularly in South Arabia and the Persian (or Arab) Gulf, while continuing to accept British and American arms and military training. To the average Libyan, President Nasser was the most admired of all foreign statesmen, and his portrait was almost as ubiquitous as the king's. A certain suspicion of foreigners, including other Arabs (not unreasonable in people with a long history of foreign rule), was ignored when it came to meeting the national need for goods and services. By the mid-1960s the kingdom had trade and other relations with eighty-four countries of all shades of political colouring. When the Higher College of Teacher Training was opened in Tripoli in 1965, its Chief Technical Adviser was an Iraqi (with an Italian secretary) and the teaching staff was recruited from Britain, France, Malta, the United Arab Republic, and the United States. In the same year, room service in a leading hotel was provided by Spanish and Sudanese nationals; Madras Indians were stringing new power wires between villages near Tripoli; a British firm of consulting engineers and Bulgarian contractors (helped by Tunisian and Italian sub-contractors) were working on the new Tripoli Sports City; Libyan naval cadets were training in Greece; Pakistani and Nationalist Chinese doctors were practising in Cyrenaica and Fezzan.

THE ECONOMY

Agriculture

The small population and large oil revenues suggested to some observers that Libya was in the 1960s becoming 'another Kuwait', in the sense of a country that can afford to import all the goods and specialised services it needs. Yet there were reasons why Libyan development could be very different from Kuwait's. Libya not only had a population five times greater and an area nearly 120 times bigger (creating problems of its own) but also a potentially sound agricultural economy, supplemented by tourism.

Up to this century, there were two main sources of income: stock-raising and (under the Romans, in particular) settled agriculture, and trade in the raw materials and manufactured goods for the most part produced outside North Africa. The great majority of the population had always been pastoralists or farmers, and the number of traders and merchants (and corsairs, who were merchants of a kind) was small. Following the collapse of the ancient trans-Saharan trade system at the end of the nineteenth century, the Italians in the early twentieth century tried to build a viable colonial economy on state-sponsored agriculture and, after the Second World War and independence, farming was still the main hope for the country's economic future. Then came the discovery of oil and, within a few years, the acquisition of considerable wealth; the effect on farming was crippling, because a serious manpower shortage was added to the traditional problems of poor soil, scanty water, and unreliable climate. The small population, which had been something of an advantage when the economy largely depended on foreign aid, became a handicap when the demand for non-agricultural labour suddenly increased. During the colonial period, the older quarters of Tripoli and Benghazi had been filled with a wage-earning proletariat recruited from the countryside to work on the ambitious Italian building and development schemes. But the Italian demand for labour was small compared with that created when serious oil-prospecting started in the mid-1950s. Farmers from northern Tripolitania, shepherds from Cyrenaica and the Sirtica, *Jebbadin* from the oases of Fezzan, were attracted to the towns and the oil camps by the prospect of high wages and better conditions as unskilled or semi-skilled labourers. The farms and the oasis-gardens were neglected, the number of livestock diminished, and the land reclaimed from the desert was again threatened by encroaching sand-dunes.

Official concern was great and the government tried to protect and develop agriculture, which was the country's most reliable long-term economic base: oil reserves, although tremendous, were not inexhaustible, and sales were subject to political uncertainties and the possibility of customer-nations developing alternative fuels or sources of supply. When the first Five-Year Economic and Social Development Plan was launched in 1963, nearly £29,300,000 was allocated to agriculture and forestry; industry, by contrast, received under £7 million and, out of the Plan's total allocation of nearly £170 million, public works was the only sector to receive more. Introducing the draft of the Plan in parliament in August 1963, the Prime Minister explained the large allocation to agriculture by declaring that it was 'deemed to represent the backbone of our national economy, not only because it is a main source of work and income for the majority of the people, but also because it is a contributory factor to the settlement of inhabitants and strengthens the social and economic interrelationships among the various sectors'. Projects outlined by the Prime Minister included land reclamation and agricultural settlement; afforestation; renovation of neglected ex-Italian farms and establishment of new ones; improvements in communications; government subsidies, loans, and grants; irrigation schemes; development of animal resources; and training.

Although the Plan proposed 'to improve the economic condition of the farmers', this was inevitably a fairly distant prospect. According to government figures, the average *per capita* income of agricultural workers was estimated at about £19 a year in 1960; the corresponding figure for the non-agricultural worker was nearly double, at about £35. The authors of the Five-Year Plan admitted that 'the difference is too great, even though relatively low *per capita* income is associated with rural populations in nearly all parts of the world'. What the Plan tried to do was to make farming a more attractive occupation, now that many Libyans were able to choose how and where they made their livings. The northern towns, with their high wages, services, amenities, and agreeable climates, offered greater, more human, and more positive attractions than any number of plans to provide outlying areas with electric light, piped water, schools, clinics, and other symbols of 'development'. The lad who abandoned the ancestral sheep pastures in the Garian hills to take a job (despite his illiteracy) as a sweeper and messenger in a Tripoli printing shop for a few pounds a week had no *immediate* alternative prospect of betterment to dissuade him from leaving the countryside. The scarcity of agricultural labour caused a drop in production and a rise in costs, and farmers had increasing difficulty in hiring casual harvesters at wages they could afford to pay. At the same time, an expanding foreign community and an improving standard of living created a demand for more and better food, a demand that had largely to be supplied by imports. In the 1960s Libya, which had previously been a net exporter of agricultural produce, became a net importer; the slaughterhouses had to turn to Sudan for cattle, and American corn oil went on sale in a country where the Italians had planted 3 million olive-trees.

In addition, farming was inefficient, largely as a result of poor methods of cultivation and traditional land tenure practice; the country suffered less from a feudal system of land ownership than from fragmentation of holdings, which resulted in many plots being too small for efficiency. In the mid-1960s, agriculture was meeting only 40 per cent of home demand, and between 1955 and 1967 food prices rose by 70 per cent.

The government was fully aware of these shortcomings and tried to increase agriculture's contribution to the national economy.

Farmers were offered low-interest fifteen-year loans by the National Agricultural Bank (founded in 1957), as well as subsidised farm machinery and equipment. (A grey Peugeot pick-up truck, among the commonest vehicles on Libyan country roads, was usually the first purchase of a farmer granted a loan.) Repayments did not start for five years and were then made in ten annual instalments. The bank also bought olive oil, almond, and groundnut surpluses, generally above world prices, to create an anti-inflationary buffer stock, and encouraged farming co-operatives. From 1961 onwards the bank was advancing more than £1 million a year in loans, and in 1966 it ceased charging interest altogether. The state-controlled National Agricultural Settlement Authority (N.A.S.A.) was set up in 1963 with an annual budget of about £1 million and in 1965 started reclaiming 15,000 hectares of scrubland in the Gebel Akhdar and renovating 1,800 ex-*Ente* colonial farms, more or less neglected since 1941–2. It was planned to plant 5 million vines, fruit-, and almond-trees and to settle 4,000 nomadic and semi-nomadic families on the new farms and train them in arboriculture. The success of the scheme, involving the conversion of tent-dwelling nomadic pastoralists into house-dwelling settled farmers, was expected to have as much social as agricultural significance for the future development of the country. In addition to the Gebel Akhdar scheme, N.A.S.A. had plans for the redevelopment of Fezzanese oases, for the creation of 250 market-garden farms near Tripoli and of fruit farms in the Tarhuna and Garian–Yefren areas, and for the renovation of former Italian colonial farms south of Misurata.

New hope for desert reclamation was given by the discovery that a mineral oil mulch, sprayed onto dunes, would hold down the sand for at least a year, long enough for tree seedlings, planted immediately after the spraying, to grow to 6 feet and effectively bind the sand with their roots. Within seven years of planting, the dunes disappeared under a healthy growth of young timber. By 1967 some 55,000 hectares of dunes had been planted with 28 million eucalyptus-, acacia-, and pine-trees, and the planting of a further 45,000 hectares within ten years was planned to protect Tripoli and its surroundings from the sands of the Gefara Plain.

Industry

It was the service industries, and not manufacturing, that created the main demand for labour. The development of manufacturing industries was slow and on a limited scale. Just before the Second World War there were some 20,000 industrial employees in the country, but the main 'industries' both then and after independence were small food-processing plants, garages, and workshops. Even in the 1960s the tobacco industry, employing about 4,000 in growing and processing, was the second-largest industry after oil. A Ministry of Industry was formed in 1961 to supervise state-owned factories and to plan the development of private and nationalised industries. In the first Five-Year Plan almost £7 million was allocated to this sector, and one of the Plan's declared aims was 'to raise the present level of production, in quantity, kind, and quality, to promote consumption of Libyan manufactured goods so as to lessen dependence on foreign goods' and to create an export market and a 'higher level of employment'. Of the allocation to industry £5 million was set aside for credits, and an Industrial Development Organisation was established; in 1965 it became the Industrial and Real Estate Bank, authorised to lend 60 per cent of its £10 million capital free of interest.

One of industry's main obstacles was the small home market. In addition, lack of experienced management, the shortage and cost of skilled labour, competition from foreign goods, and the need to import many raw materials, meant that industry needed state aid and protection for healthy survival. Export opportunities were few: Libyan manufacturers, apart from traditional handicrafts, stood little chance of competing either on quality or price in Europe, and were unlikely to be accepted in neighbouring African countries developing and protecting industries of their own. In response to the demands of the building boom, factories producing cement, gypsum, glass, paint, and other materials were opened in the 1960s, but all building hardware and fittings, and even bricks and tiles, were still imported.

The oil industry held out hopes for the establishment of petrochemical and other oil-processing industries, with the power provided by local natural gas. As of 1968, the first such projects were Occidental's planned ammonia plant, Esso's refinery and gas liquefaction complex at Marsa Brega, and a proposed Esso sulphur plant with an annual capacity of 45,000 tons. But such installations were merely subsidiary to the oil industry and were unlikely to employ many workers.

Despite such inducements as interest-free industrial development loans, most private investment was made either in housing and real estate, or in oil industry contracting – transport, servicing, equipment-hire, and catering – or in foreign trade. Not only was there a marked shortage of Libyan investment in manufacturing industry, but an absence of foreign capital. The Beirut *Commerce du Levant* thought that 'the real reason' for this lack of foreign investment was that 'any foreign hold on the national economy is repugnant to the Libyans, and they will only tolerate it in the field of oil exploration.' As a result, the government had to play the part of industrial pioneer and at the same time provide the bulk of the funds for the private sector's modest industrial development ventures.

Until the start of the first Five-Year Plan in 1963, there had been little economic planning, apart from the work done by the Bank of Libya. But planning became essential when the government began to receive, and spend, substantial oil revenues. The Plan, with its series of 'more or less carefully studied and loosely co-ordinated' investment projects, suffered from no shortage of money; indeed, it ran into difficulties because there was more money to spend than had been allowed for, such was the unexpected growth of oil revenues. Spending over the five years was probably nearer £250 million than the £169 million originally envisaged, and by 1966 it was obvious that the Plan was losing both its proportions and its objectives. It also failed to carry out some schemes because of physical limitations and the desire to get value for money. (A *Financial Times* criticism in 1965 was that 'there is a tendency in some Government quarters to seek the perfect solution rather than the quick but imperfect one.') The second Five-Year Plan, which was to have started in 1968, was postponed for twelve months to allow for the completion of unfinished projects under the first Plan and to give more time for the preparation of the second.

Communication, Housing, Public Works

The third-largest allocation under the first Plan, of £27,460,000, was made to communications. The most ambitious road works to be undertaken in Libya since the Second World War were the widening of the entire coastal highway from a nominal two lanes to a genuine three. By 1967 Libyan, French, Italian, and Yugoslav contractors were starting work on the six sections of the road. The cost was to be more than £36 million (compared with the cost of £1 million to the Italian taxpayer for the completion of the unfinished half of the road in 1935–6). Having realised that the new road would be one of the most dangerous types there is – the three-lane highway on which the middle lane is used by both streams of traffic (sometimes simultaneously) for overtaking – the Roads Department started to plan the busier sections as a dual carriageway. Other important projects included completion of the Tripoli–Nalut road and its continuation along the route of the old 'wash-board' track to Ghadames, the Brak-Edri and Sebha–Ubari roads in Fezzan, and the Agedabia-Gialo and Tobruk-Giarabub roads. With their completion, the country would have a good basic network of hard-surface highways linking all the main centres of population.

In October 1965 a national carrier, Kingdom of Libya Airlines, started international services from Tripoli and Benghazi with two French Sud Aviation *Caravelle* jets and internal services (Tripoli–Sebha) with one chartered Douglas DC-3. Due to the 'air-mindedness' of the large expatriate community and of many Libyans, K.L.A. carried 132,000 passengers in its first year of operation. The addition of two chartered Fokker *Friendship* aircraft to the fleet in 1966 resulted in the opening of the first public air services to Ghadames, Marsa Brega, Baida (previously reached only by a four-hour drive from Benghazi), Tobruk, and later, Kufra. A third *Caravelle* went into service in 1967.

A scheme that was planned to end the national housing shortage by the early 1970s was announced by the Prime Minister in August 1965. One hundred thousand homes, he said, were to be built in the next five years at a cost of £400 million; assuming an average of five people per dwelling, about one-third of the population was to be rehoused. The Idris Housing Scheme, as it was called, started eighteen months later when work began on 9,200 homes at a total cost of £52 million, an average price £1,500 higher than the original estimate of £4,000 per unit.

The largest allocation under the first Five-Year Plan, £38,662,000, went to Public Works. High on the list of priorities were water and electricity supplies, sewerage, and land reclamation, at Benghazi. After the destruction of the town of Al Marj (Barce) by earthquake in 1963, the Al Marj Reconstruction Organisation was formed as a department of the Ministry of Works.

DEFENCE

In 1968, the strength of the army was about 7,000 men, mostly British-trained, and equipped mainly by Britain and the United States. The army was outnumbered almost two to one by the armed police forces. The air force, formed in 1963, had by 1967 about 250 American-trained personnel and a few jet trainers and piston-engined transports; eight F-105 jets were delivered in 1968. The navy's first proper warship, the 440-ton British-built frigate *Tobruk*, was delivered in June 1966, whereupon the king called for a navy 'able to defend every inch of Libyan territory'. Orders for a maintenance ship (handed over late in 1968) and for three fast patrol boats were accordingly placed in Britain.

Manpower and training were the factors limiting the size of the armed forces. As of 1968, there was one Libyan soldier to every hundred square miles of the country and one sailor to every 5 miles of coastline. Until the mid-1960s, Libya, in common with other Maghrib countries, had spent less than 5 per cent of national income on 'defence', compared with an average of about 10 per cent by Middle East Arab countries. Quiet neutralism and base-leasing agreements seemed to be the best defence policy for a people not numerous enough to provide adequate forces of its own. The idea of buying missiles, and training a few specialists in their operation, instead of employing scarce manpower in conventional armed forces of unpredictable loyalties, seems to have crystallised towards the end of 1966. Eighteen months later a £100 million missiles contract with the British Aircraft Corporation was announced. (Some estimates put the final cost nearer £150 million.) B.A.C. was to supply *Thunderbird* high- and medium-level anti-aircraft missiles and *Rapier* low-level missiles for interception of aircraft attacking below radar cover. The contract included radar detection and control equipment, and the training of Libyan operators in Britain. The entire system was to be mobile for additional protection, and in obedience to the laws of desert warfare which generally abhor static defences. The system was designed to give formidable striking power against an attacker and critics who questioned its cost were also left to guess the identity of the would-be aggressor.

EDUCATION AND HEALTH

One Libyan in every six was in 1968 a full-time pupil; over 250,000 children were enrolled in the one thousand government and private schools. The school population had doubled since 1960, and in the three years 1963–6 alone a total of 457 new school buildings with over 2,500 classrooms were completed. In 1966 the Ministry of Education estimated that 70 per cent of school-age children were receiving a full-time education. Government schooling was free at all levels; students at colleges of advanced education and at the two universities (the Libyan University and the Islamic University of Mohammad bin Ali al-Sanussi) were paid up to £300 a year in maintenance grants. In 1966 the government stated in a report that 'the policy of education for the many and not for the few is leading to universal secondary education'. As a result of the teacher-training programme, there was claimed to be no shortage of teachers, except at higher levels, where foreigners (mostly Egyptians) helped to make up the numbers. Yet the 1964 census showed that only 0·13 per cent of the population had been educated to graduate level and that, while the male literacy rate had dropped from 72 per cent in 1954 to 59·6 per cent in 1964, the rate of female illiteracy was still around 95 per cent. In 1964–5 girls made up less than one-quarter of the school population, although enrolment was increasing steadily as girls, in the words of the Ministry of Education, showed their determination 'not to be impeded by the traditions and folkways that once impeded their mothers and grandmothers.' The government in 1965 announced a fifteen-year literacy programme which, at an estimated cost of £18 million, was to teach 750,000 adults to read, write, and do simple arithmetic at evening classes.

A government schools-feeding programme was started in 1955 with the help of UNICEF, FAO, and the American CARE organisation. Its object was to make up the deficiencies in child feeding by supplying half the necessary daily calorie intake and one-third of the protein. By the mid-1960s, the government was meeting the full cost of the scheme, about £500,000 annually, from which 250,000 children were benefiting.

Tuberculosis, trachoma, and malaria were the main illnesses in a relatively healthy country. In the 1960s malaria was eradicated (Libya actually claimed to be the first African state to be free of it) and the others were controlled. In 1966 there were over 400 doctors in the country, about thirty hospitals, and 300 clinics.

Libya was in the 1960s becoming a fully-fledged welfare state. The National Social Insurance Institute (or I.N.A.S., *Istituto Nazionale di Assicurazione Sociale*, the Italian organisation from which it was developed) was founded in 1957 as a public body, financially and administratively independent, to provide free medical, maternity, and dental care and old age and sickness benefits. Certain categories of employee were compulsorily enrolled and contributions were shared by employers and employees. There were plans to extend the scheme to cover the whole population and to provide wider services.

In Tripolitania, the Italian community was a source of valuable manual skills, technical knowledge, and managerial ability. Foreigners, including many so-called 'New Italians' and Palestinian refugees, went to work in the country, usually on short-term contracts, after the discovery of oil. But the shortage of skilled manual labour, particularly for building and civil engineering projects, could only be met by importing foreign workers, and in October 1966 the government signed a manpower agreement with Morocco, and plans were also announced to bring in selected workers from Tunisia and Sudan.

INFLATION

Between 1957 and 1965 prices increased by about 100 per cent, and wages rose even higher. Tripoli became one of the most expensive cities in the world and its cost of living index for Libyans (1955=100) stood at over 150 by December 1963. A new index (January 1964=100) had reached 122 by December 1967. It was estimated that the 7·4 per cent increase in agricultural production in 1966, compared with 1965, was almost entirely accounted for by price rises, as was the 10 per cent increase in industrial output. Despite attempts by the Bank of Libya to restrict credit and guide industrial investment, a continuing inflationary spiral seemed inevitable, given the economic and social conditions of the country. Proposals for graduated income tax promised to bring in yet more revenues, and with about 15 per cent of the labour force (excluding the armed forces and the police) already working for the government, there was little scope for increasing state employment; Ministries cannot have an unlimited number of janitors. It was also estimated that the oil industry could not absorb more than 5 per cent of the labour force.

Money was filtering through to the man in the street, although his standard of living was not as high as he thought it deserved to be. According to figures published by the World Bank in 1966, annual *per capita* income was still only $200, compared with $3,290 in Kuwait and $300 in Jordan. While it was obvious that fortunes were being made by some (and the *laissez-faire* economy encouraged individual enterprise) it was also clear that oil revenues were increasing rather than lessening the gap between the nomad and the semi-nomad on the one hand and the city-dweller on the other; one of the most bewildering of the problems of social reorganisation was the integration of traditional communities into modern Libyan society.

When the six-day Middle East war started on 5 June 1967, Libyans were unable to take part in the fighting, but there were big demonstrations in Tripoli and Benghazi. On 7 June Libyan oil industry workers refused to load waiting tankers, reportedly on the instructions of the government and in support of the Arab oil producers' embargo agreed at a Baghdad meeting a week before. The oil companies ordered their tankers out of territorial waters and at least one company on 14 June issued a confidential report, repeated daily, that Libya was 'on the verge of revolt' and that Libyan workers had been called on to destroy British and American installations. National morale was lowered by rumours that members of the government had slipped away to Italy, and the internal situation remained tense for many weeks. Despite a government call to union leaders to reopen the oil ports to ships of 'friendly nations', a total embargo remained in force until early July and then became selective. A return to normality started in August with the appointment of a new government under Abd-al-Kader Badri, who brought defiant oil-workers to trial.

It was at the Khartum Arab Summit Conference at the end of August that Libya's standing in the Arab world was enhanced by the new-found role of aid-donor. With Kuwait and Saudi Arabia, Libya pledged funds to help Egypt and Jordan recover from the effects of the war. The Libyan contribution was set at £30 million a year 'until the traces of Israeli aggression are removed', in addition to the £20 million given soon after the cease-fire. The decision, also taken at the Khartum meeting, to end all Arab oil export embargoes still in force (Britain, the United States, and West Germany were the only importing countries still seriously affected) allowed the commitments to Egypt and Jordan to be fulfilled without financial embarrassment.

Another outcome of the Middle East war was a renewed Libyan demand for immediate talks on evacuation of foreign bases. As a result, the small British garrison was withdrawn from Benghazi in February 1968, but detachments remained at Tobruk and the El Adem staging post. But there seemed to be no prospect of the Americans completing their withdrawal until the Wheelus Base agreement expired in 1971.

The restoration of confidence after the shocks of the summer of 1967 was consolidated at the end of October by the appointment of a young, Cairo-educated lawyer, Abd-al-Hamid Bakkush, as Prime Minister; he retained the Justice portfolio he had held in the Badri administration. Aged thirty-two, Bakkush was claimed to be the world's youngest premier in office, and he brought into his cabinet several of his contemporaries who had already proved their ability as under-secretaries or as heads of government departments. Two such men were Ali Atiga, who became Minister of Planning, and Omar Jauda who, after several years as Under-Secretary at the Ministry of Health, was appointed Minister. Bakkush was young enough, and had the ideals and the background, to understand and sympathise with the problems of the post-independence generation of Libyans. He and his self-confident young colleagues seemed to be the men to give the country a new sense of purpose and a stronger personality of its own. At home, Bakkush set up a ministerial committee, on which representatives of the universities also served, to encourage national consciousness. Ministers went on the radio to explain government policy, and the Prime Minister, in a speech to the Senate, announced his intention to encourage citizens 'to take part in providing general services instead of letting the Government do everything'. The announcement that the armed forces were to be increased to 10,000 men as a substitute for defence by Libyan-based British and American forces (referred to as 'the non-Libyan alternative') was characteristic of the new process of 'Libyanisation', and it was Bakkush who finalised the missiles contract with Britain.

Showing a degree of strength and confidence in his own authority rare in Libyan premiers, Bakkush at the beginning of 1968 brought

106 people, 94 of them Libyans and the rest of different Arab nationalities) to trial on charges of plotting subversive and terrorist activities over a period of seven years, inciting demonstrations, and organising strikes, including that of oil industry workers in the summer of 1967. The accused, most of them young, were alleged to have received their orders from the Beirut-based Arab Nationalist Movement, an extreme left-wing revolutionary organisation. Sentences, announced in February, were typically moderate: eighty-seven people were given terms of imprisonment ranging from six to thirty-two months and were fined up to £400; the foreigners were also to be deported after serving their sentences.

Growing international awareness of Libya's new-found importance was enhanced by a series of official foreign visits made by Bakkush during his eleven-month ministry. There were signs of closer Franco-Libyan co-operation and in April 1968 Bakkush, as the first Libyan Prime Minister to visit France, had a series of meetings with President de Gaulle. He was to have visited London and Washington in September, but his unexpected resignation was announced at the beginning of that month. Although the reason was reported to have been disagreement with the king over government appointments, it was suggested that Bakkush had been eased out of power by conservative elements who were understood to be critical both of his progressive zeal and the cost and purpose of his missiles contract with Britain. He was succeeded by his Foreign Minister, Wannis Gaddafi, some fifteen years his senior.

Most of Libyan history is the record of the doings of foreigners in Libya, and of domination from Tunisia or Egypt, Europe or western Asia. The cities from which the three main regions of the country have been administered in the past 2,500 years included Carthage, Alexandria and Rome, Constantinople, Damascus and Baghdad, Tunis and Cairo, Palermo, Valletta, and Madrid, London, and Paris. Changes were usually imposed from outside: it was not the *circumcelliones*, nor the Austurian tribesmen, who ended Roman rule, but the Vandals; not Omar Mukhtar and his guerrillas who drove the Italians out, but British force of arms; even independence was gained in 1951 largely through the good offices of the United Nations.

But things have gone well for Libya since 1943, and a country that achieved and consolidated independence and became one of the world's main oil-producers in less than two decades can no longer be dismissed as a 'buffer state of sand', or be remembered solely as the setting for the longest campaign of the Second World War. Libya is ready for more important things than in the days when, like Shakespeare's Bohemia, it was merely 'a desert country near the sea'.

Bibliography

Arsharuni, N., *Liviya.* Izdatyelstvo Mysl, Moscow, 1965.

Askew, William, *Europe and Italy's Acquisition of Libya 1911–1912.* Duke University Press, Durham, North Carolina, 1942.

Assan, Giorgio, *La Libia e il Mondo Arabo.* Edit. Riuniti [Rome], 1959.

Balardinelli, A., *La Ghibla. Cenni sul Territorio, Notizie Storiche.* Governo della Tripolitania, Ufficio Studi e Monografie Coloniali, N.3, 1935.

Barbour, Nevill (ed.), *A Survey of North West Africa (The Maghrib).* Oxford University Press, London, 1959.

Bennett, Ernest N., *With the Turks in Tripoli.* Methuen, London, 1912.

Bergna, P. Costanzo, *Tripoli dal 1510 al 1850.* Arti Grafiche, Tripoli, 1925.

Bignami, Paolo, *Fra i Colonizzatori in Tripolitania.* Nicola Zanichelli, Bologna, 1931.

Blunsum, Terence, *Libya. The Country and its People.* Queen Anne Press, London, 1968.

Boahen, A. Adu, *Britain, the Sahara and the Western Sudan, 1788–1861.* Clarendon Press, Oxford, 1964.

Boardman, John, *The Greeks Overseas.* Penguin, 1964.

Bodyanski, V. L., and Shagal, V. E., *Sovremennaya Liviya (Spravochnik)* (Contemporary Libya. A Guide). Izdatyelstvo Nauka, Moscow, 1965.

Borsari, Ferdinando, *Geografia, Etnologia e Storica della Tripolitania, Cirenaica e Fezzan.* Libreria Internazionale Ermanno Loescher, Turin, 1888.

Bovill, E. W., *The Niger Explored.* Oxford University Press, London, 1968.

Briggs, Lloyd Cabot, *Tribes of the Sahara.* Harvard University Press, Cambridge, Mass., 1960.

Brown, Leon Carl (ed.), *State and Society in Independent North Africa.* Cornell University Press, Ithaca, 1960.

Cachia, Anthony J., *Libya under the Second Ottoman Occupation (1835–1911)*. Government Press, Tripoli, 1945.

Carrington, Richard, *East from Tunis. A Record of Travels on the Northern Coast of Africa*. Chatto and Windus, London, 1957.

Clifford, Alexander, *Three Against Rommel*. Harrap, London, 1943.

Come Siamo Andati in Libia. Libreria della Voce, Florence, 1914.

Contini, Fulvio, *Storia delle Istituzioni Scolastiche della Libia*. Plinio Maggi, Tripoli, 1953.

Cooley, John K., *Baal, Christ and Mohamed. Religion and Revolution in North Africa*. John Murray, London, 1965.

Coro, Francesco, *Settantasei Anni di Dominazione Turca in Libia (1835–1911)*. Poligrafico Maggi, Tripoli, 1937.

Corradini, Enrico, *L'Ora di Tripoli*. Fratelli Treves, Milan, 1911.

Cowper, H. S., *The Hill of the Graces*. Methuen, London, 1897.

Dearden, Seton (ed.), *Tully's Ten Years Residence at the Court of Tripoli*. Arthur Barker, London, 1957.

Della Cella, P., *Viaggio da Tripoli di Berberia alle Frontiere Occidentali dell'Eggitto Fatto nel 1817*. Tipografia A. Ponthenier, Genoa, 1819.

Denti di Pirajno, Alberto, *A Cure for Serpents (A Doctor in Africa)*. André Deutsch, London, 1955.

Despois, Jean, *La Colonisation Italienne en Libye. Problèmes et Méthodes*. Larose, Paris, 1935.

Duveyrier, H., *Le Confrérie Musulmane di Sidi Mohamed ben Ali Es-Senousi et Son Domaine Géographique*. Ministero delle Colonie, Direzione Generale degli Affari Politici. Tipografia del Senato, Rome, 1918.

Evans-Pritchard, E. E., *The Sanusi of Cyrenaica*. Oxford University Press, London, 1949.

Fantoli, A., *La Libia negli Scritti degli Antichi*. Ministero delle Colonie, Rome, 1933.

Fioravanzo, Giuseppe, and Viti, Guido, *L'Italia in Africa. Serie Storico Militare*, Vol. II, *L'Opera della Marina*. Ministero degli Affari Esteri, Comitato per la Documentazione dell'Opera dell' Italia in Africa, Rome, 1954.

Forbes, Rosita, *The Secret of the Sahara: Kufara*. Cassell, London, 1921.

Furlonge, Geoffrey, *The Lands of Barbary*. John Murray, London, 1966.

Gabelli, Ottone, *La Tripolitania dalla Fine della Guerra Mondiale all'Avvento del Fascismo*. Vols. I and II. A. Airoldi, Intra, Verbania, 1939.

Gautier, E. F., *Geneseric Roi des Vandales*. Payot, Paris, 1932.
Gautier, E. F., *Le Passé de l'Afrique du Nord. Les Siècles Obscurs*. Payot, Paris, 1952.
Ghisleri, Arcangelo, *La Libia nella Storia e nei Viaggiatori dai Tempi Omerici all'Occupazione Italiana*. G. B. Paravia, Turin, 1928.
Ghisleri, Arcangelo, *Tripolitania e Cirenaica. Dal Mediterraneo al Sahara*. Società Editoriale Italiana. Istituto Italiano d'Arti Grafiche, Milan-Bergamo, 1912.
Goodchild, Richard, *Cyrene and Apollonia. An Historical Guide. Ghazi. The Story of a City*. Department of Antiquities, Cyrene, 1962.
Goodchild, Richard, *Cyrene and Apollonia. An Historical Guide*. Antiquities Department of Cyrenaica, U.K. of Libya, 1959.
Graziani, Rodolfo, *Cirenaica Pacificata*. Mondadori, Milan, 1932.
Graziani, Rodolfo, *Verso il Fezzan*. F. Capocardo, Tripoli, 1930.
Graziosi, Paolo, *Arte Rupestre del Sahara Libico*. Vallecchi, Florence, 1962.
Gunther, John, 'Libya, or a Child Learning to Walk' (from *Inside Africa*). Hamish Hamilton, London, 1955.
Hartshorn, J. E., *Oil Companies and Governments. An Account of the International Oil Industry in its Political Environment*. Faber and Faber, London, 1962.
Haynes, D. E. L., *The Antiquities of Tripolitania*. Antiquities Department of Tripolitania, 1959.
Herodotus, *The Histories*. Penguin, 1954.
Hollis, Christopher, *Italy in Africa*. Hamish Hamilton, London, 1941.
Holmboe, Knud, *Desert Encounter. An Adventurous Journey through Italian Africa*. Harrap, London, 1936.
Italia e Africa Mediterranea. Università degli Studi di Firenze, Sansoni, Florence, 1942.
Julien, C. A., *Histoire de l'Afrique du Nord*. Payot, Paris, 1952.
Keith, Agnes Newton, *Children of Allah*. Michael Joseph, London, 1966.
Khadduri, Majid, *Modern Libya. A Study in Political Development*. Johns Hopkins Press, Baltimore, 1963.
Khalidi, Ismail Raghib, *Constitutional Development in Libya*. Khayat's College Book Co-operative, Beirut, 1956.
Kubbah, Abdul Amir Q., *Libya. Its Oil Industry and Economic System*. The Arab Petro-Economic Research Centre, Baghdad, 1964.
Lapworth, Charles, *Tripoli and Young Italy*. Swift, London, 1912.

Lethielleux, J., *Le Fezzan. Ses Jardins, ses Palmiers.* Publications de l'Institut des Belles Lettres Arabes, Tunis, 1948.

Lischi, Dario, *Tripolitania Felix.* Nistri-Lischi, Pisa, 1937.

MacArthur, Wilson, *The Road to Benghazi.* Collins, London, 1941.

Manfroni, Camillo, *L'Italia nelle Vicende Marinare della Tripolitania.* A. Airoldi, Intra, Verbania, 1935.

Mathuisieulx, H-M de, *La Tripolitaine d'Hier et de Demain.* Librairie Hachette, Paris, 1912.

Mercatoli, Enrico, *Tripolitania-Cirenaica.* Società Editrice Sonzogno, Milan, 1932.

Merighi, Antonio, *La Tripolitania Antica.* A. Airoldi, Intra, Verbania, 1940.

Minutilli, F., *La Tripolitania.* Frat. Bocca, Turin, 1902.

Moore, Martin, *Fourth Shore. Italy's Mass Colonisation of Libya.* George Routledge, London, 1940.

Moorehead, Alan, *African Trilogy* (*Mediterranean Front – A Year of Battle – The End in Africa*). Hamish Hamilton, London, 1944.

Murabet, Mohammed, *Some Facts about Libya.* Tripoli, 1961.

Murabet, Mohammed, *A Brief History of Tripolitania.* Tripoli, 1965.

Nallino, C. A., *Norme per la Trascrizione Italiana e la Grafia Araba dei Nomi Propri Geografici della Tripolitania e della Cirenaica.* Ministero delle Colonie, Rome, 1915.

Narducci, Guglielmo, *La Colonizzazione della Cirenaica nell'Antichità e nel Presente.* Stabilmento Tipografico Frat. Pavone, Benghazi, 1934.

Norman, John, *Labor and Politics in Libya and Arab Africa.* Bookman Associates, New York, 1965.

Oliver, Roland, and Fage, J. D., *A Short History of Africa.* Penguin African Library, 1962.

Pananti, Filippo, *Avventure e Osservazioni sopra le Coste di Berberia.* Tip. della Minerva Ticinese, Mendrisio, 1841.

Passamonti, E., *I Patti Mediterranei dalla Guerra Libica al Conflitto Mondiale.* A. Airoldi, Intra, Verbania, 1941.

Piazza, Carlo, *Libia Commerciale ed Agricola nella Storia.* Giuseppe Abbiati, Milan, 1913.

Picard, Gilbert, *Il Mondo di Cartagine* (*Le Monde de Carthage*). Aldo Martello, Milan, 1959.

Picard, Gilbert, *Les Religions de l'Afrique Antique.* Librairie Plon, Paris, 1954.

Piccioli, Angelo, *La Nuova Italia d'Oltremare. L'Opera del Fascismo nelle Colonie Italiane.* Mondadori, Milan, 1934.

Provera, Ada, *Cenni Storici Sulla Libia.* La Prora, Milan, 1936.

Ralz, Odorico, *Le Operazioni Libiche sul 29° Parallelo Nord*. Sindacato Italiano Art Grafiche, Rome, n.d.

Ramusio, Giovanbattista, *Il Viaggio di Giovan Leone, etc.* Co' Tipi di Luigi Plet, Venice, 1837.

Romanelli, Pietro, *La Cirenaica Romana*. A. Airoldi, Intra, Verbania, 1943.

Romanelli, Pietro, *Origini e Sviluppi delle Citta Tripolitane*. R. Istituto Superiore Orientale, Napoli: Conferenze 1939. Edizione Universitarie, Rome, 1939.

Romanelli, Pietro, *Storia delle Provincie Romane dell'Africa*. Istituto Italiano per la Storia Antica, Rome, 1959.

Rossi, Giacomo, *I Negri della Nigrizia Occidentale e della Interna e i Mori e Arabi Erranti del Sahara e del Deserto di Libia*. Stamperia Reale, Turin, 1838.

Rowe, Alan (ed.), *Cyrenaican Expedition of the University of Manchester, 1952*. Manchester University Press, 1956.

Russell, Michael, *Gli Stati dell'Africa Settentrionale*. Società Editrice Fiorentina, Florence, 1843.

Soames, Jane, *The Coast of Barbary*. Jonathan Cape, London, 1938.

Stroppa, Francesco, *Nomadismo e Nomadi della Tripolitania*. Ministero delle Colonie, Rome, 1915.

Thrige, J. P., *Res Cyrenensium. La Storia di Cirene*. A. Airoldi, Intra, Verbania, 1940.

Tugendhat, Christopher, *Oil. The Biggest Business*. Eyre and Spottiswoode, London, 1968.

Villard, Henry Serrano, *Libya. The New Arab Kingdom of North Africa*. Cornell University Press, Ithaca, 1956.

Ward-Perkins, J. B., and Goodchild, R. G., *The Christian Antiquities of Tripolitania*. Society of Antiquaries, 1953.

Warmington, B. H., *Carthage*. Robert Hale, London, 1960.

Wellard, James, *Lost Worlds of Africa*. Hutchinson, London, 1967.

Williams, Gwyn, *Green Mountain. An Informal Guide to Cyrenaica and its Jebel Akhdar*. Faber and Faber, London, 1963.

Zartman, William I., *Government and Politics in Northern Africa*. Praeger, New York, 1964.

Journals and Bulletins

Bartoccini, Renato, 'Il Porto Romano di Leptis Magna.' *Bolletino del Centro Studi per la Storia dell'Architettura*. N. 13, Supp. A1, 1958.

Bergna, P. Costanzo, 'I Caramanli.' *Libia. Rivista di Studi Libici*. Vol. 2, 1953, Tripoli.

Brown, Robert Wylie, 'Libya's Rural Sector.' *Africa Report*, African-American Institute, Washington, April 1967.

Farrell, J. D., 'Libya Strikes it Rich.' *Africa Report*, African-American Institute, Washington, April 1967.

'La Libia in Venti Anni di Occupazione Italiana.' *La Rassegna Italiana*, Sept.–Oct. 1932.

Leva, Antonio Enrico, 'Tripoli in una Descrizione di Cent'Anni Fa.' *Africa. Rivista Trimestrale di Studi e Documentazione dell'Istituto Italiano per l'Africa*, Rome, XXII, N. 1, March 1967.

Libia. Rivista Mensile Illustrata. 1937–41.

'Libya Joins the Giants.' *Petroleum Press Service*, Vol. XXXV, No. 3, March 1968.

'Modern Libya.' *Supplement to Afro-Mideast Economic Bulletin*, Spring 1965.

'Oil Strike at Zelten.' *The Lamp*. Standard Oil Company (New Jersey), Fall, 1959.

Paribeni, R., 'Sepolcreto Cristiano di Engila presso Suani ben Adem.' *Africa Italiana*, 1927.

Pelt, A., 'The United Kingdom of Libya from Colony to Independent State.' *U.N. Bulletin*, 15 February 1952.

Power, Thomas F. Jr., 'Libya and the U.N.' *U.N. Review*, Vol. I, No. 11, May 1955.

Rodger, George, 'Desert Search.' *The Lamp*. Standard Oil Company (New Jersey), Fall, 1957.

Tripoli Times/Corriere di Tripoli. Jan.–Feb. 1943.

Reports and Official Documents

Ayoub, Mohamed, Excavations in Germa. Report, 1966.

Ayoub, Mohamed, The Royal Cemetery of Germa. Report, 1965.

Brevi Note Illustrative sulla Libia per i Partecipanti all VIII Congresso Internazionale di Agricultura Tropicale e Subtropicale, Florence, 1939.

Constitution of the Kingdom of Libya. As Modified by Law No. 1 of 1963.

Corso di Cultura sull'Arte Ravennate e Bizantina. Università degli Studi di Bologna; Istituto di Antichità Ravennate e Bizantina. Dante, Ravenna, 1965.

Economic Development of Libya, The. Report of an Economic Survey Mission Organised by the International Bank for Reconstruction and Development at the Request of the Government of Libya. Johns Hopkins Press, Baltimore, 1960.

Esso in Libya. Esso Standard Libya Inc. Tripoli (1965).

Five-Year Economic Social and Development Plan 1963–1968. Kingdom of Libya, Ministry of Planning and Development.

Handbook on Tripolitania. Compiled from Official Sources. British Military Administration, Tripoli, 1947.

Italian Colonial Empire, The. Information Department Papers No. 27. The Royal Institute of International Affairs, 1940.
Labour Survey of North Africa. International Labour Office. Studies and Reports: New Series No. 60, Geneva, 1960.
La Rinascita della Tripolitania. Memorie e Studi sui Quattro Anni di Governo del Conte Giuseppe Volpi di Misurata. Mondadori, Milan, 1926.
La Strada Litoranea della Libia. Mondadori, Milan, 1937.
Libya. Reference Division, Central Office of Information, London, R. 4640, 1960.
Libya. A Brief Political and Economic Survey. Chatham House Memoranda. Information Department, Royal Institute of International Affairs, 1957.
L'Occupazione di Cufra. Tipo-Litografia del Comando R.C.T.C. della Tripolitania, 1931.
L'Occupazione del Fezzan. Comando R.C.T.C. della Tripolitania. Tripoli R.C.T.C., 1930.
Petroleum Development in Libya 1954 through 1964. Government of Libya, Ministry of Petroleum Affairs, 1965.
Rennell of Rodd, Lord. British Military Administration of Occupied Territories during the Years 1941–47. H.M.S.O., 1948.

United Nations Reports

Annual Report of the United Nations Commissioner in Libya. Prepared in Consultation with the Council for Libya. General Assembly. Official Records, Fifth Session. Supplement No. 15 (A/1340). Lake Success, New York, 1950.
Second Annual Report of the United Nations Commissioner in Libya. Prepared in Consultation with the Council for Libya. General Assembly. Official Records. Sixth Session. Supplement No. 17 (A/1949). Paris, 1951.
Supplementary Report to the Second Annual Report of the United Nations Commissioner in Libya. Prepared in Consultation with the Council for Libya. General Assembly. Official Records. Sixth Session. Supplement No. 17A (A/1949/Add 1). Paris, 1952.
Annual Report of the Government of the United Kingdom to the General Assembly concerning the Administration of Cyrenaica and Tripolitania 1950–51 (A. 1390).
Annual Report of the French Government to the General Assembly concerning the Administration of Fezzan, 1950–51 (A/1387).
Supplementary Report of the United Kingdom of Great Britain and Northern Ireland to the General Assembly concerning the administration of Cyrenaica and Tripolitania for the period 15th October–24th December 1951 (A/2024).

Index

Printed in Great Britain by
Western Printing Services Limited, Bristol